AGAMBEN AND THE POLITICS OF HUMAN RIGHTS

AGAMBEN AND THE POLITICS OF HUMAN RIGHTS
Statelessness, Images, Violence

John Lechte and Saul Newman

EDINBURGH
University Press

Edinburgh University Press Ltd
The Tun – Holyrood Road
12 (2f) Jackson's Entry
Edinburgh EH8 8PJ

www.euppublishing.com

First published in hardback by Edinburgh University Press 2013

This paperback edition 2015

Typeset in 11/13 Palatino Light by
Servis Filmsetting Ltd, Stockport, Cheshire,
and printed and bound in Great Britain by
CPI Group (UK) Ltd, Croydon CR0 4YY

A CIP record for this book is available from the British Library

ISBN 978 0 7486 4572 5 (hardback)
ISBN 978 1 4744 0305 4 (paperback)
ISBN 978 0 7486 7772 6 (webready PDF)
ISBN 978 0 7486 7774 0 (epub)

CONTENTS

PREFACE

Today many acknowledge that the modern human rights project, which grew out of the smouldering ruins of the Second World War, is now in crisis. Despite human rights having achieved remarkable prominence over the following decades with the proliferation of international treaties and legal instruments, the most casual glance at the world around us reveals countless situations where human rights are violated, often by the very sovereign powers who claim to uphold them.

The ongoing violence in Syria at the hands of a despot who has declared war on his own people; a devastating famine in Somalia that has driven nearly one million to seek refuge in neighbouring countries; boatloads of asylum seekers drowning in the coastal waters off Australia; and the seemingly interminable 'war on terror' pursued by the West – a war which was fought ostensibly in the name of human rights and yet which has been accompanied by covert rendition, indefinite detention and torture, as well as drone strikes resulting in numerous civilian deaths. We look out helplessly on a world of suffering, violence and oppression. We also gaze on a world of camps: refugee camps in stricken parts of the world; migrant detention camps beyond the borders of wealthy nations; and the now apparently permanent terrorist detention camp at Guantánamo Bay – perhaps the most striking and ignominious symbol today of the degradation of human rights.

Why is it, then, that the prominence of human rights discourses seems to coincide with their apparent impotence?[1] We can point to various factors here: inadequate means of human rights enforcement and, of course, the hypocrisy of governments who use human rights norms as a plaything of foreign policy, even to legitimise wars, piously invoking them when it suits their interests to do so and ignoring them when it does not.

There is, no doubt, a fundamental and perhaps irreconcilable tension between the principle of national sovereignty and that of human rights, which necessarily imply a limitation on state power. This is a tension that we explore in this book. Sovereignty embodies a desire for autonomy, for what might be called *ipseity* (see Derrida 2005) – a self-enclosed solipsistic identity that refuses to recognise or answer to anything other than itself. Human rights, which in theory seek to call sovereignty to account, to make it answer to universal principles of justice, therefore invoking an alternative ontology of the human, which exceeds the order of the state, are thus an anathema to it. At its heart, state sovereignty is about security or what Roberto Esposito calls immunity (2011); it is about shoring up its borders, both real and conceptual, against whatever threatens to contaminate it. Sovereignty ultimately implies violence. Thus, human rights, even where they are at least formally part of the constitutional order, must always give way to the exigencies of security; transcendence is always trumped by fact and the situation.

Nothing better illustrates the fundamental dilemma facing human rights today than the situation of statelessness: when stateless people, whose numbers are growing exponentially, claim rights in the absence of recognition by nation-states, upon what basis do they do so? If, as many – including, most famously, Hannah Arendt – contend, human rights can only be recognised within a national polity and can only be realised alongside citizenship or membership within an established political community, then where does this leave those who are excluded from such arrangements? As we argue in this book, human rights mean nothing if they are only the rights of citizens, the rights of those within recognised and established political boundaries. Human rights, in other words, mean nothing if they are not also the rights of the stateless, the rights of the other beyond the borders of the state, the rights of those who, as Arendt put it, have not even the 'right to have rights'.

However, in making this claim, we open up a series of complications and ambiguities concerning human rights and their ontological basis. These must nevertheless be investigated and worked through if we are to have any hope of understanding the roots of the current crisis of human rights and of rethinking and renewing them today. The problem, as revealed by statelessness, is actually twofold. First, human rights have their basis in a European tradition of thinking that privileges the idea of the public space, which is seen as the genuine sphere of politics. This goes back to ancient Greek thought, particularly to the original distinction between *polis* and *oikos* (the household, domestic economy, private life) and to the division between *bios* (a particular *form* or *way* of life – political life, for instance) and *zoē* (life as mere biological existence; the fact of being alive). The former was regarded as pre-eminent over the latter: man was, for Aristotle, *zoon politikon*, a political animal, someone whose existence was defined and exalted by a certain activity or form of life – politics – rather than simply by his biological existence.

This distinction is central to Arendt's thought. For her, it is only in the polis, only by appearing in the public realm, only by participating in political life and the collective affairs of the community that one can be fully human. By contrast, the activity of labour and the sphere of private life and domestic economy – upon which, of course, the very possibility of public life depended – were nevertheless consigned to the realm of 'necessity' and 'givenness' to a form of existence, which, deprived of the dignity of full political life, was therefore barely human. Thus a division is set up in Arendt's thinking between the idea of political community and public life, on the one hand, and existence outside this sphere – that of 'necessity' and 'savageness' –which does not, as yet, qualify for full humanity. This division maps onto the distinction between the nation-state – which, in our times, has become the only apparent expression of political community – and those excluded from it. Thus, Arendt, while lamenting the plight of refugees and stateless people between the World Wars, is able to say that because they are excluded from every community and thus fall back on their 'bare' humanity, their very humanity as such is in question: 'It seems that a man who is nothing but a man has lost the very qualities that make it possible for other people to treat him as a fellow-man' (Arendt 1968: 300). For Arendt, nothing confirms this better than the impotence of human rights or the Rights of Man in giving protection and succour to those expelled from every polity.

Yet, the problem with this position, we argue, is that it seems, against its intentions, only to affirm the degradations and violence to which stateless people are subjected; they are, after all, following Arendt's logic, only barely human, and their claim to rights is thus disqualified in advance. The solution, we suggest, is not to simply argue for their integration into the nation-state order and established identities of citizenship, but rather to break down this very ontological distinction between political community and its other, between political life and bare life, which founded such exclusions in the first place; it is to affirm, in other words, that other forms of political life beyond the boundaries of the sovereign state order and the national community are possible – that, indeed, life itself, wherever it is found, is *always already* political, that there is no such thing as bare, non-political life. One of the purposes in writing this book is to challenge the line of thinking that suggests that rights can only have resonance if they are recognised within a political community, enshrined within law and enforced by the sovereign. The rights claims made by those without the 'right to have rights' must be the starting point for any renewal of human rights today.

The second major problem we address follows closely on the heels of the first – it intersects with it and, at the same time, departs from it – that is, that any encounter with human rights must grapple with the biopolitical terrain on which they are situated today. Indeed, this is the basis of Giorgio Agamben's critique of human rights. For him, human rights cannot be detached from the nexus of biopolitical sovereignty, from that infernal machine of modern and ancient power which holds life itself within its clasp. By intervening on the biopolitical terrain, sovereign power works to produce 'bare life' – biological and politically denuded life, life as objectified and calculable, above which is suspended the permanent threat of sovereign violence or the state of exception. Rather than protecting us from sovereignty, as they are supposed to do in theory, the Rights of Man, for Agamben, signify the inscription of 'bare life' through the category of citizenship within the order of the sovereign state. Agamben, like Arendt, accepts the originary distinction between *bios* and *zoē*, yet arrives at radically different conclusions: the question is not so much the political status or lack thereof of those excluded from the polity, but rather the way in which life itself is *included in the form of its exclusion*; our inclusion within the state order is ultimately or potentially in the form of the ban, where the protections of the law and thus of rights are withdrawn from us and where we are at the mercy of an unlimited sovereign power – a situation exemplified in the camp (see Agamben 1998: 166–88). In other words, even being within the polis does not in any sense guarantee our protection, so the notion of a political life within the state order takes on dark and ambiguous connotations.

Furthermore, because human rights are bound up with sovereignty and are essentially a reflection of our biopolitical condition – they are concerned primarily with the preservation of biological life – they are, according to Agamben, complicit in the continual reduction of life to 'bare life'. This is something that can be witnessed in the narrowing of human rights into humanitarianism – a phenomenon which is itself tied to, and indistinguishable from, the violent operation of sovereign power in many parts of the world today.

If we are to retrieve human rights from humanitarianism and if we are to assert their autonomy from sovereign power, we must come to terms with this terrain of biopolitics; we must, in other words, try to think life in ways that transcend the logic of biopolitics, which always seeks to reduce it to its narrowest, biological threshold, thus authorising the securitising and immunising impulses of the sovereign state, which claims to protect life at all costs, even to the point of destroying it.[2]

Yet – and this is where we find his approach more fruitful than Arendt's (and which is why he is the focus of the book) – Agamben does not, despite what many of his critics allege, leave us at a political dead end. There are ways out of the trap of sovereign biopolitics. But this cannot be without, we argue and as Agamben himself hints at, a different notion of life – life which is always a form of life and in which it is not possible to isolate a separate domain of 'bare life' (see Agamben 2000: 2–11), where even 'bare life' – life in its seemingly most diminished sense – is always already a form of life. What is being proposed here, then, is a transcendence of the original *zoē/bios* distinction upon which so much of Western political thought is based. In this book, we explore how life might be approached in a different way, through language, gesture and the image. The very act of claiming rights, we suggest – even in the absence of formal declarations and legal institutions and in the direst and most precarious of circumstances – is an instance of life lived as a form-of-life, of life as transcendent.

So what is being staked out here is a new conception of politics – one that follows and extends Agamben's suggestive, though vague, thinking in this direction. The practice of politics as it has hitherto been understood is simply not up to the task: politics is insufficiently distinguishable from power and from the notion of a project or projects to be achieved, and here we can even include revolutionary projects. As such, politics has been unable to free itself from the terrain of law and sovereignty, from the game whose rules have already been set by power.

Rather, in this book, we develop a different ontological approach to politics, formulated through notions of inoperativeness, impotentiality and the realisation of the freedom and community in which we already live. Human rights play an important part here, not in the sense that they prescribe particular norms and conditions of life – norms that seek recognition within the formal arrangements of power and law – but rather in the sense that they reveal something essential of the human *qua* human.

We do not pretend to have solved the problems of human rights here. Indeed, such a pragmatic, project-oriented, means-ends approach would be against the book's intentions. Instead, we hope to have opened up new lines of thought and enquiry, new ways of thinking about politics and the human, which may, one day, allow us to escape the tangled, violent morass that currently besets human rights.

John Lechte and Saul Newman
November 2012

NOTES

1 Here Costas Douzinas makes the rather obvious, yet vital, point that the modern era, particularly the twentieth century, which ushered in the idea of universal human rights, was witness to more genocides, massacres, violence and human rights abuses than at any previous time (see 2000: 2).
2 As Foucault says about biopolitics in the modern age: 'entire populations are mobilized for the purpose of wholesale slaughter in the name of life necessity: massacres have become vital. It is as managers of life and survival, of bodies and race, that so many regimes have been able to wage so many wars, causing so many men to be killed' (1998: 137).

NOTE

Unless otherwise stated, all translations from original French texts are by John Lechte.

Chapter 1

HUMAN RIGHTS AND STATELESSNESS TODAY

INTRODUCTION: HUMAN RIGHTS AS A PROBLEM

Today it is impossible to avoid the conclusion that if abuses such as torture, state violence and oppression in general are to be prevented, then the implementation of human rights calls for a radically new point of departure. In this regard, it is crucial that we face up to the problems of the past that have often rendered human rights impotent.

Despite being compromised, so that they are, as often as not, honoured more in the breach than in the observance, we still need to consider why human rights are at the same time implicated in many aspects of global politics today. Why is it still possible to embarrass nations with regard to their human rights record? Why is it that human rights are used as a spearhead for global economic expansion? Why are they still used as a justification for one nation-state violating the sovereignty of another, as was the case with the American intervention in Iraq? Why did Nelson Mandela once say that human rights were central to international relations?

A possible and pragmatic response might be that human rights, which are really only enforceable within nation-states, also confirm the privileging of the individual over society and the state – over the broad collectivity, in other words. Being tied to the principle of individualism implies that human rights enhance the expansion of market relations, as individuals seem to slip neatly into the shoes of the consumer. Individual rights, it can thus be claimed, are de facto consumer rights, and it is the Western market system which stands to gain most here.

Wendy Brown, summarising Michael Ignatieff's stance on human rights, thus highlights the following point: 'He [Ignatieff] claims [. . .] that rights as "civil and political freedoms are the necessary condition

1

for the eventual attainment of social and economic security"' (Brown 2004: 454). This leads Brown to the view that: 'What Ignatieff is rehearsing, of course, is not an ontological account of what human beings need to enjoy life, but rather a political-economic account of what markets need to thrive' (2004: 457). Here, Brown is reiterating the critique of political liberalism, which originates with Marx, to the effect that human rights are entirely functional to the capitalist economic system.[1] Brown's critique and others like it also emphasises the globalising drive of capitalism and how the pursuit of a human rights agenda, with its individualist focus and its protection of private property, tends to facilitate the emergence of a global market.

Securitisation/Immunisation

Moreover, 'securitisation', emerging in a much more intense form after 9/11 and the proclamation of the 'war on terror', is a clear threat to human rights. Indeed, it is the idea of 'security', we argue, that, above all, renders human rights implementation ineffective. Thus, in the name of security, human rights must be sacrificed. Guantánamo Bay would be the most striking exemplar of this sacrifice.

Indeed, the securitisation of nation-states and all the border control and surveillance measures that this entails is what Roberto Esposito has identified under the term 'immunity' (2008: 9; see also Esposito 2011). He points to moments in the history of modern political thought where immunity becomes the central tenet of Western politics. Hobbes' idea of a 'Leviathan' – a political body founded on fear – is a key example of this (see Esposito 2009). Fear compels people to seek protection in the arms of the sovereign; they come to see that the fundamental purpose of the polity is to provide security to ensure the preservation of the community, including protection from external and internal forces, whose intentions are to appropriate the political body for their own benefit and enjoyment. As a metaphor, immunity includes the idea that the 'contagion' in the midst of the political body can be used to stimulate 'antibodies' to fight and rid the body of the intruder.

Whatever the terminology chosen, however, and whatever metaphors are invoked, Esposito enables us to see that the political climate of the second decade of the twenty-first century often imposes a stark choice: security or human rights; preservation of the existing form of the nation-state or open democratic community; a system based on exclusion or inclusion.[2] As logic would have it, one can enforce human rights, but only at the expense of security; one can have security, but only at the price of giving up on human rights.[3]

But if all this is true, how is it that the invocation of human rights often accompanies claims that it is necessary to go to war to defend human rights (cf. the Iraq War)? That it is necessary to impose security in the interest of defending a people's human rights? Esposito's explanation is that political action has become caught up in a paradox whereby, in order to preserve life, it is necessary to destroy life. Biopolitics is thus always shadowed by thanatopolitics. The project of securing life, of protecting the lives of some – citizens of a nation-state, for instance – is always at the expense of others, whether through their exclusion or even their elimination.[4] Therefore, to get at the crux of the problems related to defending human rights requires an engagement with the issues raised by both Esposito and Agamben. As Giorgio Agamben has argued in a much-recited denunciation, human rights, rather than limiting biopolitics and sovereign violence, actually participate in the production of 'bare life', which is power's very basis and terrain of intervention. A key part of this book will be devoted to exploring this allegation and to seeing whether or not human rights are redeemable in light of this.

As Agamben suggests, law – as it relates to life – has never been entirely separate from fact. Thus, the *ius soli* ('place of birth') and *ius sanguinis* ('birth from citizen parents') already in Roman law implied the 'primary inscription of life in the state order' (Agamben 1998: 129). This implies that the law as such has, for a very long time, made way for its own suspension in light of an arising situation (for example, a state of emergency). Or, more broadly, what is true in fact has never been separate from what is true by right. The figure of *homo sacer* ('sacred man – the one who is pure life and can be killed without the perpetrator committing homicide') becomes the real basis of a totally non-transcendent sacred. As this ancient – and yet still present – figure of *homo sacer* shows, the terrain of biopolitics, which refers to power's regulation of life itself, is not simply a feature of modernity as Foucault contended, but goes back to earliest antiquity.

Nevertheless, Agamben indicates that the process of life being inscribed within law accelerates enormously in modernity, as is signalled by the intensification of the logic of security and immunity. Since the era of Nazism, in particular, the application or suspension of the law has been driven by particular situations. The law is waived if security is threatened. This is the basis of a state of emergency/state of exception, which is itself foreshadowed by the law. The law, in such a situation, is viewed as an ideal that must be suspended in light of the real state of affairs. Referring to the work of Carl Schmitt, Agamben says that: 'concepts such as "good morals", "proper initiative", "important motive", "public security and order", "state of danger", and "case of necessity" [. . .] refer not to a rule but to a situation' (1998: 172).[5] The 'situation' is what a state of emergency is intended to address. But if the situation is always prevalent, when it coincides with the norm – as is the case with the security of the state – law, in a fundamental sense, is continually suspended. This is what enables Agamben to argue (in a manner too extreme for some) that the camp – the prime instance of the suspension of the law – has increasingly become the norm: 'The camp', Agamben thus says, 'is the space that is opened when the state of exception begins to become the norm' (1998: 168–9). He sees in the camp 'the space of this absolute impossibility of deciding between fact and law, rule and application, exception and rule, which nevertheless incessantly decides between them' (1998: 173). In an even more extreme version of his thesis, Agamben argues that: 'the birth of the camp in our time appears as an event that decisively signals the political space of modernity itself' (1998: 174). Seen in this way, modernity becomes radically beholden to a realist and totally non-transcendent form of law and politics as the power of sovereignty – a form giving rise to the dominance of 'immunity', as outlined by Esposito. Here, too, violence enters the picture. For, above all, power works by the threat or application of violence and the use of force in the state of exception.

Idealism and every form of transcendence are thus shattered by the dominance of the politics of fact and situation. Even ontology begins to be swallowed up by empirical reality, so that the thing as such becomes what it is empirically in the here and now, in the present. How can human rights survive in any significant way in such an environment?

For Agamben, in *Homo Sacer*, the answer to this question is that human rights effectively cannot survive, because they, too, have become contaminated by the logic of fact and situation, so that the human has become the factual biological entity without any transcendence. In short, human life is reduced to 'the figure of bare life or sacred life, and therefore, despite themselves [humanitarian organisations] maintain a secret solidarity with the very powers they ought to fight'

(Agamben 1998: 133). Because human rights supporters also have a realist and *factual* view of the human and because they, too, like the state, reduce *bios* to *zoē*, they become complicit with the power they are supposedly opposing.

THE HUMANITARIAN HORIZON

One of the problems highlighted by Agamben is the way that human rights are increasingly subsumed within the discourse of humanitarianism in which they are circumscribed and depoliticised. While it is important, of course, to conceptually distinguish between human rights and humanitarianism, we must also recognise the way that the former has, in practice, largely been reduced to the latter. When one thinks of human rights violations today, one usually thinks of the humanitarian spectacles of suffering and catastrophe that we see regularly on our TV screens – the pitiful images of the ragged, harried victims of wars, massacres and famines, together with the appeals for humanitarian aid and Western intervention. The face of human rights today is, as Agamben puts it: '[t]he "imploring eyes" of the Rwandan child, whose photograph is shown to obtain money . . .' (1998: 133). Such humanitarian images projected instantaneously around the world become the focal point for human rights; they are situations in which the violation of human rights – the massacring of innocents, the severing of limbs, forced starvation – could not be clearer. We are called upon to act – to stop the atrocities and to defend the innocent. Celebrities lead campaigns for humanitarian aid, visit refugee camps in Darfur and Somalia, have photos taken with emaciated children and lobby politicians.

The ideology of humanitarianism also becomes a legitimising discourse for actual military interventions, which are today conducted in the name of 'humanity'.[6] The NATO operations in Kosovo in the 1990s, the US wars in Afghanistan and Iraq and the recent intervention in Libya were all at least partially justified on humanitarian grounds – protecting the lives and human rights of civilians against genocidal dictators and repressive regimes. There has been a blurring of the distinction between the principles of humanitarianism and the principles of warfare: not only has war become 'humanitarian' (in the most cynical sense of the term, with, for instance, the rhetoric of targeted or 'surgical' strikes designed to spare civilian casualties), but also, humanitarianism has become militarised.[7] Indeed, today, the conduct of military campaigns is often indistinguishable from humanitarian operations (or vice versa) – aid parcels are dropped, along with bombs and guided missiles, and humanitarian aid workers accompany soldiers into war zones. Military campaigns deliver both life and death, confirming Foucault's thesis on modern biopolitics – that it is the power 'to foster life or to disallow it' (1998: 138). Indeed, the indifference of the powerful towards mass suffering in some situations and their readiness to intervene in others is not merely illustrative of their self-interestedness and hypocrisy. More precisely, it reveals the perverse logic of biopower, in which the impulse to secure and foster life finds its counterpart in the production of death – something which can be seen in the zones of indifference which prevail over large parts of the planet, in which millions of 'expendable people' are simply allowed to die. We are not suggesting, of course, that such suffering is ignored by humanitarian NGOs and human rights groups. On the contrary, these groups work hard to bring these situations to the attention of the world and to exert pressure on governments to act. Rather, it is the ambivalence of states that is at issue here, along with the way in which humanitarian ideology conceals a highly inconsistent policy of intervention on the part of states. The discourse of humanitarianism – with human rights in tow – becomes part of a global biopolitical regime, which allows power to intervene in certain select situations in the name of the preservation of life, while turning a blind eye to other injustices and atrocities.

For various aid agencies around the world, human rights have become another tool in the attempt to change the material situation of people. Images of catastrophes turn the victims into the objects of our compassion. Yet this is not the same as fighting for human rights. Human rights have to be understood as more than a means to an end. Thus it is not a matter of being moved by images of the oppressed Afghan woman, the Somali refugee in Kenya or a rape victim in the Congo. It is not a matter of responding to a situation where the people involved are perceived to be nothing other than victims of circumstances, albeit terrible circumstances. Rather, it should be a matter of recognising the human *qua* human, despite the situation.

The problem of the reduction of human rights to humanitarianism and human protection centres on the figure of 'bare life', or life stripped down to its mere biological existence, and survival. In the syntagm 'Man and the Citizen' from the French Declaration, 'Man', giving way to the more contemporary 'human', was thought to be entirely external to civil society and, in recent times, especially since the work of Arendt, it was thought, as a result, to be impossible to do justice to the human as human. In Agamben's scenario, however, it is precisely the fact of the human as essentially the biological body (the biological being equivalent to a pure, material, non-transcendent life) that qualifies it to be included in the civil sphere. Yet paradoxically, while it is through rights that we are included in the civil sphere as citizens, this inclusion coincides with the growing weakness of rights and the readiness on the part of the state to sacrifice them in the name of security.

Agamben's fundamental point (which he often does not pursue rigorously or unequivocally enough) is not, then, that the whole of democratic society is identical to a concentration camp or that the human is, in truth, nothing but a body, but rather that the absolute primacy of fact and situation and the total erasure of transcendence, which gives precedence to sovereignty, renders the human similar to the body in the camp; this body is the absolute incarnation of this non-transcendent reality. Fact, to reiterate, dominates right. And this entails that sovereignty or power (not law or rights) is to be always protected at whatever cost.

Is it really, then, Agamben's point that rights as such are complicit with power? Let us again acknowledge that Agamben is often ambiguous here and that this issue will need further attention at a later stage. However, Ayten Gündoğdu believes that there is, in Agamben's argument, a clear complicity between power and rights: 'the more we invoke rights, the more entangled we become with sovereign power . . .' (2012: 9).

Indeed, it is true, as Gündoğdu points out, that at one point Agamben explicitly writes in *Homo Sacer* that '*it is almost as if*' (our emphasis) rights and liberties only won in a battle with sovereign powers

> simultaneously prepared a tacit but increasing inscription of individuals' lives within the state order, thus offering a new and more dreadful foundation for the very sovereign power from which they wanted to liberate themselves. (1998: 121)

It is precisely this point that will require further analysis at a later stage. For now, we note the following. First of all, there is the 'almost as if' qualifier prefacing Agamben's remark, suggesting uncertainty as to the point being made. Second, if rights are implicated in the power that they oppose, this is, at best, in a highly complex, tenuous and paradoxical way – indeed, only in the sense that the suspension of the law is itself foreshadowed by the law. This is founded on a paradox, because the suspension of the law – as in a state of emergency – occurs, for the most part, in order to protect the populace from disorder, insecurity and violence – the very aspects, as popular opinion would have it, that need to be controlled if the enjoyment of rights is to take place at all. The problem, of course, is that threats can be presented as ongoing, so that the point where rights are enjoyed is never actually reached. Third, why does the law need to be suspended if rights are already implicated in sovereign power? It just does not make any sense to claim, on the one hand, that the state of exception and the suspension of the law, including the 'normal' respect of human rights, is equivalent to the assertion of sovereign power and, on the other hand, that rights are implicated in this power – that somehow the defence of human rights furthers the interests of power. This is simply to attribute an omnipotence to sovereign power, an omnipotence which is highly questionable. At worst, we could say that the discourse of rights is used – or, rather, misused – by sovereign power in an ideological way to legitimise itself, even as it goes about suspending and curtailing those very rights; in other words, governments say, perversely, that it is because they respect rights and adhere to the rule of law that they have the moral authority to suspend those rights when faced with a threat to security (the Hobbesian justification); that, in other words, they can curtail rights without losing their moral legitimacy as good liberal democratic regimes, which otherwise respect rights and law under normal circumstances (the problem being, of course, that the emergency is omnipresent and that we are never in a 'normal' situation)[8] or that in an equally perverse logic of the 'trade off',[9] some rights have to be sacrificed so that others can be protected. Either way, the problem relates to the way that the discourse of human rights is misused, manipulated and traduced by sovereign states, rather than an actual complicity that the idea of human rights itself shares with power.

It is nevertheless true that Agamben is often ambiguous on this point, as he is on the relationship between *zoē* and *bios*. When he argues that *zoē* is actually a form of life (= *bios*), he is consistent with the position that there is no life distinct from a form of life. However, there are times when he gives the impression that *zoē* is separable from *bios* and that, as such, it can be appropriated by sovereign power. Similarly with rights: when these are taken in hand by institutions closely aligned with the state, they tend to serve the interests of the state as the harbinger of sovereign power. However, when rights are linked to the exposure of the human (something we shall explore later in the book), rights reflect a form of life – one that, as we shall suggest, resists power.

Furthermore, as we will show, the whole argument regarding the priority of immunity is brought into question if too much weight is attached to claims that rights are complicit with power. That is, Agamben would need to argue that the defence of human rights is entirely complicit with concerns about the security of the state – that the state of exception would not be about the withdrawal of rights – an argument that seems to be highly implausible. Instead, it is more important to argue that agencies which fight for these rights are complicit because they participate so fully in the scenario of non-transcendence[10] – something that is no doubt exemplified and affirmed by Michael Ignatieff's pragmatist approach to human rights (see Ignatieff 2003).

Thus, in accepting that Agamben has identified a genuine problem for the defence of human rights, Anthony Burke has argued that it is only by reaffirming a sacred as transcendent,[11] that the cause for human rights can be renewed. It is precisely this theme that we will address in later chapters. For now, we will further examine the growing tension between human rights and security, as well as its implications for those who are stateless, those who have not even the 'right to have rights'.

Human Security?

The operation of exceptional spaces today, as well as the general ubiquity of mechanisms of security and surveillance, clearly has important consequences for human rights, highlighting their apparent ineffectiveness in the face of an increasingly powerful state. The question arising here is whether the ethical, legal and political terrain can be reclaimed for human rights. One possible approach to this is the discourse of human security, which claims that the narrower, traditional logic of national security (defined primarily in its police and military functions) should be broadened to include humanitarian and human rights concerns. Yet, from our perspective, the prominence today of this discourse of human security,[12] even if well-intentioned, is symptomatic not of the triumph of human rights, but rather of their weakness and ambiguity. The project of moulding security around human rights concerns does not signify the pre-eminence of human rights, but rather the centrality and hegemony of security or, as we stated above, the dominance of the drive for immunity (Esposito) and the dominance of fact over right (Agamben). This has raised the question whether there is a convergence between these two principles and thus a lack of a genuinely autonomous politics of human rights.

Mary Kaldor, one of the chief academic exponents of human security, talks about a new paradigm of international politics that is emerging – one based around humanitarian intervention, human rights, global civil society and international law. This is the paradigm of human security, which she defines as 'being about the security of individuals and communities rather than the security of states, and it combines both human rights and human development' (Kaldor 2007: 182). The aim here is to rethink security beyond the traditional state-centric paradigm of national security and situate it around individuals, incorporating economic, food, health and personal and political security elements. Security, in this interpretation, 'is about confronting extreme vulnerabilities, not only in wars but in natural and man-made disasters as well – famines, tsunamis, hurricanes' (2007: 183). According to Kaldor, human rights are primary and serious human rights violations are grounds for various forms of humanitarian and even military intervention, although here she is careful to say that military intervention should only be used as a last resort. For Kaldor, it is important that military intervention, if it is used, should be conceived of in terms of policing and human rights enforcement, rather than in terms of traditional warfare, and it should be carried out in a multilateral fashion on the basis of broad international consent.

In challenging the state-centric (= sovereign power) approach to security and in having as its focus the security of the person as individual beyond his or her membership of a nation-state, the human security perspective would seem like a worthy aspiration for international policymaking. In calling for a critical interrogation of this concept, we certainly have no intention of reasserting the supremacy of the state-centric 'realist' paradigm or of supporting the various critiques of human security on the grounds of its 'idealism'.[13] The problem, as we see it, is more complex than that and relates to the power relationships obscured behind the idea of human security, as well as the ontological bind that security imposes on life. Security – whether imposed by states or international organisations – constrains and limits the autonomy and potentiality of being human, closing off its possibilities and subjecting it to biopolitical government. Human security therefore suffers from the same pitfalls as humanitarian action generally – in caring for the victim in a given situation or set of circumstances, it establishes a power relationship over the victim, reducing him or her to a politically irrelevant form of 'bare life', incapable of political agency and autonomous action. Foucault has taught us to be cautious of the idea of 'care' – to be alert to its dangers and the subtle forms of domination that it involves. The seemingly innocuous care of doctors over patients, psychiatrists over the mentally ill, social workers over the needy and teachers over pupils are all, perhaps inevitably, power relationships, which, according to Foucault, should be both interrogated and challenged. At the very least, we should be constantly aware of their potential dangers.[14] Indeed, we might see human security as a contemporary globalised pastoral power – a form of power which Foucault traces from the origins of the Christian pastorate through to modern rationalities of government (see Foucault 2007: 135–85). The government of the 'one and the many' or of the shepherd over his flock, as Foucault describes it, no longer consists of the salvation of souls, but of the securitisation of bodies.

Securitisation in protecting bodily integrity and preserving human life at the same time constrains the autonomy of the human. We should be aware of the potential damage that securitisation does to the thing that is being secured. As Michael Dillon puts it: 'securing is an assault on the integrity of whatever is to be secured' (1996: 122). Human security, in this sense, is depoliticising. Not only does it establish a power relationship in the form of salvation and care, but it risks shutting down the constitutively open ontological space that is necessary for politics. While proponents of human security would argue that one first has to have security before one can have politics, this puts us back into the Hobbesian paradigm, whereby the ontological primacy of security over politics leads to constraints and limitations on politics. Once again, we are not suggesting that proponents of human security do not desire anything less than the possibility of full political lives for the suffering masses of the planet, and, indeed, we give them full credit for seeking to transcend the narrow, state-centred, sovereign conception of security. However, the ontological priority given to security is, at the same time, a danger to politics. As Jacques Derrida argues, democratic politics, in particular, necessarily implies openness to risk and the dangers of freedom.[15] So in evaluating the emancipatory potential of human security, we should enquire as to the ultimate compatibility between human rights and security and ask why the cause of human rights today seems acceptable only if it is attached to, constructed around and packaged within the signifier of security.[16] Our claim would be that for human rights to be explored to their full radical potential, they must ultimately exceed the language and practices of security.

THE PARADIGM OF STATELESSNESS

So far we have suggested that human rights have become problematic in two key senses: the first is that they have been used as a cover for national self-interest, particularly for the dominant powers. This push to defend human rights often occurs in the context of less visible national attempts to bring about a global marketplace and the attendant dominance of market relations that this entails. The second problem, as highlighted by Agamben, is the dominance of fact and situation over rights. Here, the state of exception is predominant, and the situation comes to subsume the properly transcendent dimension of rights. The human, as such, has fallen into this totally non-transcendent abyss, as proposed by secular modernity. Because what is essentially human is deemed to be the biological body, we see that, if understood in this way, the body becomes the pure plaything of sovereign power within the terrain of biopolitics.

It is in this context that we must explore the problem of statelessness and the ambiguous question of the rights of the stateless. The condition that stateless people find themselves in around the world today, as they languish in detention camps, migrate from place to place or live a precarious and clandestine existence under constant fear of deportation, seems to conjure up all the ambiguities and tensions confronting human rights that we have thus far evoked. The generally appalling treatment by states of asylum seekers and 'illegal' migrants and the vicious measures of border control, policing and surveillance are a concretisation of the dominance of fact and situation over transcendent rights in international politics. In other words, the barbaric treatment of stateless people is a condition or symptom of the immolation of transcendence on the altar of sovereign exigency.

In addition, stateless people seem to constitute a certain blindspot for nation-states and public opinion, which fail to acknowledge the full catastrophe that is currently taking place. The Afghan asylum seekers drowned in the coastal waters off Australia or incarcerated in a detention camp in the Australian desert or the Iraqi, Iranian, Afghan or Sudanese migrants forcefully cleared by French police from their makeshift camp (the Calaisis 'jungle')[17] or the image of two drowned Roma Gypsy girls, who had recently been fingerprinted by the Italian authorities and whose bodies washed up onto a Naples beach, ignored by the sunbathers sitting calmly by – all of these images should not just raise feelings of indignation in support of the 'victims', but should also acknowledge the non-recognition of the transcendence of the human that takes place at the same time.

These situations are brutal and shocking and yet they do not seem to evoke deep reflection or concern about the human as human. Although this catastrophe is closer to home, it is somehow less visible and less likely to elicit compassion – indeed, quite the opposite. Such is the perversity of this situation that the very victims escaping oppressive regimes that we, in the West, declared war on – in the name, let it not be forgotten, of human rights – find themselves barred from entry into our societies and incarcerated in detention camps, where their rights – which, again, we supposedly defend – are now denied to them. The perception of statelessness as a threat takes precedence over the defence of human rights. While human rights form the post-ideological ideology of Western societies, many in these societies are horrified by the spectre of statelessness, 'illegal' migration and demonstrations in detention centres. As a result, there is an acceptance of human rights violations where force is inflicted on others, in order to protect the social order and national identity.

Through these fears and concerns over security, we must recognise the biopolitical horizon of statelessness. While sovereign power, wherever it is enforced, tends to reduce everyone – citizen and non-citizen – to a kind of biological entity (to a natural fact) in relation to which a technocracy manages their needs and behaviours, the stateless person, as non-citizen, is at the forefront of this development. For refugees, asylum seekers and 'illegal' migrants, due to their lack of legal and political status, are precisely reduced to 'bare life'; they are anonymous, nameless, faceless, and they wait, in many cases for years, while their fate is determined by governments and tribunals, like the man from the countryside in Kafka's parable, who waits eternally outside the door of the law, only to have it finally shut in his face. Moreover, the subjection of stateless people to an array of demeaning and intrusive examinations and surveillance – such as fingerprinting and medical inspections – points to the biopolitical management of 'illegal' migration in the interest of security, so that the body of the stateless person becomes the site for state surveillance and control.[18] Furthermore, if we understand biopolitics as operating on the terrain of immunisation, then we can see border controls as a strategy of immunising the fearful body politic through the exclusion of the body of the threatening outsider – the body who may not only pose the threat of contamination in a physical sense through disease, but also weaken the cultural integrity of the nation, spreading the virus of Islam or terrorism.

Perceived security threats are thus attributed to the asylum seeker who not only threatens to disturb the identity of the national community, but might pose a risk to state security. Indeed, we have seen a growing securitisation of migration, particularly in the years following September 11, and the spilling over of concerns about terrorism into concerns about 'illegal' migration – a growing 'zone of indistinction', as Agamben might put it, between the two. The entirely ungrounded fear that some asylum seekers might be 'Islamic terrorists' has been used, for instance, by the Australian Government in order to provide a rationale for ruthless border control measures. Similar fears are observable in the United States following 9/11 (see Tirman 2006). Indeed, a sense of insecurity about terrorism, immigration and other perceived threats to national identity all seem to blur into the same abstract fear – a fear which is deliberately manipulated in the media and exploited by governments. Statelessness becomes a site of (in)security for national governments, thus authorising more intense border controls.[19] New powers of search and detention given to border agencies, draconian laws and restrictions on asylum seeking, the centralisation of surveillance and information-gathering systems at a European-wide level, the clearing of makeshift camps by police and the offshoring of spaces of detention are all instances of this attempt to contain and control statelessness. Didier Bigo describes the effect of measures such as those entailed in the Schengen Agreement to create an internal security zone within the EU:

> The consequence of this extension of the definition of internal security at the European level is that it puts widely disparate phenomena on the same continuum – the fight on terrorism, drugs, organized

crime, cross-border criminality, illegal immigration – and to
further control the transnational movement of persons, whether
this be in the form of migrants, asylum seekers or other border
crossers – and even more broadly of any citizen who does not cor-
respond to the a priori social image that one holds of his national
identity (e.g. the children of first-generation immigrants, minority
groups). (2008: 19)

The most visible manifestation of these immunising practices is the
migrant detention camp, which occupies, as we have pointed out, a
space of biopolitical exception, in which sovereign power functions in
excess of the law (and in tandem with it) and where those detained in
such spaces are denied the rights and legal protections normally given
to citizens. It is argued that the situation demands such measures. Thus,
these camps and facilities operate as sites of exclusion, where the logic
of bordering and the condition of statelessness – in all its precarious-
ness and vulnerability – are made concrete. To further emphasise this
exclusion and policy of the exception – as if the barbed wire, prison-like
walls and surveillance cameras were not enough – some of these camps
are located offshore and are outsourced to the management of private
security firms. For instance, we have the detention centres that have
been opened on islands in the South Pacific, which are run on behalf
of the Australian Government, or the camps and border zones situated
in Libya, Tunisia and Morocco, which are designed to control the flow
of 'illegal' migration from sub-Saharan Africa into the EU. Spain, for
instance, has rediscovered a use for its colonies in Morocco, constructing a border fence around Ceuta, so as to prevent border crossings into
Spanish territory.[20] We can also point to the use of ad hoc, temporary
spaces for detention, such as transit zones in airports. The proliferation
of these extra-territorial processing zones around the world is emblem-
atic of the condition of statelessness and the increasing lengths to
which states will go to control this situation.

Moreover, the daily life of those detained in such spaces combines
the intervention on a minute level of the disciplinary regime of sovereign power with the virtual absence of legal protection and rights recognition. Detainees, who often languish in such places for years only
to have their asylum claims rejected, sometimes on a technicality, live
an existence where enforced boredom is combined with the constant
anxiety of deportation, as well as with petty administrative cruelties and

arbitrary rules. A first-hand account describes this disciplinary regime, which is all the more terrorising, in a Kafkaesque way, for its lack of regularity and normality:

> All the rules are enforced arbitrarily, without any rhyme or reason. The rules change all the time, and the inmates are not told about the changes, because if they know the rules they might consider themselves to have some rights. (ICFI 2002)

'*Being in force without significance*' is how Agamben characterises the situation of the law in the sovereign ban (1998: 51 [emphasis in original]) – something which aptly captures this anomic condition of the detained asylum seeker and, indeed, the condition of statelessness in general.

THE RIGHTS OF THE STATELESS

The question that arises here, in all its urgency, concerns the sort of protections that are available to people in such circumstances. They are offered little or no protection under national laws, and, indeed, the practices of detention that we have described are designed to deliberately isolate and exclude the stateless person and to remove him or her from such protections. Therefore, the stateless person has nothing to fall back on but human rights principles, as well as various international frameworks and conventions. And, indeed, many current practices of detention and border control not only violate human rights principles as set out in the 1948 Declaration – which, for instance, forbids subjecting people to 'cruel, inhuman or degrading treatment' and which grants people the right to asylum[21] – but also contravene various international protocols on the treatment of refugees, especially the 1951 Refugee Convention. Yet, for the most part, such practices continue in a seemingly unrestricted fashion, driven by the exigencies and prerogatives of state power.[22] We are forcefully confronted here with the apparent impotence of human rights and even of international law in the face of state sovereignty. At the very least, there is major tension between the principles of universal human rights and those of state sovereignty. As Seyla Benhabib puts it: 'There is not only a tension, but often an outright contradiction, between human rights declarations and states' sovereign claims to control their borders and to monitor the quality of and quantity of admittees' (2004: 2). And, as has been indicated, in most cases, national sovereignty prevails.

Here we are reminded of Hannah Arendt's poignant illustration in *The Origins of Totalitarianism* of the futility of refugees and stateless people seeking protection on the basis of the rights of man:

> If a human being loses his political status, he should, according to the implications of the inborn and inalienable rights of man, come under exactly the situation for which declarations of such general rights provided. Actually the opposite is the case. It seems that a man who is nothing but a man has lost the very qualities which make it possible for other people to treat him as a fellow-man. (1968: 300)

Arendt's crucial challenge to human rights is an essential starting point for any serious study of human rights and will be dealt with at greater length in the following chapter. However, what is revealed here is the tension between two different orders of rights – universal human rights, bestowed on mankind in general, and the rights of citizens within bounded political communities, in other words, between human rights and civic rights. Arendt's point is that only the latter offer genuine protection, in so far as one is included within a particular political community. By contrast, the former order of universal human rights exists only in the abstract, offering no real protection and, indeed, confirming one's very exclusion from community and, through this, from humanity itself; for humanity is defined here as essentially the political community. Invoking the abstract rights of man simply reduces the claimant to 'bare life', to the simple fact of biological existence, leaving him vulnerable to be marked as an outsider and less than human.

There is real conflict between these two ontological orders of rights and two different understandings of belonging – one which is intrinsic to the tradition of Western political philosophy itself. For not only is this tradition indebted to Aristotle's distinction between *zoē* and *bios*, where bios includes membership and participation in politics as a condition of a 'good life', but the politicisation of *zoē* as the fact of biological life is implicit in the theory of the social contract, which is so influential in the modern era.

As regards the stateless person, it is not that he does not have rights;

rather that within the order of sovereign states, such rights become meaningless, because political life is dominated by the fact of situations, and there is little interest or concern in giving the transcendence that is the basis of rights its due. In this regard, we need to fully investigate the condition of what we have described as 'biopolitical exceptionalism', where it may be that the division between statehood and statelessness, belonging and exclusion, rights and rightlessness is less clear-cut, to the point where it could be that we are all increasingly reduced to a condition of statelessness.

Were the claim made by Arendt correct – that the only rights worth having are those bestowed by a political community as opposed to abstract universal human rights – we would then be forced to confront a number of essential questions. Can it be that the human is only fully expressed and confirmed within a political community? We believe that the answer to this question is no. For political community inevitably means – at least, currently – the community established by the nation-state, and we believe that this is as much part of the problem as it is part of the solution. If political community is not an adequate indication of the essential human, what is the ontological status of the human *qua* human as the bearer of human rights? If, for instance, Elspeth Guild is correct in her contention that 'refugees are neither victims nor Homo Sacer; they are struggling for their rights' (2010: 25), we need to better understand the ontological basis of this struggle for rights. If we want to insist on an understanding of human rights which transcends the idea of particular political communities, then how can these human rights be enforced in the absence of adequate international mechanisms of enforcement? Moreover, if we are to defend the idea of universal human rights – or rights that transcend the particularities of nation-states – and if we are also to insist on a conception of humanity that is always already politically valid, then this raises the challenge of thinking the human and community entirely differently. Humanity and community and the relationship between them are given new resonance and meaning through the condition of statelessness. Can there be a conception of humanity that, on the one hand, transcends 'bare life' and, on the other, finds its fulfilment in forms of community and collective political life that no longer take the form of the nation-state?

In this light, one of the objectives of our examination is to explore Agamben's enigmatic claim that:

given the by now unstoppable decline of the Nation-State and the general corrosion of traditional political-juridical categories, the refugee is perhaps the only thinkable figure for the people of our time and the only category in which one may see today – at least until the process of dissolution of the Nation-State and its sovereignty has achieved full completion – the forms and limits of a coming political community. (1996: 158–9)

For Agamben, who radicalises, updates and goes beyond Arendt's problematic, the figure of the refugee or stateless person, precisely by virtue of his or her radical exclusion from the nation-state and from the categories of citizenship and rights that derive from it – in other words, precisely because of what Arendt saw as his abject and politically disqualified existence – is the harbinger of a new horizon of political existence. However, the question we are left with is what might this new form of political life, this 'coming political community', actually be? And, moreover, would it be a form of politics in which human rights have any role to play? Agamben is notoriously vague about the shape of this 'coming political community', and it is unclear from his allusive writings whether he believes human rights can be redeemed – whether they can be radically reformulated and detached from sovereignty – or whether they would simply be transcended and made superfluous in future forms of community.

CONCLUSION

Whatever the case, we suggest that it is necessary to reconsider the very being of the human, if a new form of community is to be envisaged. This, as has been reiterated, has to be the human as transcendent, not as the 'natural' biological body – the body of the Greek *zoē*. In this context, human rights would be a way of encountering this transcendent human and would mark the space through which the human, as such, is articulated. In this way, rights could be understood as a threshold through which we must think in order to imagine new forms of political existence.

Notes

1 See Marx's famous critique of the Rights of Man in 'On the Jewish question' (1843), where he said that: 'None of the supposed rights of man, therefore, go beyond the egoistic man, man as he is, as a member of civil society; that is, an individual separated from the community, withdrawn into himself, wholly preoccupied with his private interest and acting in accordance with his private caprice' (in Tucker 1978: 26–52, 43).

2 See Bataille's notion of community as what defies self-preservation (a biologically driven notion) (1988: 10–30). See also Esposito's discussion of Bataille (2011: 112–34).

3 Of course, another question to be posed here is whether the so-called 'war on terror' and the security measures it implies have, in reality, increased our security or left us more vulnerable. Indeed, many security experts have raised serious queries about this, believing that, if anything, such extreme measures have only antagonised many around the world and have served as fertile recruiting ground for terrorism. However, our general point is that even if such measures *were* effective, the sacrifice of human rights involved would still not be justified.

4 For Esposito, moreover, the immunising paradigm always ends up destroying or sacrificing part of what it seeks to protect. In this sense, we can point to the way, for instance, that security measures against terrorism – supposedly implemented to protect our liberal democratic way of life – end up constraining important elements of this way of life. See Derrida's notion of 'autoimmunity' – the self-destructive impulse at the heart of democracy, which destroys democracy in the very attempt to protect it (2005: 40).

5 The supreme irony of Schmitt's position is that, beginning with theology, it ends up privileging the non-transcendent contingent moment, which is the exception as situation. Let it be affirmed here that every form of political pragmatism confirms Schmitt's thesis privileging the situation, which, in the end, is always geared to the defence of sovereign power.

6 In 1999, Tony Blair announced a new moral doctrine of the humanitarian 'just' war, of which the campaigns in Kosovo, and later in Afghanistan and Iraq, were seen as examples.

7 Here we should remember, as Didier Fassin and Mariella Pandolfini counsel us to, that: 'Even dressed up in the cloak of humanitarian morality, intervention is always a military action – in other words, war' (2010: 22). See also Eyal Weizman's analysis of the way that humanitarian law, which ostensibly seeks to limit harm and suffering, at the same time provides a normalising discourse for military operations that are now conducted according to the dubious morality of the 'lesser evil' (Weizman 2011).

8 Thus, in believing that such suspensions can be authorised while leaving the liberal–democratic constitutional order essentially intact, Ignatieff shows a certain naivety (see Ignatieff 2005).

9 See Jeremy Waldron's critique of the notion of the 'trade off' between liberty and security (2003: 191–210).

10 'Non-transcendence' here refers to the material situation in the here and now, one that must be managed and not changed. Thus, when agencies minister to people in dire situations – such as famine or war – the aim, in the first instance, is to enable the bare survival of those individuals in need. Mere aliveness is the only aim, regardless of any concern about the power relationships this may entail or the way that the autonomy of the 'client' is completely negated.

11 Here we acknowledge that the term 'sacred' should be used with some caution. While we want to link it to what is transcendent, it is often linked specifically to organised religion. An anthropological approach to the sacred as an ambiguity of borders, as found, for instance, in the work of Mary Douglas or, after her, Julia Kristeva, seems to run the risk of secularising the sacred, that is, of turning it into something that is really an effect of the mundane world, not something that is truly sacred. Bataille's approach is much more promising. For while he does make an attempt to give the sacred content, his chief interest is in opposing the reduction of the world to the mundane world – the world of the restricted economy. Instead, Bataille argues that there is another world – the world of the general economy, a world of loss, of risk and destruction for its own sake; in short, a transcendent world – one that cannot be easily captured in the social sciences. Agamben, too, recognises the difficulties and elsewhere invokes the exposure of the human through language and gesture – a human that, like the sacred, is not open to objectification.

12 After first being mentioned in UN Development Program's 1994 report, the notion of human security has come to form one of the main planks of UN policy. Principles of human security were set out as part of the UN mission in a letter from the then Secretary-General Kofi Annan to the UN General Assembly, which stressed the importance of human rights to collective security (see United Nations 2005).

13 See, for instance, David Chandler's critique of human security (2008: 427–38).

14 Here Foucault refers to a 'genealogy of problems, of *problematiques*', which is close to our own approach to the question of human security and humanitarianism. He says: 'My point is not that everything is bad, but that everything is dangerous [. . .] If everything is dangerous, then we always have something to do. So my position leads not to apathy but to a hyper- and pessimistic activism' (2000: 253–80, 256).

15 See Derrida's discussion of autoimmunity and the 'war on terror' (2005: 40; see also Derrida in Borradori 2004: 94–102).

16 Here we remain skeptical of Ken Booth's association of security with human emancipation: the freedom entailed in the notion of emancipation is seen to equate with security as freedom from certain threats. Again, however, it is the ontological assumptions of security which, for us, pose certain problems and limits for freedom (see Booth 1991: 313–26).

17 See the moving description of the terrible conditions of the Calaisis 'jungle', including the story of an Eritrean man who drowned while washing himself in the English Channel, because of the lack of showers (Dembour and Martin 2011: 123–45).

18 In this way, the body becomes a biopolitical site for both resistance, as well as control, as do various practices of self-mutilation by camp detainees, such as lip-sewing. See Patricia Owens' article on lip-sewing amongst detainees in an Australian refugee detention camp, which is enacted as a kind of biopolitical protest against the condition of 'bare life' (2009: 567–82). Also on this subject, see Edkins and Pin-Fat (2005: 1–24).

19 Jeff Huysmans talks about the framing of immigration as a security concern in European societies and the way that this constitutes the identity and autonomy of the political community in opposition to existential threats: 'Securitizing immigration and refugee flows thus produces and reproduces a political community of insecurity' (2006: 51).

20 In trying to break through this fence, a number of border-crossers were killed in 2005, caught in a no-man's land between the Spanish and Moroccan borders – a no-man's land, which quickly became a shooting alley.

21 Although this is always to be subordinate to the priorities of nation-states, thus highlighting, once again, the problem with the UNDHR.

22 This is, of course, not to diminish the importance of the numerous campaigns on the part of refugee advocacy organisations, lawyers and human rights groups to challenge practices of border control and detention, nor is it to ignore the successful legal challenges to detention in certain individual cases.

Chapter 2

HUMAN RIGHTS IN HISTORY

An examination of 'human rights in history' will enable a better under-standing of the context in which modern notions of rights arose and thus outline the terms of what we see as the central question facing human rights today: how might it be possible to defend the rights of those who have lost the 'right to have rights'?

Generally, what passes for the history of modern human rights focuses on the period after the Second World War – on the aftermath of the Nuremberg Trials and on the Universal Declaration of Human Rights (UDHR) confirmed by the United Nations General Assembly (UNGA) in December 1948. Thirty human rights were specified and expressed as a set of abstract moral claims or aspirations. However, while these rights supposedly enshrined the sanctity of individuals, at the same time, they depended upon the goodwill of nation-states to uphold them, thus consigning human rights to a crippling contradic-tion and an uncertain future.

It is true that, in light of the brutality of the Nazi regime, the Nuremberg Tribunal did constitute a step forwards in the defence of human rights from a legal point of view. As David Chandler explains:

> Where the tribunal broke new legal ground was in using natural law to overrule *positivist* law, to argue that the laws in force at the time in Germany were no defence against the retrospective crime of 'waging an aggressive war'. This was justified on the grounds that certain acts were held to be such heinous crimes that they were banned by universal principles of humanity. Human rights frameworks were used to undermine positivist law, to cast the winners of the War as moral, not merely military, victors. (2009: 118 [emphasis in original])

However, despite this loosening of the grip of positivist law in light of universal principles, the Nuremberg Trials, as many have pointed out, were conducted by the United States as the occupying power in Germany, not by any supranational authority – a fact which reinforces the primacy of nation-states as the chief agents for protecting human rights. It has emerged, then, that the protection of the human rights of individuals depends entirely on the good will of governments, the irony being that it is almost invariably governments as the incarnation of sovereign power, who are the main violator of human rights. While the latter have been cast as having an essentially legal basis, it is this very basis which is part of the problem, because it assumes the primacy of the nation-state as chief enforcer.[1] Another way of putting it – a way which accords with Agamben's insights, as outlined in Chapter 1 – is to say that sovereign power, as both the violator and enforcer of human rights, thus determines the nature and mode of implementation of these rights. Thus, sovereign power is double-edged in the most negative sense. For even when human rights are protected, it can only be at the behest of sovereign power.

Studies which have failed to take into account the absolute nature of sovereign power and the problematic legal emphasis placed on the notion of 'rights' have endeavoured to find historical precursors to human rights, most often in the context of ancient Greece and Rome. In such studies, it is sometimes pointed out that, although the word 'right' may not have come into existence in Europe until between the twelfth or fourteenth centuries, other terms (such as the Greek *dike*, often translated as 'justice', or the Latin *ius*, referring to 'law', 'right' or 'justice') existed which convey a similar meaning, so the absence of the word 'rights' does not entail the absence of the concept. However, given the current legal emphasis, it seems to be stretching things in the extreme to argue that, in fact, the origins of human rights go back to Greece and Rome. Moreover, if it is judged that the legal basis of rights fails to evoke the full sense in which rights violations need to be prevented, such a genealogy is demonstrably inadequate. For it equates the evolution and emergence of the nation-state, most notably in the nineteenth century, with the emergence of the protection of human rights – a view which sets out to prove what is already accepted as true.

If, indeed, we were to follow Andrew Vincent's call and refuse to reduce human rights to a moral sphere which transcends politics (2010: 31–2), it behoves us, nevertheless, to keep actual macro political structures in view and to point out their limitations. While Vincent, to his credit, recognises that genocide is embedded within the very structure of the nation-state (2010: 106–8), there is a certain sense that he, like many others, does not go far enough in analysing the origins and nature of this Western mode of political and social organisation.[2] Here, it is worth noting Anthony Smith's characterisation of the centrality of the nation-state in modern political organisation: 'The nation state [now] is the norm of modern political organization and it is as ubiquitous as it is recent. The nation state is the almost undisputed foundation of world order, the main object of individual loyalties' (1971: 2, cited in Vincent 2010: 116 [Vincent's insert]).

While it is clear that rights declarations and legislation since 1945 bear no formal resemblance to what has gone before in this field – while, as a matter of current practice, human rights defences tend to be about the individual citizen self (thus, a self or subject within a nation-state), who may claim human rights insofar as they are recognised within a particular legal system (as is the case, for example, with the European Convention on Human Rights) – there is a history (or, more accurately, a genealogy) in the Western tradition, which can serve as an important lineage for deepening our understanding of human rights. To pick up this genealogy, however, requires that the notion of the human return to centre stage in the debate. No doubt scholars like Vincent would see this as an attempt to return to a version of natural rights based on the necessary concomitant of human nature. However, to return to the human is not to return to a notion of human nature, nor, indeed, to any fixed human essence; it is also to refuse to reduce the human to its biological being (Greek *zoē*) or, as has become familiar after Agamben, to 'bare life'. To begin on the path indicated, it is only necessary to evoke the most popular definition of human rights (even if this also is an almost wilful misrecognition of the predominance of the legal status of rights), which is: 'the rights one has simply because one is a human being' (see Donnelly 2003: 1). What, we may ask, does it mean to be a 'human being'? And what are the implications of this for an understanding of human rights?

NATURAL RIGHTS AS A PRECURSOR TO HUMAN RIGHTS?

It is sometimes suggested that the real origin of the contemporary notion of human rights is the seventeenth- and eighteenth-century idea of natural law and natural rights. The plausibility of this no doubt derives from the fact that, in both contexts, there is deemed to be a given and essential humanness called human nature, which is expressed in human rights. There are rights pertaining to a given and natural humanness, whether this be founded on the idea of human nature (which would include a capacity for reason and language) or on the idea of an essential biological being. In both cases, it could be said that such rights always already exist in virtue of being human; they are not in any way acquired. The newborn are just as much the bearers of natural or human rights as any adult human.

Despite appearances, however, there is, as Vincent shows (2010: 37–103), a fundamental discontinuity between two categories of rights: natural rights (based in the idea of nature) and human rights (based in the idea of civil society and the nation-state). This is not to deny that, in human rights debates, it can often seem, especially as echoed in the phrase 'in virtue of being human', that what is at issue are rights that derive from the mere fact of being born, that there is somehow a natural dimension that clings on in the modern era. As Vincent puts it: 'What we have in the late twentieth century are ghostly echoes of a largely redundant vocabulary or, alternatively, odd transmutations of an older terminology' (2010: 37).

Thus, after Hannah Arendt, many others (including Agamben, albeit from a critical perspective) have claimed that any articulation of human rights in the post-Enlightenment era is only possible in the context of the institutions of the nation-state. This is why stateless people are often unable to find redress for their situation. By contrast, we are proposing an alternative reading of human rights – one that is based neither on natural rights, nor on the civic instantiation of human rights within a state order as proposed by Vincent – but which transcends this altogether by revealing something about the ontology of the human itself.

Another decisive reason why natural law and natural rights no longer have any real connection to contemporary human rights campaigns is that such rights were founded in theism. Even Rousseau – guardian of the secularly oriented French Revolution – subscribed to deist principles when it came to the origin of nature. Famously, Rousseau writes, in his *Profession of Faith of a Savoyard Vicar*, as his first 'article of faith': 'I believe, therefore, that a will gives motion to and animates nature' (1969: 576). And later, he adds: 'This Being who can do what he wills, this Being who is his own act, this Being who, finally, whatever it may be, who gives motion to the universe and commands all things, I call God' (1969: 581). So nature, for Rousseau, might be the arbiter of all things, but God is the arbiter and origin of nature.[3]

Thus, it is the religious – or, at least, the theistic – basis of natural rights which distinguishes them from human rights. As Vincent puts it, for natural rights adherents: 'Nature without God made little or no sense' (2010: 71). Thus, a discontinuity, not continuity, reigns between the classical and modern era when it comes to the question of rights. And yet, it must be admitted that the concept of rights that one inherits as part of nature reminds us of the problem of human rights today, which is: on what basis can human rights be defended outside the framework of both the nation-state and biological life (bare life)? When it is said that the notion of human rights refers to those rights that one has in virtue of being human – even if this also implicit in the eighteenth-century *Declarations* and thus might be thought to give the human a certain dignity – the impression gained is that this is the very minimum one can hope for and that to be the recipient or bearer of such rights implies that one is on the brink of collapse. If, on the other hand, to be nothing but human is, in fact, to open the prospect of revealing the complexity of one's humanity, a very different conception comes into being. It is this that we shall elaborate on in later chapters. But now, we turn to the ambiguous place of human rights in the modern European political tradition.

'FREEDOM AND NECESSITY', 'PUBLIC AND PRIVATE'

Let us recall Arendt's point, that the:

> Rights of Man [. . .] had been defined as 'inalienable' because they were supposed to be independent of all governments; but it turned out that the moment human beings lacked their own government and had to fall back upon their minimum rights, no authority was left to protect them [. . .] (1968: 171–2)

In the history of European political thought since the Second World War, and especially in light of Hannah Arendt's work, the primacy of being a member of a political community arose as a key principle in human rights discourse. This was because to not be a citizen, to not be a member of a political community, was to be in a position in which one had nothing but one's humanity to call upon as a justification for having one's human rights recognised. Arendt points out that the 'Rights of Man', in the absence of citizenship, were, in effect, unenforceable because no one knew precisely what rights someone had who was no longer a member of any sovereign state. This leads to Arendt's well-known conclusion that only those who are members of a political community (of a public sphere) can have their rights protected. On this basis, it is clear that stateless people are also 'rightless' people:

> The calamity of the rightless is not that they are deprived of life, liberty and the pursuit of happiness, or of equality before the law and freedom of opinion – formulas which were designed to solve problems *within* given communities – but that they no longer belong to any political community whatsoever. Their plight is not that they are not equal before the law, but that no law exists for them; not that they are oppressed, but that nobody wants even to oppress them. (Arendt 1968: 175–6 [emphasis in original])

For Arendt, though, as for the tradition of European thought, statelessness does not just mean the absence of the means for protecting human rights; in other words, it is not just a pragmatic situation which is at issue. Rather, to not be part of a political community is to be expelled from humanity itself – it is to cease to be fully human:

> Not the loss of specific rights, then, but the loss of a community willing and able to guarantee any rights whatsoever, has been the calamity which has befallen ever-increasing numbers of people. Man, it turns out, can lose all so-called Rights of Man without losing his essential quality as a man, his human dignity. Only the loss of a polity itself expels him from humanity. (1968: 177)

There is an ambivalence (if this is the term) in Arendt's thinking when it comes to the plight of stateless people. This is evident when Arendt, on the one hand, argues that stateless people are unavoidably at the mercy of individual nation-states. Protection for them can only come from this source. For the fact is that there is no supranational or other institutional arrangement available in the era of modernity to lend succour to the stateless – to those who cannot claim any link with a political community. This is why, for stateless people between the two World Wars, it was often better to commit a crime and thus be inserted into a national legal system, than to remain in a condition of stateless-ness and live under the continual threat of expulsion from whichever country one happened to be in at the time (Arendt 1968: 166–7). To be part of the legal system is to be the beneficiary of whatever rights are integral to that system – access to a lawyer, the rule of *habeas corpus*, the right to a speedy trial and so on.

But for Arendt, on the other hand, the nation-state – although in decline, due to international power imbalances and to the drawing-up of national borders that took no account of the differences between peoples who were entrapped within such borders – is nevertheless an entity to be revered and sustained at all costs, as the only viable vehicle of political community. Thus, the *faute de mieux* argument – where stateless people can only have recourse to the nation-state for protec-tion, even if, ideally, it would be better to have a way of defending human rights in virtue of one's humanity independently of the nation-state – gives way to the argument that valorises the nation-state as the vehicle of political community. And it is the latter, above all, which is important, for it is what constitutes the human as human. As we have seen, one cannot be fully human outside of a political community. On this basis, the real decline and disappearance of the nation-state would be a terrible tragedy.

It is worth returning to the words that Arendt uses to reinforce her argument regarding the importance of political community for being human, because none of Arendt's commentators have picked up on the full significance of the position expressed at the end of part two of *The Origins of Totalitarianism*. Whether or not Arendt, later in her *oeuvre*, continued to subscribe to what she writes here is less impor-tant than the fact that she puts into words a position that has become hugely influential, touching as it does on the role of the public sphere in modernity and on the importance in European thinking of the opposi-tion between 'freedom and necessity'.

What, then, are we to make of those who are part of a social or cul-tural set-up where, in the commonly held European view, there is no viable political community? Or where people are unable to escape the travail of necessity and remain rooted in a struggle for sheer physical survival?

In a number of passages, Arendt sets out the implications for those in this predicament, those whose claim for protection in the absence of political community consigns them to nothing but 'the abstract naked-ness of being human' (1968: 179) – of being nothing but 'bare life'. Such people also exist in the sphere of what Arendt defines as the 'merely given' (or what, in other places, will be called 'necessity'). The 'merely given' – which is also *zoē* – is, in fact, a 'permanent threat to the public sphere' (181). The 'public sphere' is equivalent to political community. It is thus based in the legal structure of society and is constitutive of formal equality, whereas the sphere of *zoē* is one of natural differences and inequalities. It is only in the public sphere that political life proper can take place and actors can experience freedom. Arendt also calls this sphere pure artifice and creativity. What is crucial here is that the public sphere must be clearly demarcated, if not totally cut off from the private sphere, lest the realm of necessity comes to destroy the public sphere's basis in equality and freedom.

Here we should also recall Arendt's criticism of the French Revolution – that it brought questions of survival and necessity onto the centre of the political stage. Driven by the bodily needs of the poor and pity for their plight, the French Revolution – unlike the American Revolution, which preserved a properly political domain in the form of a stable constitutional framework – led to the domination of the politi-cal by social and moral concerns, something that ultimately produced the Terror (Arendt 2009). This denigration of the social as a domain of necessity, of bare life, that must be resolutely separated from the domain of the political forms the background to Arendt's scepticism regarding the revolutionary French *Declaration of the Rights of Man*: such rights were not properly political, as they were driven by the emotion of pity for the suffering masses. They thus expressed the illegitimate intrusion of bare life into the world of politics (see Rancière 2004: 298).

The problem, particularly if one is not part of the Western tradition, is that political community and freedom, relative to all those who might make a claim on them, are in short supply. A very significant propor-tion of the world's population thus cannot qualify as being fully human on Arendt's account, just as a slave, who, having no civil status (and often not even a name) and existing entirely in the sphere of necessity, cannot be fully human. As though recognising the possible implica-tions for the slave populations of the past, Arendt makes the following concession:

[I]n light of recent events it is possible to say that even slaves still belonged to some sort of human community; their labour was needed, used and exploited, and this kept them within the pale of humanity. To be a slave was after all to have a distinctive character, a place in society – more than the abstract nakedness of being human and nothing but human. (1968: 177)

As we can read in *The Human Condition*, however, there was 'contempt toward the slave, who had been despised because he served only life's necessities' (Arendt 1958: 316). Even though it is possible to say that Arendt herself might have had a wavering attitude towards the slave and was prepared to admit him into humanity, there is no doubt that, on a broader plane, public life – the life of the polis and political community; the life of freedom and the *vita activa*; this life raised out of all necessity – is the only truly human life. Human rights, therefore, can only be based on *this* life and are so for essential, not contingent, reasons.

Furthermore, Arendt says that rights deriving from the fact of being human are distrusted on the grounds that such rights 'are granted even to savages' (1968: 180). Moreover, not to be part of a political community (and this is why it needs to be brought to everyone) means – as we have pointed out elsewhere (see Lechte and Newman 2012) – that 'the dark background mere givenness' risks breaking 'into the political scene as the alien which in its all too obvious difference reminds us of the limitations of human activity' (Arendt 1968: 181). Such a panoply of terms reminds us of what threatens to undermine and usurp our humanity as established in the *polis*: 'difference'; 'mere givenness'; 'savageness'; 'necessity'; 'the abstract nakedness of being human'; nature; 'mere existence'. Above all, the 'great danger', says Arendt, is that people will be 'thrown back, in the midst of civilization, on their natural givenness, on their mere differentiation' (182). As such, people will forfeit all the civilising aspects of political community – most notably, a chance to experience freedom. As such, 'they begin to belong to the human race in much the same way as animals belong to a specific animal species' (182). Finally, the danger is that humanity might 'produce barbarians from its own midst by forcing millions of people into conditions which, despite all appearances are the conditions of savages' (182). Moreover, for Arendt, existence for 'savages' is existence without history – lives lived without having left anything to the 'common world'; people 'thrown back into a peculiar state of nature' (180).

The question is: in what sense can 'savages' be human – if at all? They would seem to be that part of humanity which is excluded from humanity. Here we might ask: is it simply a question of seeing these excluded people as included in the category of humanity? Or, perhaps more interestingly, is it precisely their exclusion that constitutes their humanity in a positive (and political) sense, contra Arendt? Are these excluded people, to put it in Agamben's terms, a remnant, neither majority nor minority, but a subject irreducible to these categories and not coinciding with itself (2005b: 57)? Here, we can recall Rancière's idea of politics as the dissonance created by the claim by some excluded group to inclusion and equality on the basis of a universality, which is, paradoxically, denied to them (see Rancière 1999).[4]

Thus, on one level, such people are excluded because they simply exist and achieve no more than a subsistence level production, which barely enables them to reproduce. This, in Arendt's terms, is necessity writ large – the domain which counts for nothing other than physical survival, but which must be conquered if freedom and full humanity are to be realised. The key point is that, for Arendt and the European/ Western tradition which she represents, there can be no freedom or political action, no humanity in the fullest sense and no equality in the realm of necessity. The latter is always to be transcended. Arendt's clearest statement of this is to be found in her discussion of ancient Greece in the chapter of *The Human Condition* devoted to the distinction between the public and private realms. Here, 'public' equates with '*polis*' or politics and 'private' equates with the *oikos* or economy as household. As Arendt explains:

> [In Ancient Greece] the very term 'political economy' would have been a contradiction in terms: whatever was 'economic', related to the life of the individual and the *survival of the species*, was a non-political, household affair by definition. (1958: 29 [emphasis added])

Of course, without attending to physical needs, such as shelter – the realm of survival – no political life is possible: 'without owning a house a man could not participate in the affairs of the world because he had no location in it which was properly his own' (29–30). By way of bringing this point to a close, our author goes on to say that: 'What all Greek philosophers, no matter how opposed to *polis* life, took for granted is that freedom is exclusively located in the political realm, that necessity is primarily a prepolitical phenomenon' (31).

While much continental thinking has now begun to take a different tack on the notion of *oikos* (see Agamben, Derrida and Mondzain, for example), seeing in it the ideas of relation, distribution and administration, as well as the very basis of political life, Arendt's thinking is part of a generation for whom freedom and necessity were opposing poles. There can never be any freedom in necessity.

If a public sphere based in a political community can only ever be the endpoint in human destiny and never its beginning, and if in order to arrive at this endpoint one must first endure necessity, clearly some (whether individuals, peoples or groups) are not going to make it. Arendt's 'savages' are not going to make it. Although it was thought in the abstract and, in particular, at the time of the French Declaration, that the human as human was a relatively unproblematic notion, possibly because it implied a degree of transcendence, the advent of modernity has shown that this is no longer the case. For modernity, the primitive in all of us must be caged and given succour before politics proper can be realised and before human rights can, in any sense, be implemented.

AN EVALUATION OF ARENDT'S EUROPEAN ARGUMENT

Before moving on to examine slavery as an example of the human in a condition of absolute servitude and necessity, we draw attention to the problematic nature of several points raised by Arendt in her discussion of 'public and private' in ancient Greece (Athens).

First, let us address the claim that it is pointless beginning with a notion of the human as such in defending human rights, because such a being is not fully human. One must start with the campaign for the 'right to have rights', that is, to be admitted into a political community. On what basis, however, can such a campaign take place? Presumably only on the basis that those who deserve the 'right to have rights' are, in some essential sense, human. There is a cruel circularity here, a catch-22, whereby stateless people are trapped in an ontological (and real) no-man's land between humanity and non-humanity. Contra Arendt, we argue that unless the notion of the human independent of the *polis* is addressed, the whole idea of the 'right to have rights' does not makes sense.

Second, for Arendt – and, no doubt, the tradition of which she is a part – difference (which Arendt calls 'natural' difference or 'mere given-ness'), far from being the bane of the *polis*, has to be seen as the very basis of all rights and, most importantly, human rights. If there were no differences (and these do not have to be only racial or ethnic, as Arendt implies), the rationale for the enforcement of rights against prejudice and injustice would melt away. In short, if freedom in the *polis* can only take place in the *suppression* of original difference, it cannot be said that difference is not an essential part of being human.

Third – and this has been said before – to reduce the fully human to the form found in civil society runs the risk, as sociologists such as Pierre Bourdieu have shown, of erasing the difference between formal freedom and equality, and substantive freedom and equality.

Fourth, if the human is only fully realised in a political community, as described by Arendt, and as political community as a fully-fledged public sphere has only been realised in the West and particularly in Europe, the implication is that, at best, a question mark hangs over the heads of those who are not part of this tradition. And, as even Arendt herself acknowledges, it is these peoples most of all who should be the beneficiaries of human rights protection.

Finally, as we shall see, the Arendtian and European conception of Athenian society as being essentially structured around the private *oikos* and public *polis* is largely ideological. Indeed, most ancient historians would agree (see Finley 1980) that life in ancient Athens was not driven by the *Hauswirtschaft* (household economy) and that the economy was also part of the public domain, with, for one thing, slaves being used by the state on various public works. However, Arendt gives the impression that only chattel slavery within the household existed.

For their part, Austin and Vidal-Naquet indicate that the Greek term *oikonomia*, from which *oikos* derives, means:

'management of the household' (the *oikos*) in its broadest sense (domestic economy, one might say), and not only in its strictly economic sense. It can also mean 'management, administration, organisation' in a more general sense and be applied to different spheres; thus one may talk of the '*oikonomia* of the affairs of the city'. (1977: 8–9)

Thus, it is not possible to find a clear-cut instance, in practice, of the opposition between so-called freedom and necessity.

Scholars in the field of human rights research almost invariably take as valid Arendt's version of the relation between necessity and freedom, as understood since Aristotle, as the basis of politics and the nation-state. In other words, this whole field of scholarship more or less takes over, holus-bolus, the idea that politics only becomes possible once basic needs have been satisfied, even if it is acknowledged that the attempt to realise the 'right to have rights' raises a problem regarding the status of stateless people (see Vincent 2010: 173–5).

SLAVERY – OR FREEDOM AND NECESSITY REVISITED

'Natural community in the household therefore', Arendt says, 'was born of necessity, and necessity ruled over all activities performed in it' (1958: 30). And to continue the summary, she adds:

> The realm of the *polis*, on the contrary, was the sphere of freedom, and if there was a relationship between these two spheres, it was a matter of course that the mastering of the necessities of life in the household was the condition for freedom of the *polis*. (1958: 31)

The issue raised here, with regard to the question of human rights, is that while many contemporary analysts want to find a formal lineage in the evolution of legal rights, such as may be possible with the history of citizenship, the legal basis of rights, as we have seen, is of a strictly recent origin. However, what is evident from a survey of the historical record is that situations like chattel slavery, which raises the question of the nature of the human, are not difficult to find. In other words, while a history of political community will almost certainly not be, formally speaking, about the history of rights, human history nevertheless includes many substantive situations – situations which were considered too undignified to be accorded any proximity to the domain of politics – where the protection of human rights would have been relevant. If human rights cannot be fully understood without an appreciation of the nature of the human, then it will, at least in part, be within the realm of what European thought calls 'necessity' that the true nature of the human will emerge. In short, the history of the human is the best indicator of the evolution of human rights. This is why we need to turn to slavery as it occurred in ancient Athens and Rome.

Athenian and Roman Slavery

The general consensus is that slavery in Athens and Rome served both an economic (in the modern sense) and social function. Economically, the societies in question could not, without slavery, have been able to produce the wealth necessary to enable educated men to have the time available to engage in politics.[5] Moreover, broad cultural achievement (for example, in the arts) was only possible on the basis of slave labour. Socially, slavery (or unfree labour) sustained the key formal division in society between free and unfree members. It therefore constituted the basis of social status. As it is generally presented, labour itself was of low social status, and the slave was the incarnation of this. On the other hand, to own slaves (Aristotle apparently owned thirteen) was also a mark of elevated social status.

According to Yvon Garlan: 'The fact is that, in the eyes of the Greeks, slavery was relevant only to the economic sphere, that is, to the art of managing a family unit, an *oikos*' (1988: 15). A slave was considered to be human (*anthropos*), but was also a possession, the main point being that an unfree person could never become a citizen and, thus, a political actor. In sum, the rule was: once unfree, forever unfree. At least, this may have been the case in Greece. When the Roman situation is considered, manumitted slaves could apparently vote in Roman assemblies (see Finley 1980: 83, citing Livy 7.16.7). This serves as a reminder that even if freedom is not realised, the human is essentially invested with the potential to become free. This is because slavery cannot be understood to be an essential quality of the human, but is always a contingent thing. Consequently, there is no slavery without enslavement. There is no 'slave nature', despite Aristotle (and Nietzsche) (Aristotle 1995: 1291a, 8).[6]

Almost invariably, it is made to appear that as the division between free and unfree is the key to Athenian and Roman society, slavery becomes the incarnation of unfreedom, as citizenship becomes the mark of freedom. Furthermore, unfreedom and a concern for necessity are also inextricably linked.

If we turn to the work of M. I. Finley, a key point for this historian of generally recognised formidable erudition in the field is that Athenian and Roman societies were 'slave societies'. That is, unlike the situation in the southern United States, where slavery was but one element in the economy, slavery in Athens and Rome was both integral and essential to the very structure of these societies. We are talking, if Finley is to be believed, about societies founded on slavery (1980: 67–92). Some important implications follow from this:

1. By far, the most significant labour in the productive process is done by slaves (the existence of some free labour notwithstanding).
2. Such slave labour cannot be viewed as 'labour power' (where labour, as such, becomes a commodity), but is to be understood as equivalent to the body of the slave – for the slave, and not his labour, is owned by the master and is, therefore, an object to be bought and sold.
3. Slave labour is under the complete control of the master, who is not subject to any external monitoring or impediment with regard to what he requires of his slave.
4. Slave labour is entirely labour 'for others' and not, to any extent, labour 'for oneself'.

Finley reiterates the key point that in 'all Greek or Roman establishments larger than the family unit, whether on the land or in the city, the *permanent* work force was composed of slaves' (1980: 81 [emphasis in original]).

The implications of the latter point are as follows: slaves are present in Athenian economy and society not as, for example, craftsman are still incidentally present in the capitalist economy, but as white collar labour is now the dominant form of labour in today's capitalist economy, based in the service and information technology industries. Moreover, the dominant social division in ancient society is between those who are free and those who are unfree. Understood in this way, the very notion of the *polis* must evoke the notion of slave – something which is almost universally overlooked when considering this topic. What conventional wisdom attempts to do is to acknowledge that there were slaves, but that the latter were an incidental historical fact which did not change the true quality of the *polis* as based in freedom and equality. This, then, is to go beyond the simplistic idea that slaves provided the leisure time that made it possible for educated men to engage in politics. For labour provided by debt-bondage – or, indeed, free labour – could equally provide this outcome. The *polis* was not the incarnation of freedom, because any freedom worth the name must be universal (as Hegel said).

The ambiguity of being a slave is captured by the following statement by Finley:

> If a slave is a property with a soul [Aristotle], a non-person and yet indubitably a biological human being, institutional procedures are to be expected that will degrade and undermine his humanity and so distinguish him from human beings who are not property. (1980: 95)

In another text, Finley gives a more cryptic, but still revealing, characterisation: a slave is both a person and property. As a person, 'slaves were human in the eyes of the gods, at least to the extent that their murder required some form of purification and that they were themselves involved in ritual acts, such as baptism' (Finley 1985: 62). The scandal of slavery, then, is that a person (human) can be treated as property. The paradox of slavery is that this property is also a person and therefore fully human. The prevailing and widely held contemporary view that full humanness can only be achieved in the *polis* thus breaks down.

To the extent that someone is a person, they can be individuated, identified, have a personality and, of course, be punished and victimised. Personhood, indeed, is a very significant element in being human. When it comes to labour in Graeco–Roman times, then, a person, whether slave or free, performed the labour. Not only, as we have seen, is there no abstract concept of labour–power, but as Finley points out: 'Neither in Greek nor in Latin was there a word with which to express the general notion of "labour" or the concept of labour "as a general social function"' (1985: 81).

ARISTOTLE AND SLAVERY

As is well-known – without the full significance being fully appreciated – Aristotle devotes a large portion of Book I of the *Politics* to a consideration of slavery as it exists within the state apparatus. Here it is acknowledged that the household is divided into a number of parts, including the division between slaves and freemen (1995: 1253b1), and that there is an argument that slavery is founded on convention, not on the natural predisposition of those who end up as slaves. Aristotle will later make quite clear that, for his part, this argument is fallacious and that some are born slaves, while others are born free.[7]

Quickly, Aristotle arrives at the point where the necessaries of life are crucial, so that without the necessaries being satisfied, nothing of significance can be achieved, least of all politics. In this context, the slave is that form of property which is an instrument and crucial to production. Life in the full (*bios*), of course, is 'action and not production, and therefore the slave is the minister of action [not the subject/author of action]' (1254a7–8). In terms of belonging, the slave belongs to the master, while the master can never belong to the slave. And this occurs according to nature: 'he who is by nature not his own but another's man, is by nature a slave; and he may be said to be another's man who, being a slave is also a possession' (1254a13–15). Thus, we see, and Aristotle is moved to further confirm this (13254a20–3), that as one is essentially and by nature a slave, one is also a possession and an instrument to be used to satisfy the need for the 'necessaries' of life. In other words, for Aristotle, it is impossible for a slave to ever become free. Indeed, it would be going against nature to try to bring about such a thing.

A doubt then seems to creep into Aristotle's thinking. For although nature would like to distinguish between the bodies of freemen and slaves, so that slaves would have bodies appropriate for work and freemen would have bodies appropriate for a life in the *polis*, 'the opposite often happens', so that slaves often have the bodies and souls of freemen (1254b33–4). Perhaps unsurprisingly, Aristotle manages to get around this problem by pointing out that it is a natural fact that body differences in humans (and the slave *is* still human) are not extreme, but that, in any case, the real differences occur with the soul, which remains invisible. This is where natural inferiority is located. Whereas the soul of a freeman is very pronounced, that of a slave is virtually non-existent. So Aristotle can still conclude that: 'It is clear, then, that some men are by nature free, and others slaves, and that for these latter slavery is both expedient and right' (1255c1–2).

In his hierarchy of categories at the end of Book I, Aristotle raises the question of the 'excellence' that a slave might have, as compared to a freeman. Household management, to be sure, attends more to men than to things and to 'human excellence more than to the excellence of property which we call wealth and to the excellence of freemen more than to the excellence of slaves'. A question, says Aristotle, 'may indeed be raised, whether there is any excellence at all in a slave beyond those of an instrument and of a servant' (1259b20–2).

Here, Aristotle has to do some very fancy footwork, for he wants to attribute minimal excellence to the slave, so that the slave can be defined as human, but, at the same time, be as close as possible to necessity, having 'no deliberative faculty at all' (1260a12–13). So the slave is qualitatively unable to rule over a freeman, just as he is qualitatively mired in necessity and can never attain to the realm of freedom or deliberative thought, yet, despite all this, he is fundamentally human and has a soul. The slave is the lowest category of the human and constitutes a necessary element of the qualitative hierarchy, which, for Aristotle, is the very condition of the possibility of conceptualising the human as human.[8]

Malcolm Bull has added a further dimension to the argument by suggesting that the issue turns on the incomplete nature of a slave's soul – a fact which enables him to be ruled by another, but at the same time be defined as human, albeit an incomplete human, because endowed with an incomplete soul. As Bull says: 'If slavery is the rule of the slave's body by a soul of another, then the very possibility of slavery depends upon the slave's body not being governed by the slave's own soul' (1998: 101). The problem, as Bull well shows, is to know how a slave's soul can have the necessary autonomy that it must have in order to be human, while at the same time being naturally disposed to be governed by a master.

Clearly, the issue of slavery in Aristotle would be of little more than exotic interest if the *Politics* was not such an influential text in the history of Western political thought and if, furthermore, slavery was not so intimately connected to the distinction between freedom and necessity, which serves as the Enlightenment and post-Enlightenment definition of politics as essentially located in the public sphere of nation-states. It needs to be made clear that we have not sought to interpret the meaning of slavery over the whole of Aristotle's *oeuvre*, most notably in the *Nicomachean Ethics* and the *Economics*. Our task has simply been to interpret the meaning and significance of slavery in Book I of the *Politics*. In this regard, and although the analogy is not absolutely perfect, it is important to recognise that especially in terms of life chances and social status, today's stateless people closely approximate yesterday's slaves as the latter which are described in the *Politics*. Thus, if Aristotle's text is foundational, it is so in the sense that it marks a distinction that goes to the very heart of the problem of contemporary politics, which concerns how it might be possible to defend the human rights of those bereft of the 'right to have rights'. Thus far, our presentation indicates that a total rethinking of the Western tradition in political and social theory is required if any headway is to be made in improving the situation of those who are external to, and excluded from, every possible *polity*.

While many readings of Book I of the *Politics* are ready to concede that Aristotle's is an ideological presentation of slavery, few have noted the exact basis on which a slave was considered a slave, namely, that he ministered to the physical needs of the community and, in particular, the household; for, so it goes, one must first solve the problem of physical survival before actual freedom is possible. From a Western perspective, whoever is forced to work to solve the problem of mere survival tends to assume the lowly status of a slave. In the nineteenth century, the survival problem was seen to be solved through free labour or labour power. Neither Marx nor Aristotle differ one iota on this point. For both of them, the solution to the problem is essentially prior to the realisation of freedom. Where they differ is simply with regard to the *way* that this problem is solved.

It is not, therefore, just a matter of whether or not Aristotle sought to confirm the superiority of one class over another, but of recognising the lowly status that work had, insofar as it was associated with pure survival (*zoē*). In the Western tradition, such work has always been denigrated, so that those societies which were thought to have to devote all their energies to producing/finding enough to enable 'bare life' ('subsistence' societies) have always been ranked low on the world hierarchy, where it has been a matter of 'First World' nations versus 'Fourth World' nations, now called 'developed' and 'developing' nations, respectively. In light of such prejudicial categories, is it really conceivable that stateless people whose origins are often in 'Fourth World' nations will be allowed just access to 'First World' nations? This is the question that any human rights campaign worthy of that name must address. And in addressing it, the nature of the human must be uppermost in one's thinking.

ANTIGONE

Much has been written about the struggle presented in Sophocles's tragedy *Antigone* between the 'ethical' law of kinship and the law of the state or between, as Hegel puts it, 'the unwritten and infallible law of the gods' (Hegel 1979: 261) and the state. In one sense, the drama is about the existence or otherwise of the *right* to oppose sovereign power in light of a duty that transcends the laws of the *polity*. As King Creon says: 'He whom the State appoints must be obeyed' (Sophocles 1974: 144, ln 665). For Creon (and perhaps for all sovereign power), the mere fact of commanding, irrespective of what is commanded, should elicit obedience. In Creon's terms, obedience for its own sake is what ensures that the state will endure. As well as Antigone, surrounding Creon in the play are his son, Haemon, the blind prophet, Teiresias, and Creon's wife, Eurydice. Each is there in both word and deed to impress upon Creon – and, no doubt, upon all sovereign power – that pure obedience does not suffice and, indeed, can lead to the undoing of even the most totalitarian of regimes. Whether or not this is simply a version of poetic justice or relates to something intrinsic to the wielding of state power is the key issue.

Creon orders that Antigone be put to death for attempting to bury her brother, Polynices, slain in an attempt to overthrow Creon's rule. As a traitor, Creon declares, Antigone's brother has no right to a ritual burial, whereas her other brother, Eteocles, who defended the state is to receive a full and honourable burial. Haemon and then Teiresias try to counsel Creon from carrying out such a harsh punishment – the first because he has heard that the people think the action unjust and against the law of the gods; the second because such action will bring calamity to the state, not ensure its survival.

Here some remarks are warranted with regard to the status of Antigone in Sophocles' tragedy. In this regard, it is clear, as has often been said, that Antigone herself is high-born, being the daughter of Oedipus. Even though Creon says: 'We'll have no woman's law here, while I live' (Sophocles 1974, line 558) and, 'Better to be beaten, if need be, by a man, / Than let a woman get the better of us' (715–16), he recognises that Antigone is not someone who can be lightly dismissed, that even though, formally, Antigone could never be a full member of the *polis*, substantively, she is a force to be reckoned with. If she were not, the play itself would not have emerged as a key tragedy in Western culture. Almost despite it, therefore, the drama shows that being a full member of the *polis* (or its equivalent) is not the indispensable condition for realising one's humanness and that women, even in light of severe discrimination, are capable of asserting their humanity. The principle brought to light here, then, in relation to the slave and to women, is that discrimination can never erase one's humanness. On this point, it is important to note that both women and slaves were drawn to the cult of Dionysus and often achieved a rich religious life outside the *polis* (see Jean-Pierre Vernant 1978: 80–1). As we will see later, the degradation of Polynices in light of Creon's order does not detract from the fact of his humanness. The principle to be fully acknowledged here is that victimage, no matter how ferocious it might be (and those in Nazi death camps come to mind), can never erase humanness, but even, in fact, reinforces it.

From a modern perspective, however, it might be said that Creon fails to treat Polynices as human, because a traitor to the state cannot be the beneficiary of justice and deserves no more than to be totally destroyed, much as the terrorists today who oppose the hegemony of Western states are deemed only worthy of destruction. However, it is precisely because Polynices is human that the failure to allow a proper burial creates such a scandal, just as we saw that it was the fact that a slave *is* human that creates a scandal. Even as a traitor, Polynices signals his humanness, and, implicitly, Creon, like any contemporary audience to the play, knows this. So in being 'left unburied, left to be eaten / By dogs and vultures, a horror for all to see' (205–6), the impact of Polynices' humanness comes across to the audience even more strongly.

Moreover, as Andrew Benjamin (2010) shows, a key passage by the Chorus introduces the enigma of the human, even if some translations brush over this.[9] Benjamin focuses on the key Greek terms – '*ta deina*', which he translates as 'astounding/wonderful', but points out that Heidegger translates the same terms as '*das Unheimliche*', which literally translates to 'unhomely', and they are famously translated in Freud and elsewhere as 'uncanny' (Benjamin 2010: 99). The point is that the human cannot be definitively pinned down and remains an enigma or a question mark to be pondered, perhaps endlessly. Such a notion of the human would transcend any simple division between *oikos* and *polis*, private and public, necessity and freedom.

There may be an objection that today the state is not the personal fiefdom of a single individual, but is, in Western-style democracies, in the hands of many representatives acting as the executives of the people. And, of course, the structure of the modern state is very different from that presented in *Antigone*. But the words of Creon could easily be transposed into a modern context: 'He whom the State appoints must be obeyed' (665), for he is supposed to be the legitimate ruler. Indeed, we could say that absolute authority is afforded to the sovereign precisely by virtue of it being formally democratic; the sovereign derives its legitimacy and authority to act from the will of the people (no matter how flimsy and implausible the mandate and no matter how decrepit our democratic processes actually are).[10] As a result, everyone must, for example, submit to biometric scanning at airports, because the state demands it in its perpetual reduction of transcendence to fact and situation.

It remains to indicate, now, that the modern state, especially in light of Hegel's philosophy, maintains a clear distinction between those who are members and those who are not members of the *polity*, with all the disadvantages that the latter entails – disadvantages most clearly signalled in the figure of the stateless person.

Hegel and Slavery/Necessity

Our main concern now is with Hegel's interpretation of *Antigone* and his view of the relationship between tragedy and slavery. However, it is worth noting, by way of introduction, some aspects of Hegel's view of slavery in the section of the *Phenomenology of Spirit* (1979), translated as 'Lordship and Bondage'. Thus, after each has staked his own life, the bondsman (or slave) *qua* bondsman ends up working for the Lord. Of course, for Hegel, work, on one level, is an indication of the way that the subordinated self-consciousness recognises the master as master. Although, as many have pointed out, Hegel's text is not a sociological treatise, it is worth considering the status of work here. Would it be similar, for example, to the forms of work done in ancient Greece to enable the class of masters to engage in politics and all the pursuits that freedom entails?

The difficulty in finding confirmation of such an argument – at least initially – is that, unlike Aristotle, Hegel sees slavery as but one phase of the dialectic of World History, within which the struggle for recognition takes place and finds its apogee in the recognition that all humans are free, not that one is free (as with Oriental despotisms) and not that some are free (as in Greece and Rome). Freedom is universal or it is not at all. So, finally, the well-known outcome is that while the slave recognises the master as master, the master ultimately recognises that his freedom and self-certainty are tied to the work of the slave. But more than this, the master recognises that through work, the slave becomes his equal; for recognition from a dependent consciousness cannot give the self-certainty of *'being-for-self'* (Hegel 1979: 117 [emphasis in original]). Only when recognition occurs between equals is it a worthwhile form of recognition.

It is difficult to do justice here to the complexity of Hegel's philosophical position. However, three things can be noted. The first is that work (and its object) is the medium through which recognition takes place. In no way is work to be understood as an end; it is not, therefore, to be valued in its own right. This is similar to Aristotle's position. The second point is that work as necessity is to be sublated or transcended, so that it forms the foundation of freedom. In Hegel's words: 'To be sure necessity as such is not yet freedom; but freedom presupposes necessity and contains it sublated within itself' (1991: 233). The third point is that where work has difficulty in providing for basic needs, freedom is also difficult. As Hegel says in *Lectures on the Philosophy of World History*, 'Aristotle has long since observed that man turns to universal and more exalted things only after his basic needs have been satisfied' (1993: 155 [emphasis in original]).

Even allowing for the dialectical sophistication of Hegel's notion of work in the *Phenomenology*, it is clear that there is no freedom *in* work, for work can never be an end in itself. Work, for Hegel, can never be an authentic *way of life*. Rather, it is the foundation of freedom that enables it to be sublated. What, then, does Hegel have to say about tragedy and slavery? And what is its relevance for human rights?

Hegel on Tragedy and Slavery

Tina Chanter, in her commentary on Hegel and tragedy, cites key passages on tragedy from Hegel's *Aesthetics*, in order to show that the condition of slavery can never give rise to tragedy. This is because tragedy can only arise from the free actions of individuals, not from those oppressed by an external power. She elaborates on this by saying that:

Hegel is able to maintain tragedy as a site of reconciliation by admitting only those conflicts that can be said to be ethical as the locus of collision, thereby purifying in advance the contents of tragedy, such that slavery is excluded as a tragic theme. To include slavery within the orbit of tragedy would be to contaminate it with a contradiction that remains unthinkable and irresolvable by Hegelian logic: slavery becomes the excluded unthought ground of tragedy, and Antigone is decipherable as a figuring of its exclusion. (2010: 64)

Furthermore, as Chanter sees it, Hegel's position is that, '[d]ue to its injustice, slavery is not a topic that tragedy can purify through artistic presentation' (65). The view that slavery (and, no doubt, oppression in general) cannot be part of art's engagement only serves to reinforce the actual tragedy experienced by the slave. For to the European mind that Hegel represents (at least in large part), no words etched on his shackles, no figures gouged into the walls of his abode, no object fabricated in moments of unsupervised time – none of these could be heart-rending and poetic evocations of the human of which the slave is the incarnation. For Hegel, a slave cannot even express the agony of his own servitude. The slave can only remain silent. The dialectic thus breaks down when it comes to slavery; for the actual condition of slaves offers no way out, no path to freedom generated by the very fact of necessity.

As Chanter also notes, in Hegel's interpretation of *Antigone*, the drama is played out in Creon's terms: private family ethical obligations can be played out, but only in so far as they do not put the state at risk. Antigone cannot enter the political realm unless she obeys that realm's strictures. In Chanter's words: 'Hegel takes for granted that the only representation of the political that *Antigone* offers is the one that Creon represents' (2010: 66).

CONCLUSION

It could thus be argued that, structurally speaking, little has altered since Sophocles' day, when he cast Creon in the role of sovereign power and had him proclaim that everything must work towards the security and integrity of the state as the realm of politics. What the history of the human reveals – if not the history of 'rights' as such – is that the distinction between the political and the non-political, defined according to whether or not one is a member of a political community like a state, has fundamentally contributed to making the difficulties faced by stateless people almost insuperable.

Because it became clear that the history of human rights, in the sense that we are familiar with this expression today, cannot be forged on a genealogy of rights, we saw that, by contrast, the human provides a rich tapestry upon which to highlight the key issues faced by any defence of human rights. With the history of slavery, we saw that the key to maintaining servitude is the rigorous policing of the division between *oikos* and *polis*, private and public, religion and politics. To be excluded from the *polis* entails an exclusion of the human from the human or, to put it in Agamben's terms, we have an exclusion which is also an inclusion.

It now remains to investigate, in the following chapter, the dynamics of Agamben's critique of human rights and, in particular, the notion that he presents of 'bare life'. For it is the human presented as essentially the pure biological existence that is bare life which goes to the heart of the way that the modern nation-state functions today, particularly in relation to stateless people.

Notes

1 See Andrew Vincent, who writes: 'Many have regarded rights as just positive legal facts' (Vincent 2010: 13).
2 For Vincent, human rights should be viewed as political, rather than legal or moral concerns. They invoke the idea of a civil state or political community based on public law, citizenship and the recognition of certain standards of civic behaviour. They are, as he puts it, a vocabulary of the civic state. While acknowledging the paradox that it is also the state which is the main violator of human rights – and here he makes a distinction, albeit a somewhat tenuous one from our point of view, between the nation-state and the civic state – he maintains, following in many ways Arendt's argument, that the basic aspects of our humanity, as reflected by human rights, are realised only through citizenship, through membership of a constitutionally self-limited civil state.
3 The principles of the theory of the Social Contract – an Enlightenment idea, which had Rousseau as one of its signatories – are also, we should recall, founded on the presupposition of the state of nature given by God as the origin of society. Natural law and natural rights would be based on a similar foundation, which makes them very different from a post-Enlightenment view of things, where verification of the historical veracity of foundations becomes the order of the day.
4 See also Rancière's critique of Arendt on human rights (2004).
5 As Austin and Vidal-Naquet put it: 'servile labour [. . .] appeared to the Greeks to be the unavoidable precondition of civilized life' (1977: 18).
6 There is no doubt that Arendt would agree with this, so that, theoretically,

a slave or those mired in necessity can escape their condition. The point, however, is that such people must escape their condition, in order to qualify to be fully human. For, to repeat, only members of a political community are fully human for Arendt.

7 Given the astonishingly weak arguments that Aristotle presents regarding slavery and given that the majority of what Aristotle has to say on this subject is to be found within the opening Book I of the *Politics*, it has to be wondered why this text has been so seminal in the history of Western political thought. Our suggestion would be that the answer has to do with the strategic place, as we shall see, that necessity occupies in Aristotle's thought – a place in relation to which slavery is fundamental. Not that there are not those amongst contemporary classicists who, as Finley says, have tried 'to argue this section of the *Politics* away; Aristotle was being tentative, it is said, and was himself dissatisfied and aware of the flaws in his demonstration. The apologia', Finley quickly points out, 'cannot be substantiated' (Finley 1980: 119).

8 Although women (in relation to men) and children (in relation to parents) also manifest qualities of essential subordination, they do so, Aristotle claims, in ways very different from those of the slave (1260a10–41; 1260b1–20).

9 For example, in the opening lines uttered by the Chorus in the Penguin edition of *Antigone* (1974), anthrópou is translated as 'man', rather than as 'the human': 'Wonders are many on earth, and the greatest of these / Is man' (339–40, 135).

10 Indeed, as Agamben shows, the acclamations and rituals that once glorified sovereigns and authoritarian leaders are no less present in modern democratic societies in the form of 'public opinion' transmitted by the apparatus of the media (see 2011: 255–6).

Chapter 3

AGAMBEN AND THE RISE OF 'BARE LIFE'

> In the era of biopolitics, there is no transcendence: substance (life in general) is not independent of the different modes (forms of life), but the *unlimited – or 'anarchical' – totality of the modes themselves*, different merely according to their degree of intensity and power. (Ojakangus 2005: 12 [emphasis in original])

As we proposed in the previous chapter, to exclude human beings from humanity does not erase their humanness and, indeed, may actually confirm it. In large part, this and the following chapter set out to verify this statement by pinning down the key elements in Agamben's approach to power and politics in contemporary Western societies. Once clarified, these points shall put us in a much better position to appreciate and evaluate the significance of the notion of the 'camp' as the key tendency, according to Agamben, in democratic politics today.

Of course, we now know that Agamben is indebted to Aristotle's distinction in defining life in terms of *zoē* (life as mired in necessity and the satisfaction of basic needs, but also life as natural life or as aliveness) and *bios* (life as a *form* or *way* of life). *Bios*, as a political life, was a way of life; as such, it was the way of freedom. This freedom is possible to the extent that the exclusion of bare life founds the 'city of men' (= the *polity*). In our view, this is similar to Arendt's position in relation to ancient Greek society, where the exclusion of pure necessity founds the realm of action as freedom and creativity – the political realm proper. Agamben's focus is on the paradoxical nature of this exclusion – a paradox that arises in an analogous way, as we shall see, in relation to the exception. For it is not a matter of the exclusion of bare life being radical or absolute, so that there would be no contact at all between what is excluded and the sphere from which it is excluded; rather, this is an exclusion which is also, on one level, an inclusion, such that it can, in some sense, also 'belong' to the realm of politics from which the exclusion takes place: 'There is politics because man is the living being who, in language, separates and opposes himself to his own bare life and, at the same time, maintains himself in relation to that bare life in an inclusive exclusion' (Agamben 1998: 8). We have already seen a similar *modus operandi* in relation to the slave and in relation to those who, like stateless people, are on the threshold between the human and the inhuman. Not to be human in any way would make the slave entirely outside any possible status hierarchy. The natural slave, in Aristotle's terms, must still be human, otherwise slavery has no meaning. The slave, in other words, has to be included as human, in order to be excluded from every existing form of social life.

Bare life is the driving force and 'protagonist' of Agamben's book, *Homo Sacer*. In particular, it is a matter, for our author, of demonstrating how that which was excluded from the *polity* is now the very basis of politics. This point is intimately connected to the exception. For, like bare life, the exception is both external to the law and also that which makes the law as law possible. Along a line of thinking that Agamben derives from Carl Schmitt, the exception, which implies the suspension of the law, is at the same time fundamentally related to the law, not only because the suspension of the law has to be signalled within the law itself, but also because the law participates in the nomination of what counts as an exception. As Agamben puts it:

> the decisive fact is that, together with the process by which the exception everywhere becomes the rule, the realm of bare life – which was originally situated at the margins of the political order – gradually begins to coincide with the political realm, and exclusion and inclusion, outside and inside, *bios* and *zoē*, right and fact, enter into a zone of irreducible indistinction. (1998: 9)

Does this really imply that there is now a *bios* of *zoē* – *zoē* as a way of life? Certainly, if politics still means freedom and creativity, *zoē* must now be equated with a way of life. For our part, however, there is a profound ambivalence in Agamben's theory when it comes to a definition of politics. To the extent that the issue regarding the exception brings *two* realms into consideration – bare life and politics – it is quite possible that Agamben simply follows tradition and accepts that human life is divided into necessity and freedom, with the latter founding the political order. There is, at the same time, a gesturing in Agamben's work towards a new understanding of life as a 'form-of-life' – a life no longer based on the distinction between *zoē* and *bios* and which becomes the figure for a new kind of post-sovereign politics.[1] It must also be admitted that there is a certain vagueness here that raises the question of whether there can be a positive biopolitics. On the other hand, if we were to accept Ewa Ziarek's interpretation of bare life, bare life would always be *post factum* and a remnant in relation to the *polity*. Thus, Ziarek says, bare life is: 'a disjunctive inclusion of the inassimilable remnant' (2008: 91). And she adds that there are problems here: 'First of all, as argued by several commentators and critics [cf. Ernesto Laclau] . . . what is lacking in Agamben's work is the theory of "emancipatory possibilities" of modernity' (92–3).

For our part, as we have previously shown (see Chapter 2), modernity is part of the problem, for it brings with it the very division of necessity and freedom that relegates certain people to the status of less than fully human. Arendt's 'right to have rights' can never enable anyone external to the so-called political realm to find a way in to it; in particular, this is so for refugees, asylum seekers and, more broadly, stateless people.

At certain points in *Homo Sacer*, Agamben gives the impression that what he is really criticising is the attempt to incorporate bare life, as the excluded element that founds the political order and as equivalent to pure humanness (the 'Man' of the French Declaration), into the sovereign order through the category of citizenship. Or rather, he opens our eyes to the fact that bare life and sovereignty become continuous with each other, so that it becomes difficult to separate the political order from the order of sovereignty: '*homo sacer* presents the originary figure of life taken into the sovereign ban and preserves the memory of the originary exclusion through which the political dimension was first constituted' (1998: 83).

Perhaps the clearest expression of this in a contemporary context might be in the following passage from Agamben:

The refugee must be considered for what he is: nothing less than a limit concept that radically calls into question the fundamental categories of the nation-state, from the birth-nation to the man-citizen link, and that thereby makes it possible to clear the way for a long overdue renewal of categories in the service of a politics in which bare life is no longer separated and excepted, either in the state order or in the figure of human rights. (1998: 134)

Peg Birmingham considers, amongst other things, how the essentially human for Agamben is intimately entwined in language as, in Benveniste's terms, *énonciation*: the act of language itself (Birmingham 2011: 139–56). We shall return to this. But first, it is important to state the substance of Birmingham's approach to Agamben and human rights. In Birmingham's view, human rights, for Agamben, can never be 'proclaimed', so that the victims or those hitherto outside the *polity* might then be admitted into the political community. Rather, it is clear for Birmingham that Agamben has demonstrated the inadequacy of linking the human to the 'nativity' of the nation-state and to the Arendtian principle of the 'right to have rights'. For such an arrangement enshrines exclusion at its very heart – an exclusion which only serves to foster doubt as to the humanness of those in such a predicament. Above all, though, Birmingham agrees that the human as such cannot be equated with bare life and the operation of biopower (2011: 149). For the latter reduces the human to something entirely lacking distinction. As we have previously stated (see Chapter 1), such a notion coalesces fully with true reality as complete material contingency without transcendence. In Birmingham's presentation of Agamben, then, bare life effectively becomes a tool in the arsenal of sovereign power. It does not give access to the human as such.

EXCURSUS ON LIFE

'Today politics knows no value (and consequently no nonvalue) other than life' (Agamben 1998: 10). To appreciate the full import of this statement, it is necessary to go into more detail, not just about bare life, but about the notion of life as it emerges in the nineteenth century with Darwin. Although Agamben often gives the impression that bare life only has significance in relation to the origin of the law, it is our contention that the true significance of life is its inscription within biopolitics or biopower – a process that began in earnest in the nineteenth century. To begin, then, we first ask: what is the meaning of bare life outside its juridical framework in which Agamben inscribes it? In other words: what is intended by the notion of minimal life in a biological, biopolitical sense?

Bare or minimal life is that which is coterminous with all forms of living organisms. It is the closest that we can get to the notion of the pure organism as an exclusively physical entity, whose only defining quality is it is alive. Animal life, sea life, even vegetative life all appear on a continuum when it comes to bare life, strictly speaking. Bare life brings us to Darwin and to the notion of pure survival, as well as to Canguilhem's discussion of the distinction between the normal and the pathological – a distinction opening onto the opposition between 'life' and 'death', albeit in a complex way. For disease could be said to be part of life in the broadest sense, and, in the narrower sense, could enhance the life of the individual understood physiologically as an open system in which the overcoming of disease and even the risk of death could be interpreted as life-enhancing (see Canguilhem 1979: 118–34).[2] Above all, it should be recognised that bare life gives rise to – and is in complete harmony with – a quantitative approach to existence. Life, understood thus, is never a *quality* of life, never a *form* of life.

Roberto Esposito points to a lack of 'categorical exactitude' when attempts are made to define *zoē* and *bios* within the realm of biopolitics. For, strictly speaking, so-called biopolitics is really *zoē*-politics – a politics (or, more correctly, relations of power) which deals with the management of life as a purely biological entity. But in this respect, Esposito raises a question that resonates deeply with Agamben's approach, even if the theorist of *Homo Sacer* does not sufficiently elaborate on the issues raised here. Thus, Esposito writes that: '[z]oē itself can only be defined problematically: what, assuming it is even conceivable, is an absolutely natural life?' (2008: 15). For Esposito, what disrupts the smooth relation between *zoē* and *bios* – what, in other words, renders a pure *zoē* impossible – is technology: 'the human body appears to be increasingly challenged and also literally traversed by technology *[technica]*' (15). As we shall see, in more than one place, Agamben argues that there is no life (*zoē*) that is not also a way of life (*bios*) (2000: 3–12). And it would seem that 'way of life' comprehends technics and the technical more than the reverse is the case.

Despite the lack of theoretical and scientific rigour in defining and conceptualising *zoē* – given that life as pure aliveness, as it were, is well-nigh inconceivable, as Esposito says – how has it come to be that the notion of bare life (even if this is not the usual designation) has become so influential? In order to throw light on this question, we suggest that it is necessary to examine aspects of the notion of life as it emerged in the nineteenth century, particularly in Darwin's theory, but not only there. For the nineteenth century, as we know, is also the century of the birth of political economy – a field which makes 'life' a key element in the development of economic theory.

An Archaeology of Life and Labour

In taking an 'archaeological' approach to economics, as set out by Foucault, we find labour and life intertwined. Thus, Foucault presents life emerging in nineteenth-century political economy with its concepts of need (what is the minimum satisfaction needed to sustain life?), scarcity (how can the evident mismatch between finite resources and infinite desire be addressed?) and survival (when is life extant and when does death supervene?). Scarcity brings into view the limits of material existence, conditions which 'become increasingly more precarious until they approach the point where existence itself will be impossible' (Foucault 1982: 261). Life, for labourers, becomes increasingly more precarious: 'Thrust back by poverty to the very brink of death, a whole class of men experience, nakedly, as it were, what *need*, and hunger and labour are' (261 [emphasis added]). Whether we are dealing with the more conservative and 'pessimistic' views of Ricardo on 'perpetual scarcity' or with 'Marx's revolutionary promise' (261), the underlying framework based on notions of need and scarcity are the same: the human must, above all, have enough to survive and to sustain existence before embarking on the road to freedom.

When we turn to life as such, a concern with life as material existence is in evidence – a concern that dominates, Foucault says, the whole of nineteenth-century thought:

> [T]his imaginative status of animality burdened with disturbing and nocturnal powers refers more profoundly to the multiple and simultaneous functions of life in nineteenth-century thought. Perhaps for the first time in Western culture, life is escaping from the general laws of being as it is posited and analysed in representation. [. . .] [L]ife becomes a fundamental force and one that it opposed to being in the same way as movement to immobility, as time to space, as the secret to the visible expression. Life is the root of all existence, and the non-living nature in its inner form, is merely spent life; mere being is the non-being of life. For

life – and this is why it has radical value in nineteenth-century thought – is at the same time the nucleus of being and of non-being: there is being only because there is life. (1982: 278)

Instead of the abstract concept of being, we have the more material, non-transcendent, 'this-worldly' concept of 'life'. It is life that opens the way for the measurement of aliveness, as opposed to the supposed emptiness of 'being'. Foucault continues:

The experience of life is thus posited as the most general law of beings, the revelation of that primitive force on the basis of which they are; it functions as an untamed ontology, one trying to express the indissociable being and non-being of all beings. (278)

Ultimately, he argues: 'in relation to life, beings are no more than transitory figures, and the being they maintain, during the brief period of their existence, is no more than their presumption, their *will to survive*' (278 [emphasis added]).

The Nineteenth Century and the Rise of Darwinism

The notion of the 'will to survive' or what Darwin called the 'struggle for existence' (1981: 60–3) in the nineteenth century and, more broadly, in modernity points to an interest and focus on existence as the pure physicality of life – a notion of aliveness indicated by the beating heart, the pulsing blood, the breathing lungs, the dilated pupil and the skin's moisture. Each of these aspects can be quantified and, indeed, only have meaning in being more or less present. Life, as such, becomes an aliveness that can be measured.

Clearly, then, the nineteenth century, as the century in which the Industrial Revolution really got underway, is the era in which quantification, generally, and statistical theory, in particular, began to become pre-eminent, most notably, of course, over values and over quality. The age of nihilism, as Nietzsche foreshadowed, leads to a revaluation of all values – one that gives rise to a *devaluation* of value. For we are dealing with the value of non-value – an exclusion of value, which like bare life, in a sense, is the excluded inclusion in the scheme of quantification. Quantification dominates nineteenth-century thermodynamics and the impact of entropy as the loss of energy from a system. Indeed, the recognition of the necessary input and output of energy and the need for energy renewal distinguishes the thermodynamic from Newtonian mechanics, where energy always remains constant. There is no disorder or real contingency in the Newtonian scheme of things. In principle, a perfect repetition of events is possible, because time is reversible (see Mason 1962: 496), whereas, in the Industrial Revolution, time, as an index of contingency, is irreversible. There is, then, more or less energy available, depending on the situation. In the twenty-first century, as we know, energy supplies are rapidly dissipating. Ways have to be found, in order to meet the shortfall and thus sustain the standard of living attained by the West. Therefore, it is a question, above all, of quantity and utility. At least, this is so at the level of modernity's self-understanding (see Luhmann 1998). Value must give way to disenchantment, as Weber said.

Measurable Life

Although the exact relationship between the development of the field of biology in the nineteenth century and the notion of 'bare life' is difficult to establish in all its aspects, a number of points can be mentioned.

1. As the French biologist Francois Jacob points out, the very concept of life as encompassing all living things is very much a nineteenth-century phenomenon. Thus, in referring to the entry for 'life' in the *Encyclopédie,* Jacob finds that the only information given is that life is 'opposed to death' (1970: 103).
2. As is well-known, and as we have already mentioned in passing, Darwin refers to life in the broadest sense as a 'struggle for existence' (1981: 62). By this phrase, Darwin means that each species and each individual (phenotype) within a species must call upon inherited characteristics in the competition for survival with other species and other individuals. From this comes Darwin's emphasis on the 'usefulness' of character traits and various organs. 'Usefulness' means the extent to which something aids survival. Darwin, moreover, refers to the arguments by some naturalists 'against the utilitarian doctrine' (1981: 199). Such opponents 'believe that very many structures have been created for beauty in the eyes of man, or for mere variety. This doctrine, if true, would be absolutely

fatal to my theory' (199). In order to 'save' the utilitarian thesis, Darwin resorts to the concept of inheritance. This means that while 'many structures are of no direct use to their possessors' (199) in present conditions, they would have been of use at some time in the past, and they will – if they are, indeed, of no use – eventually disappear through the process of evolution at some point in the future (199). Adjustment through inheritance entails that things do not just change overnight, as it were. To put it another way: the environment does not have a direct, but rather an indirect, impact on the character of beings, because it is a matter of inheritance. For Darwin, inheritance ensures the retention of the notion of utility, and the latter has meaning only in relation to the struggle for existence or for survival. In this sense, too, we can say that 'bare life' also corresponds to the notion of survival, pure and simple, or, as Jacob expresses it, in the eyes of Cuvier or Bichat, 'life is nothing other than the struggle against destruction' (1970: 104).

3. Usefulness to survival is the key Darwinian notion when it comes to evolution. This also entails that chance variations will occur – that, in Darwin's terms, the 'conditions of existence' are what drive the evolutionary process. Although he may have started out as a believer in God's design for the universe, by the 1860s, Darwin was convinced that chance and contingency held the key to understanding the evolution of life. Adaptation, therefore, should be understood to be an index of the real conditions of the existence of the species and not in any sense as part of an essential or transcendent scheme of things. Thus:

> For Darwin, the evolutionary *implications* of chance varia-
> tion had to do with (1) the contingency of the outcomes of
> evolution by natural selection of chance variations, which
> could in turn lead to (2) chance divergence. He argued
> that two closely related, even initially identical lineages,
> inhabiting identical environments, may by chance give
> rise to different variations. (Beatty 2006: 630 [emphasis in
> original])

It is thus no surprise, then, that Darwin's emphasis on chance and contingency as crucial to evolution makes him a thinker who is also in harmony with changes in the idea of time and with the promotion of the importance of thermodynamics and statistical theory. Thus, evolution and thermodynamics both turned their attention towards the 'conditions of existence' as the essential basis of political economy. Marx's materialism is, indeed, firmly inscribed in this mode of thought, which makes it no accident that the much talked of dedication of one of the three volumes of *Capital* to Darwin would have been appropriate, even if it never happened (Ball 1979).[3]

4. With the emergence of thermodynamics in the nineteenth century, contingency and chance are recognised as being part of nature (life) itself. Rather than such phenomena being thought of as resulting from the limited nature of human knowledge, as was the case with Newtonian mechanics, they come to be recognised as being intrinsic to the life process. This is so, even if the behaviour of populations is the focus of study over the behaviour of individuals. Bare life thus becomes equivalent to the survival, both actual and probable, of populations. The latter, of course, was the major focus of Foucault's version of biopolitics (see 1998: 135–59; 2008: 41, 43). Populations also became the focus of attention, to the extent that statistical theory attains a greater level of validity when applied to populations (that is, to large numbers of individuals) and not to specific individuals. 'It is no exaggeration to say', Jacob concludes, 'that the way we now look at nature has in large measure been fashioned by statistical thermodynamics. The latter has transformed objects as well as the attitude of science' (1970: 220).

Within the context we have been describing, little effort is made by Darwin and others to isolate the human within the life of creatures. Indeed, the clear implication is that the human shares the same orientation towards life and death as all other living beings. Humans, too, then, can be understood essentially in terms of the behaviour of populations – that is, the human can be understood essentially in terms of statistical probability. Survival and the struggle for existence mark the human, just as they do every living thing. Thus, the foundation of the human becomes survival and nothing else. Perhaps the ultimate expression of this is the popularity today of genetic determinism, where our DNA is said to explain every aspect of human existence and behaviour and legitimise every form of human inequality, translating into a barely disguised social Darwinism, where superior genes are seen as the main determinants of a successful and happy life, whereas inferior genes result in one occupying a lower rung in the social hierarchy.

The impact of this reductionist view of human life as survival on human rights has been twofold. On the one hand, we see, as we pointed to in the first chapter, a reduction of human rights to the paradigm of humanitarianism and a narrowing of the conception and implementation of human rights to a simple protection of biological life. On the other hand, there is a potential threat to human rights emerging from genetic engineering. If a human life is simply bare biological life, and if survival and utility become the imperatives of human existence, then this opens the door to genetic manipulations; the human comes to be seen as a site of constant improvement and modification through biomedical technologies. For some time, there has been a growing concern about the excesses of genetic engineering and its implications for our understanding of ourselves as human, as well as over the new forms of biological exclusion – indeed, eugenics – that it might give rise to. This concern was reflected in the 1997 UNESCO Declaration of the Human Genome and Human Rights, which drew attention, amongst other things, to the risks of discrimination based on genetic characteristics, something which infringed human rights, freedoms and human dignity. The uneasiness about the reduction of humanity to biology is reflected in Article 2 of the Declaration (UNESCO 1997):

(a) Everyone has the right to respect for their dignity and for their rights regardless of their genetic characteristics.
(b) That dignity makes it imperative not to reduce individuals to their genetic characteristics and to respect their uniqueness and diversity.[4]

A similar uneasiness is expressed by Jürgen Habermas, who is concerned about the implications of genetic research and embryonic cloning on accepted understandings of human autonomy and reflective ethical self-understanding. He considers whether 'the instrumentalization of human nature changes the ethical self-understanding of the species in such a way that we may no longer see ourselves as ethically free and morally equal beings guided by norms and reasons' (2003: 40–1). For this reason, according to Habermas, genetic manipulation and eugenics have serious consequences for human rights, eroding the moral autonomy and equality of persons, which is the very basis of rights (2003: 79). Here Habermas considers various forms of legal protection for human integrity and autonomy, including a 'right to a genetic inheritance immune from artificial intervention' (2003: 27). The problem, as he sees it, is to do with the way in which eugenics seeks to predetermine an individual's life chances by interventions on the physical body at the genetic level, thus interfering with our sense of ourselves as situated within our own natural body:

> The capacity of being oneself requires that the person be at home, so to speak, in her own body [. . .] And for the person to feel at one with her body, it seems that this body has to be experienced as something natural – as a continuation of the organic, self-regenerative life from which the person was born. (2003: 57–8)

So it is the 'natural' integrity of the body – the sense in which is it not interfered with, manipulated or engineered by outside forces – that endows us with some sense of autonomy and self-ownership and, indeed, with a sense of a common humanity. Habermas is no doubt right here. But what must be also considered is the way that 'bare life' – life without any significance, without transcendence – while on the one hand designates the naturalness of life and of the body, at the same time reduces the human to an objectified body that is open in the name of greater health, efficiency, performance and even happiness to manipulation and engineering by alien forces. Such interventions take place on the terrain of 'nature' itself. The reduction of the human to merely a biological body, to bare life, at the same time robs him – potentially, at least – from the very sense of having his own body. Therefore, any consideration of human rights today must not only find ways of defending the integrity and autonomy of human life, but must also explore new understandings of what it means to be human – ways which transcend the reduction to biology and bare life and which open up the possibility of the sacred.

SACRED LIFE

A key difficulty in reading Agamben on bare life, however, is to be found in the fact that *homo sacer*, to which the notion of bare life is linked in the era of modernity, evokes all the ambiguity (or non-ambiguity – we must be careful with our terms here) of the sacred. Of course, it has long been known that a religious experience of the sacred as what inspires reverence and awe differs from an anthropological understanding, especially as presented in Durkheim and Robertson Smith (1894). For the latter, the sacred assumes an ambivalent status and tends to evoke situations of ambiguity in cultural life – situations where identities are threatened and states of being are unclear. Thus the borders of the body, especially with regard to hair, nails and saliva, are subject to rituals and taboos. Liminal states, such as childbirth, menstruation and adolescence (see initiation rites) also figure prominently. Agamben, however, finds this anthropological approach to the sacred to be inadequate for his purposes. Instead of relying on a discourse about the sacred, Agamben looks to the actual effects of the sacred within European culture as such, especially with regard to the origins of Roman law and sovereignty. It is within these two contexts that he sees the notion of the sacred arising as something profoundly ambivalent – an ambivalence captured in the notion of *homo sacer* as the one who can be killed without this being homicide. Here there is no clear identity that can be attributed to the victim. Somehow, *homo sacer* is nothing: 'an outcast, a banned man, tabooed, dangerous' (Agamben 1998: 79), being neither inside nor outside the social and judicial realm, yet being the latter's condition of possibility. On this reading, *homo sacer* would be even less than bare life as the figure of pure necessity, even if Agamben appears to accept this reconciliation later in his argument.

As far as sovereignty is concerned, the sacred assumes its full ambivalence in relation to the death of the king or actual sovereign. To clarify what is at stake, Agamben, like Foucault before him, refers to Ernst Kantorowicz's book *The King's Two Bodies: A Study in Mediaeval Political Theology* (1957). Kantorowicz investigates the tradition according to which the kings in the late Middle Ages and beyond were deemed to be invested with their estate by God and were thus touched by a certain immortality. Problems, of course, arose when the king's 'natural' body died – the natural body functioning as the support for the king's eternal sovereign state. As sovereign, Agamben says, following Jean Bodin: '[t]he king never dies' (Agamben 1998: 92). In order that this myth is perpetuated, two burials take place: 'first *in corpore* and then *in effigie*' (Bickermann 1929, cited by Agamben 1998: 94 [emphasis in original]). Thus does the image, in relation to sovereignty, come into play. The image (see '*in effigie*') begins to function like a ghost or a spectre which must be laid to rest, but which is extremely difficult to deal with because it is neither fully of the land of the living nor of the dead. The ambiguity is captured by Bickermann in the following words: 'the image functions as a substitute for the missing corpse; in the case of the imperial ceremony, it appears instead beside the corpse, doubling the dead body without substituting for it' (1929: 6–7, cited by Agamben 1998: 95). Bickerman also relates this to the funeral rites required for the soldier who dedicates himself to the gods before going into battle, as if he were about to die, and yet who does not die. In light of this, Agamben is moved to write, not without obscurity, that: 'it is here that the body of the sovereign and the body of *homo sacer* enter into a zone of indistinction in which they can no longer be told apart' (1998: 96).

Agamben notes that another figure, the *devotus* (devotee), 'who consecrates his own life to the gods of the underworld' (1998: 96), has also been approximated to the figure of *homo sacer* – again because he is between worlds, as it were. For '[i]nsofar as he incarnates in his own person the elements that are usually distinguished from death, *homo sacer* is, so to speak, a living statue, the double or the colossus of himself' (1998: 99).

Within these figures of extreme ambivalence – ghostly figures or images – figures of 'sacred life', 'something like a bare life makes its appearance in the Western world' (1998: 100). Bare life is so because it 'has been separated from its context and that, surviving its death, so to speak, is for this very reason incompatible with the human world' (100).

The difficulty Agamben throws up for the study of power and politics in contemporary society – especially in relation to biopower/ biopolitics – is that of knowing the precise relationship between bare life and *zoē*. Indeed, in the following italicised passage, we could suppose that bare life is not *zoē*: '*Not simple natural life, but life exposed to death (bare life or sacred life) is the originary political element*' (1998: 88 [emphasis in original]). For her part, Catherine Mills argues that:

> The category of bare life emerges from within this distinction, in that it is neither *bios* nor *zoē*, but rather the politicized form of natural life. Immediately politicized but nevertheless excluded from the polis, bare life is the limit-concept between the *polis* and the *oikos*. (2004: 46)

Yet, it is difficult to imagine that bare life could be removed entirely from the *oikos*, given that this sphere has to do with necessity as such (and therefore, at one end of the spectrum, also with mere survival) – the sphere that is excluded from the *polis*. What must be admitted, however, is that *homo sacer* as image is less easy to assimilate to any notion of *zoē*.

BARE LIFE

It may be possible that two forms of bare life thus present themselves: the first which is linked, as we know, to the Greek *zoē*, with the intention of evoking pure biological life. This is basis of 'biopolitics' as the management of individuals, peoples and populations viewed entirely as biological entities. Such management is the work of power itself – a power which exploits a pre-existing biological condition of the human. The second is the human as reduced to bare life after being dispossessed of rights and the equivalent of a civil identity; this is life in a state of 'ban' and in the 'state of exception', where an individual or group is 'marked', as Andrew Benjamin says,[5] for the erasure of civil identity (the Jew under Nazism and the terrorist in the contemporary 'war against terror' are two examples). Only with regard to the second form of bare life does a zone of indistinction operate, where, as Agamben says in relation to the state of exception, any division into public or private becomes inoperative.[6] In other words, what would remain of the human after the erasure of civil identity is unclear. Or rather, what would remain is the murkiness of a zone of complete indistinction, neither human nor non-human.

With *homo sacer* as the basis of the law (an exclusion which is included), a clear division must exist between it and its other. That is, only the one who is reduced to bare life as bare biological existence – who is *marked* as such – can be killed without this being homicide. The division between inclusion and exclusion is thus founded on the idea that only the one outside the polity/law can be killed, even if this outside is included in the polity as an outside. Such is the way Agamben presents his version of the Arendtian classical division in political discourse between necessity and freedom.

We can accept, then, that while the state of exception does not reinforce the classic division of private and public,[7] bare life nonetheless lends itself to this distinction if it is defined in terms of what Baudrillard designates as the 'bio-anthropological postulate' of '"primary needs" – an irreducible zone where the individual chooses himself, since he knows what he wants: to eat, to drink, to sleep, to make love, to find shelter, etc.' (Baudrillard 1981: 80). In this regard, so-called 'societies of scarcity' (81) are only ever able to partially satisfy 'primary needs'. In terms of the ideology underpinning this view, 'societies of scarcity' are those still mired in necessity – societies which have not overcome the problem of satisfying primary needs. Only societies of abundance are able to transcend necessity and thus experience freedom. Agamben, at least implicitly, recognises what is at stake here. The difficulty for him is that he often uses terms that evoke the tradition he may well be opposing.

Even more importantly, though, whatever Agamben's position implies in relation to Arendt and the tradition of European politics, the one bereft of a civil identity – the one marked out for exclusion as bare life – is at the same time bereft of any potential for political action. For Agamben, as for Arendt, the crucial characteristic of the asylum seeker is a complete incapacity for political action understood in the traditional sense of participation in an established political community. It is this so-called incapacity which human rights activity endeavours to refute when it says that to be human is not nothing: it is never bare life in any absolute sense, and, moreover, human life is always a form of life. Ironically, it is the potential for political action that such recognition opens up that could be an important element in Agamben's radical post-sovereign rendering of politics, which shall be explored in a later chapter (see Chapter 6).

THE DEADLY PRESERVATION OF LIFE

In Nazi Germany, as Agamben shows, it was proposed that a monetary figure be given to the people as 'living value' and that biology and economy be brought into a 'logical synthesis' (1998: 145, citing Verschuer 1942: 48). A passage cited by Agamben states: 'Fluctuations in the biological substance and in the material budget are usually parallel' (1998: 145, citing Verschuer 1942: 40). Here, economy, as the measure of value, applies without qualification to human life *qua* 'living wealth'. From this perspective, it is always the case that people are more or less alive. This 'aliveness', this state of health of a people, which has a monetary value is immediately political, according to Agamben.

Peoples are assessed according to whether they can measure up to the biological criteria deemed to be most desirable. In this sense, there are more or less degenerate peoples or 'races'. A degenerate people, should it exist, becomes a fundamental political problem. In this regard, just as bare life becomes the basis of human rights (the rights which one has simply in virtue of being born), so, more broadly, we find that *'the biological given is as such immediately political, and the political is as such immediately the biological given'* (1998: 148 [emphasis in original]). This is biological life, let it be recalled, as quantifiable and measurable, not life as a way of life, as *bios*. Such is the way that politics becomes 'biopolitics'.

What has been said so far leads to Agamben's clearest statement yet of what is at stake:

> When life and politics – originally divided, and linked together by means of the no-man's land of the state of exception that is inhab-ited by bare life – begin to become one, all life becomes sacred and all politics becomes the exception. (1998: 148)

In contrast to Agamben, we would argue that bare life becomes the subject and object of modern politics, not because such a zero degree of aliveness in itself exists, but because modernity furnishes us with a politics that is based on quantification and a devaluation of value. Quality, then, can never really be part of the modern practice of politics (and this surely has implications for the implementation of justice), for quality can never be measured, it is always the subject of a value-judgement. With the devaluation of value, a whole range of things along with justice no longer have a clear basis for being defended and preserved – things which would include truth, beauty, the sacred (despite Agamben), equality, the good – or, as many peoples of the world would have put it, a life that is pleasing to the gods. While bringing the contest of values of under control in order to preserve life seemed like a good thing, it becomes something else entirely when it serves the interests of sovereign power. For sovereign power uses the 'threat to life' as the basis for ignoring value. Without preserving life, there can be no pursuit of values. Life must therefore be preserved at all costs, even if the measures used to preserve life might require invoking the state of exception, which may or may not be strictly legal. Legality, as transcendent, must be put aside when it is a question of protecting bare life. Here we encounter Esposito's thesis of immunity, where the state must be preserved at all costs; for it is the state which, in turn, preserves the lives of the people or, more correctly, the life of a people.

LAW AND/OR ORDER

While for Agamben the law and the situation are coterminous with each other, so that the state of exception and bare life exist as the other of the law, for Esposito, the law is preceded by the non-judicial sphere, famously exemplified in Hobbes as the 'state of war'.[8] For Agamben, inspired by Walter Benjamin on this point, violence, too, while not reducible to the law, emerges with the appearance of the law, so that there is no law without violence and no violence without law. For Esposito, the law only exists to the extent that violence is held in check. It is not the law as such which can bring this about, but force. Force brings order so that the law might flourish. Law and order are not, therefore, coterminous for Esposito, nor for Foucault, as it turns out, at least if we listen to what he wrote in 'Le citron et le lait'. *Citron* (lemon) and *lait* (milk) or, colloquially in English, 'chalk and cheese'; law and order are thus like chalk and cheese. As Foucault points out: 'the highest value for civilizations such as ours: social order' (2002: 437–8). Thus:

> It is for the sake of order that the decision is made to prosecute or not to prosecute; for the sake of order that the police are given free reign; for the sake of order that those who aren't 'desirable' are expelled [. . .] This primacy of order has at least two important consequences: the judicial system increasingly substitutes concern for the norm for respect for the law; and it tends less to punish offences than to penalize behaviours. (2002: 437–8)

In this review of a book by Philippe Boucher, Foucault unambiguously pointed out that 'order', not the 'law', was the prime concern of the state today (see 2002: 435–8). Only a concern for order above all else can explain the non-application of the law where it should be applied. Of course, another way of putting it is to say that sovereign power is above all concerned with its own self-preservation and not with respecting the law above all else. In a passing remark, Foucault also has something to say regarding human rights:[9]

'Law and Order' is not simply the motto of American conserva-
tism, it is a hybridized monster. Those who fight for human rights
are well aware of this [. . .] Just as people say milk or lemon, we
should say law *or* order. It is up to us to draw lessons for the future
from that incompatibility. (2002: 438 [emphasis in original])

Thus, those who fight for human rights know well that law, as the
mechanism for protecting human rights (assuming that these can be
defined), will be undermined by the need for order or, as we could say
in light of Esposito, it is undermined by the need for immunity and
securitisation, which, in practice, is often the opposite of the implementation of the law.[10] Indeed, in many human rights declarations themselves, including the Universal Declaration of Human Rights (UDHR)
and the European Convention on Human Rights (ECHR), there is a
clause – the clause that foreshadows the exception – concerning the prerogatives of security and public order, which, in the last instance, limits
and trumps the proclaimed rights. For example, Article 29 of the UDHR
states:

(2) In the exercise of his rights and freedoms, everyone shall be
subject only to such limitations as are determined by law solely for
the purpose of securing due recognition and respect for the rights
and freedoms of others and of meeting the just requirements
of morality, *public order* and the general welfare in a democratic
society. (emphasis added)

We find almost exactly the same exceptional clause appearing on a
number of occasions in the ECHR. For instance, in Article 9: 2:

Freedom to manifest one's religion or beliefs shall be subject only
to such limitations as are prescribed by law and are necessary in a
democratic society in the interests of public safety, for the *protection of public order*, health or morals, or for the protection of the
rights and freedoms of others. (emphasis added)

Article 1 of Protocol 7 of the same Convention says:

An alien may be expelled before the exercise of his rights under
paragraph 1.a, b and c of this Article, when such expulsion is

necessary in the interests of *public order* or is grounded on *reasons of national security.* (emphasis added)

What is this obscure, vague and dangerously ambiguous notion of 'public order' that lurks behind the edifice of human rights – a void waiting to engulf and nullify rights in moments of the 'emergency' – moments which are determined and defined by the sovereign state? 'Public order' is the rock against which human rights and, indeed, the prescriptive dimension of the law itself are dashed. It is almost as if human rights declarations have their own inbuilt self-destruct mechanism and are deliberately erected on the edge of an abyss. Any resurrection of human rights today cannot, therefore, proceed, unless they are unfastened from their moorings in 'public order' and security, which otherwise renders them meaningless.

Order is not law's harmonious bedfellow, as many believe, but its opposing counterpart – a counterpart which acts in the interest of sovereign power, not in the interest of the human as such. Or as sovereign power acts in relation to the situation and, indeed, is wedded to existence as the situation in the here and now, order is intimately related to the exception.

Foucault's insight into the distinction between law and order would, then, seem to be a necessary precursor to the possibility of the suspension of law signalled, for instance, in Agamben's notion of the state of exception. The condition of possibility of the state of exception, which is instituted in the name of security and the order that is deemed to be inseparable from it, would be the distinction between law and order (and not law and chaos, as some hastily conclude). This is because law, unlike order, has an essential content that is often characterised as justice, but includes all those ideal transcendent principles which are necessary, not for the protection of human or animal life, but for what might called the enhancement of life, also understood as a specific way of life (*bios*).

While Agamben, following Schmitt, sees law and the exception as dependent upon one another, so that it is the law itself which makes way for the sovereign who decides on the exception, the implication of Foucault's approach is that the exception as a call for order is not dependent on the law, even if the law exists in parallel with it and even intersects with it from time to time. Perhaps Agamben recognises this, for he writes:

When life and politics – originally divided, and linked together by means of the no-man's land of the state of exception that is inhabited by bare life – begin to become one, all life becomes sacred [in the sense of *homo sacer*] and all politics becomes the exception. (1998: 148)

Here, bare life, politics – as it is currently practised – and the state of exception are inseparably entwined. Within the terms of our argument, politics becomes the exception to the extent that politics is misleadingly equated with sovereignty, power and the concern with order and security.

The Factical and Contingency

In what is probably one of the most demanding chapters of *Homo Sacer*, Chapter 4 of Part 3, Agamben pays significant attention to Heidegger's concept of 'facticity'. According to Agamben, it is impossible to understand Heidegger's relationship to Nazism if one ignores the way that each, respectively, treats the reality and concept of life. The point Agamben makes is that it is through the notion of 'life' that Heidegger and Nazism come together, even if it is also in the notion of facticity that life in the Heideggerian sense diverges from Nazi biologism, based on an objectified 'bare life'.

For many commentators, Agamben included, facticity goes to the very heart of Heidegger's philosophy of Being. Unlike the category of 'fact', facticity is not an object to be observed from an external position by a subject. Indeed, it is not the object of any science or even of reflection. From this, it has been concluded that Husserl's idea of contingency, made extant by a reflective phenomenology, where entities would already exist in a given time and space is not equivalent to facticity, which Heidegger argued could only be revealed in a 'hermeneutical phenomenology' – a phenomenology that did not become mired in the subject–object relation, a relation central to epistemology.[11]

Here, we recall that, for Heidegger, Dasein is that entity for whom its own being is an issue. In his lecture course of 1924, considered to be part of the foundation of *Being and Time*, Heidegger explains that:

Dasein is not a 'thing' like a piece of wood nor such a thing as a plant – nor does it consist of experiences, and still less is it a subject (an ego) standing over against objects (which are not the ego). It is a distinctive being [*Siendes*] which precisely insofar as it 'is there' for itself in an authentic manner is not an object. (1999: 37)

Indeed, the mode of Dasein's 'being there' evokes both Agamben's notion that there is not a *zoē* that is not also a 'way of life'. In an illuminating elaboration of this, Heidegger specifies in the text just cited that:

> In connection with this [the being-there of Dasein] stands the task of clarifying the *fundamental phenomenon of the 'there'* and providing a categorical–ontological characterization of Dasein's *being-*there, of its *being*-this-there. (1999: 52 [emphasis in original])

This fundamental orientation of not being an object and of raising the question of *how* it is a 'being-there' – the *way* that it is there – is part of Dasein's 'factical' life. There is no obvious transcendent realm with which Dasein need concern itself. Thus, in beginning his analysis of the 'political meaning of the experience of facticity', Agamben says:

> For both Heidegger and National Socialism, life has no need to assume 'values' external to it in order to become politics: life is immediately political in its very facticity. Man is not a living being who must abolish or transcend himself in order to become human – man is not a duality of spirit and body, nature and politics, life and *logos*, but is instead resolutely situated at the point of their indistinction. (1998: 153)

Even though Agamben seems to attribute the notion of facticity equally to Heidegger and National Socialism, we would have to be aware that the implications are very different in each case, which is not to deny that Heidegger's thought swims, at certain points, in the same pool as that of National Socialism.

Even though Agamben wants to link facticity and the state of exception, it seems clear that if this condition is about Dasein, assuming it is a state of being or situation of fully being what it is at a given historical moment, this is very different from the processes of the objectification of life that tend to characterise modern science, particularly Nazi science. Dasein, it can be recalled again, is never fully given, but is fundamentally its possibilities. This point is clearly set forth in Agamben's extensive analysis in 'The passion of facticity' (see 1999a: 185–204). There, facticity refers to the way Dasein is 'to its manner, its "guise"' (1999a: 194).

A different way of expressing facticity is with the phrase 'way of life' to refer to a life that is essentially human. This means that there is no life that is purely and simply biological, as was the case for Nazi ideology, and, according to Agamben, for modern biopolitics (1998: 153). As we saw, the biological state of life was, for Nazism, also an immediately political form of life. Here, a given state of human biology becomes an end in itself. Nothing else matters for this mode of political order.

For National Socialism, bare life was an end in itself. The health or otherwise of every human being was of political concern here. An example of this was the way that 'VPs (*Versuchspersonen*, human guinea pigs)' were experimented on by German physicians in order to test the limits of human endurance in situations ranging from altitude pressure to the length of survival in ice-cold water and the possibilities of reanimation (1998: 154–5). However, the biopolitical imperative driving such experiments and the use of the results was not, Agamben shows, limited to Nazi Germany. In fact, there had been similar experimentation on prisoners and death row inmates in the United States (156). In answer to the question of how the medical profession in a democratic country could have agreed to participate in such experiments, Agamben's answer is, in effect, that VPs were treated as bare life and as not being part of the political community. Thus, VPs:

> were persons sentenced to death or detained in a camp, the entry into which meant the definitive exclusion from the political community. Precisely because they were lacking almost all the rights and expectations that we customarily attribute to human existence, and yet were still biologically alive, they came to be situated in a limit zone between life and death, inside and outside, in which they were no longer anything but bare life. (1998: 159)

VPs thus highlight the very real problem that the notion of political community brings for a defence of human rights. Those sentenced to death or in a camp or those of the wrong cultural origin have an entirely problematic existence within the borders of the nation-state. Certainly, the task of defending the rights of such people becomes Herculean when it should be automatic. The reason why this is so is, we continue to stress, that in modernity the defence of sovereign power is paramount, not rights and certainly not the care of the human *qua* human.

THE CAMP

Even though it is clear that biopolitical imperatives dominate the practice of power and the economy in the modern era, particularly in the West, it is still not clear how one can argue, as Agamben does, that the camp is the *'nomos* of the political space in which we are still living' (1998: 166). In responding to this question, it should be said, first of all, that the argument is not that every political space has been turned into the equivalent of a concentration camp. Rather, in looking back at the National Socialist precedent, Agamben argues that the exception itself begins to take on the force of law, rather than being its suspension, much as the Führer's command came to be indistinguishable from the promulgation of the law itself. More specifically, in the actual German concentration camps, 'fact and law' became 'completely confused' (170), so that the application of the law begins to follow the trajectory of a given situation, rather than being the institution which stands against the facts in light of the abstract legal case. The extreme form of this would be when a situation is given the status of an emergency in light of the suspension of the rule, instead of the other way around.[12] Another reason for the confusion of the two domains is that the state of exception itself becomes part of the juridical order:

> Insofar as the state of exception is 'willed', it inaugurates a new juridico-political paradigm in which the norm becomes indistinguishable from the exception. The camp is thus the structure in which the state of exception – the possibility of deciding on which founds sovereign power – is realised *normally*. (1998: 170 [emphasis in original])

The recognition of a 'given factual situation' under the Weimar Constitution and in other legal systems, then leads to the factual situation itself being determined by the law – what, in any event, leads to the camp becoming a *'hybrid of law and fact in which the two terms become indistinguishable'* (170 [emphasis in original]).

It is not difficult to see that law can be suspended in light of a 'given factual situation'. Nor is it difficult to understand that events might overtake the law, so that a concern for security (whether paranoid or not) might begin to dominate, leading, as Foucault indicates, to the rule of order over a strict adherence to the law. What is more difficult to conceive of, and also more problematic, is Agamben's claim that law and situation or law and event become indistinguishable. Agamben's position is, however, unambiguous:

> The situation created in the exception has the peculiar character-istic that it cannot be defined either as a situation of fact or as a situation of right, but instead institutes a paradoxical threshold of indistinction between the two. It is not a fact, since it is only created through the suspension of the rule. But for the same reason, it is not even a juridical case in point, even if it opens the possibility of the force of law. (1998: 18–19)

The state of affairs that Agamben outlines is given further impetus by the tendency of modern polities to be driven by executive deci-sions having the force of law, rather than by the legislative actions of parliament – something which is also in keeping with the growing indistinction between fact and law.

While some have objected to the excessiveness of Agamben's claims about the camp being our contemporary *nomos*, it is more accurate to say that Agamben intends to evoke the idea that the *conditions for the emergence* of the camp – not the camp as such[13] – are beginning to become ascendant in Western-style democracies. This is indicated by the more pervasive and subtle measures of securitisation and border control that we see increasingly all around us, such as the body scan-ning of all airline passengers and other biometric procedures, including retinal identification, becoming readily accepted as normal, as well as giving security services the power to decide, without making the evidence public, who is a security threat[14] and who should be allowed to settle in the nation-state. Such measures point to the ascendancy of the 'situation' and the exception becoming the norm. Esposito puts it this way: 'That the obsessive search for security in relation to the threat of terrorism has become the pivot around which all the current gov-ernmental strategies turn gives an idea of the transformation currently taking place' (2008: 147). Esposito goes on to point out that the 'protec-tion of biological life' has become the key question for both 'domestic and foreign affairs' (147). Indeed, we could point to refugee camps and migrant detention centres themselves as concretisations of the logic of security and immunisation. Not only do these sites reify the bordering function of the nation-state and mechanisms of inclusion and exclusion that are embodied in sovereignty; they are also sites of screening and biopolitical surveillance, where those detained within are subjected to intrusive medical inspections, in order to weed out those dangerous bodies – carriers of disease – that threaten the biological health of the population.

CONCLUSION

As we have suggested, such measures of securitisation and immunisation operate on – and are only possible within – the terrain of 'bare' biological life, which has become the dominant category of life in our biopolitical modernity. Thus, to base human rights simply on the protection of biological life means that they become complicit in the same biopolitical logic that so often renders them ineffective. It is therefore crucial for any reconsideration of human rights today that the notion of life itself is rethought in terms of a *form* or *way* of life that is irreducible to its biological substratum and that the human can reveal that part of itself that transcends mere existence. In the next chapter, we will explore these possibilities through Agamben's understanding of language and gesture.

Notes

1 As Agamben puts it: 'A political life, that is a life directed toward the idea of happiness and cohesive with a form-of-life, is thinkable only starting from the emancipation from such a division, with the irrevocable exodus from any sovereignty. The question about the possibility of a nonstatist politics necessarily takes this form: Is today something like a form-of-life, a life for which living itself would be at stake in its own living, possible?' (2000: 7–8)

2 Here it should be acknowledged that, for Canguilhem, life is not simply reducible to its biological meaning, rather it has a social and an existential meaning (1992: 155). On the other hand, when he proceeds to elaborate on the notion of life in order to clarify the meaning of 'normal', Canguilhem's first port of call is Bichat (1771–1802) and then Claude Bernard – two nineteenth-century representatives of the physiological (to do with healthy life) and medical (to do with disease) views of life. Also, the existential meaning aside, it is clear that from a social perspective, the

dominant view of life today is that it is primarily biological.

3 Now the real link here is to the notion of use in Darwin and use-value in Marx. As Baudrillard says: 'There is no way of getting around this. Marxist labor is defined in the absolute order of a natural necessity and its dialectical overcoming as rational activity producing value' (1975: 42).

4 See also Uppendra Baxi's discussion of the effect of biotechnological developments, cloning and cybernetics for human rights (2008: 269–72).

5 'Those identified, the victims who become bare life, are positioned in advance. Bareness, therefore, is always a determination as an after effect. It operates by producing those who have already been identified as being subject to that process (i.e., to the process of subjectification). This determination means that sovereignty necessitates the capacity to discriminate' (Benjamin 2008: 82). However, it is also possible that these are simply figures of *homo sacer* as an extreme form of bare life (in other words, at the extreme end of the continuum, rather than a separate category).

6 Also see Agamben (2005a: 50), where he talks of the public–private distinction being 'deactivated' in the state of exception.

7 In fact, as we have seen above (note 6), it 'deactivates' this distinction.

8 Hobbes' sovereign, Agamben recognises, is the remnant of the state of nature.

9 See also Foucault's references to human rights in 'Confronting governments: human rights' (Foucault 2002: 474–6).

10 While it is true that security and public order measures are often authorised through law, legislation – although often, too, they are not – there is nevertheless a tension that can be identified between the essentially prescriptive character of law, which is supposed to impose limits on power in the name of principles such as rights and justice, and securitisation, which embodies an entirely different logic of exigency, pragmatics and 'situation', or what Agamben would call the exception.

11 For an analysis of the difference between 'reflective' and 'hermeneutical' phenomenology in relation to facticity, see Zahavi (2003: 155–76).

12 In the past, law, as we have noted, has not been considered to be a description of the world (fact), but more prescriptive. Andrei Marmor, a philosopher of law, puts it this way: 'The law is, by and large, a system of norms. Law's essential character is prescriptive: It purports to guide action, alter modes of behaviour, constrain the practical deliberation of its subjects; generally speaking, the law purports to give us reasons for action' (2011: 1). As a former student of law, Agamben no doubt plays on this understanding of the law in pointing to the ironical indistinction between fact and law in the state of exception. This would explain the opening point of *State of Exception*, where it is claimed that, in effect, the law is now being determined by the situation rather than the reverse, which was supposed

to be the case. Thus, there is a 'no-man's-land between public law and political fact' (Agamben 2005: 1).

13 Although Agamben does, of course, make reference to more recent examples of actual camps, such as concentration camps during the Bosnian War.

14 Melbourne's *Age* newspaper of 24 May 2012 reported a High Court challenge to the 'indefinite detention of 51 refugees deemed to be threats to national security by ASIO [Australian Security and Intelligence Organisation], including Ranjini, the pregnant mother of two young boys'. On the one hand, it could be suggested that this is an indication of public concern. On the other hand, it could be seen as the very last resort of people in an ongoing and perilous situation and that lack of political pressure is what forced the case to go to the High Court as the last avenue of appeal.

Chapter 4

LANGUAGE, THE HUMAN AND BARE LIFE: FROM UNGROUNDEDNESS TO INOPERATIVITY

A number of commentators have argued that a full understanding of Agamben's approach to modern politics is not possible without an appreciation of at least some aspects of his work on language (see Watkin 2010; Birmingham 2011). When we think of language as the key attribute of the human, this opens up the question of the relationship between language and human rights. Certainly, human rights have traditionally been couched in language, and certainly language is constitutive of community. Traditionally, it has been said that to use language is to be in a community of fellow users. This seems to be a much more open approach than that taken by political discourse, where it is a question of determining what a public sphere is and who can be a member of it. If the 'savage', in Arendt's terms, cannot be a member of a public sphere, we know (as Arendt already knew) that the savage is nevertheless already part of a community, or at least a plurality, of speakers, who, in virtue of this fact, can communicate across every cultural divide. This is to say, too, that in order to facilitate such communication, language has no a priori content. Eventually, we must recognise that, in light of this, and in light of Agamben's analysis, human rights similarly have no a priori content. To be human is to be able to give content to language. To be human is, by extension, to be able to give content to human rights in allowing their exposure.

As if to signal its relevance for what is to come in his work, one of Agamben's key works on language – *Language and Death* (1991) – concludes with passages on the sacred, which foreshadows the figure of *homo sacer* in his major work on politics (1998). Thus, in *Language and Death*, we first encounter the principle underpinning the thesis in *Homo Sacer* that he 'who has violated the law, in particular by homicide, is excluded from the community, exiled, and abandoned to himself, so that killing him would not be a crime' (1991: 105). What will become the key motif in the later work is here made to signify that the:

> ungroundedness of all human praxis is hidden here in the fact that an action (a *sacrum facere*) is abandoned to itself and thus becomes the foundation for all legal behaviour; the action is that which, remaining unspeakable (*arreton*) and intransmissible in every action and in all human language, destines man to community and tradition. (1991: 105)

How, then, does Agamben arrive at this point of the 'ungroundedness' of human praxis? Broadly speaking, Agamben argues that:

1. Humanity is distinguished by the fact that it must *acquire* language (it does not have language).
2. Humanity, *as* an animal – as bare life – is not essentially political.

This is the case even if it is also true that Agamben is wary of the human/animal distinction.[1]

In *Language and Death*, Agamben develops a complex argument about the experience of language as Voice, as the basis of humanity, being non-foundational. Can Agamben's notion of the experience of language as *énonciation* – as the act of stating/uttering, as the negative element which can never be represented – offer us certain insights into a possible reconstruction of the notion of human rights, even if this is against Agamben's explicit intention? This is to say that human rights, as an act of discourse, would function when they are invoked. The act of invoking human rights would thus be more important than a pre-existing legal text.[2] The advantage of this approach is that it does not depend for its validity on the division of humanity into those inside and those outside the polity. He or she is essentially human who can invoke human rights in any given context.[3] Human rights normally function, however, at the level of the *énoncé* – a text to be read/interpreted where the reading would be independent of any specific context – where reference is made to a pre-existing subject of these rights, a subject who, historically, has been 'man and citizen', thus raising the dilemma about membership of the polity, which was opened up by Arendt. Agamben's approach to the essential human experience as captured in the notion of an act of discourse deepens our understanding of what is at stake, while not necessarily providing an answer as to how human rights can be supported.

The innovation of *Language and Death* comes from its appropriation of Émile Benveniste's now increasingly well-known notion of *énonciation* as an act of discourse, where meaning and significance are entirely contextual (existential) and, we might add, contingent.[4] It is this which, for Agamben, will come to constitute the basis of what it means to be human. Benveniste begins defining the *énonciation* – exemplified by pronouns and other contextual markers such as 'here' and 'now' – by asking the following question:

> What then is the 'reality' to which *I* or *you* refer? It is uniquely a 'reality of discourse', something quite singular. *I* cannot be defined in terms of a 'locution', nor in terms of objects, as is the case with a nominal sign. *I* signifies 'the person who utters [*énonce*] the present instance of discourse containing *I*'. This instance is unique by definition, and has validity only in its uniqueness. (1966: 252)

The 'reality of discourse' means that the idea of a transcendental subject making the statement or discourse to which it refers is no longer operational. If such were the case – that the statement was essentially the index of a speaker – the statement could only be a singular act, whereas language as *énonciation* is what enables the repetition of this act ('I', 'you' and so on can be appropriated by anybody in a new context). As a result, Agamben agrees that it is not the living being, but language, that is speaking. Such is the price for being human. Agamben points out that the same status as applies to pronouns is also valid for other 'indicators of utterance' – what Jakobson called 'shifters' – such as 'here', 'now', 'today', 'tomorrow' and 'yesterday'. Benveniste's 'act of discourse' and Jakobsen's 'shifter' are taken over by Agamben and defined as an 'event of language' (1991: 25). The latter is uniquely captured by the notion of Voice. Voice, as the event of language, evokes the unique experience of what it means to be human. The profundity of this insight is confirmed for Agamben by the fact that the thought of both Hegel ('This' [*Diese*] in relation to sense certainty) and Heidegger (*Da-sein*: literally 'there-being') turns on the meaning of the shifters: 'this', 'that' and 'there'. A further point is that shifters or acts of discourse open out onto negativity, because they cannot be captured or preserved in writing, for example, as an *énoncé* (statement made). In other words, as an *énoncé*, 'now' has already become the past. Similarly, *Da-sein* cannot be captured in an *énoncé*. It can only be alluded to negatively as a kind of loss. This is the 'event of language' showing itself, and if, for Heidegger, language is the 'house of being', language is to be understood, according to Agamben's reading, as an act of discourse. Being, then, is ensconced in language as an act of discourse. Voice, in its real and apparent contingency, thus best alludes to the truth of being as contained in the act of discourse. Voice is the voice of the living being. But this means, for Heidegger and for Agamben, that:

> Dasein – since language is not its voice – can never grasp the taking place of language, it can never be its *Da* (the pure instance, the pure event of language) without discovering that it is already thrown and consigned to discourse. (Agamben 1991: 56)

Dasein always speaks through the voice in the place of language, but the place of language has no voice, in the sense that it cannot be marked out, represented or defined. It is the place of Being – the place where we are as human beings. Another way of putting it is to say that 'being-there' cannot be represented, just as the level of an act of discourse or the event of language cannot be represented. As soon as an attempt is made to represent it (in an *énoncé*), the act or event as such evaporates.

At the risk of oversimplifying, we say, in light of Agamben's invocation of Heidegger and the instance or event of language, that it is impossible to objectify or to represent an actual act of discourse, apart from it being an experience of language.[5] In terms of human rights, this means that the subject of human rights is the one who invokes such rights in a given act of discourse. The right is in making the claim – in the very act of claiming (which can be variable, for example, simply being on the high seas in a fragile craft; it does not have to be legal and formal)[6] – which is equivalent to being exposed, as Birmingham would say. It does not exist a priori in a statute book, for example. Such rights, then, are not to be understood as those attributed to a pre-existing sentient being deemed to be either inside or outside the political community. Neither are these rights an *expression* of such a being.

Thus, through the notion of the ungroundedness[7] of the human as encapsulated in the 'act of discourse' (*énonciation*), Agamben seeks to valorise action. It is this link between 'ungroundedness' and action that leads to violence and sacrifice:

> The fact that man, the animal possessing language, is, as such ungrounded, the fact that he has no foundation except in his own action (in his own 'violence'), is such an ancient truth that it constitutes the basis for the oldest religious practice of humanity: sacrifice. (Agamben 1991: 105)

What might seem ironical is that this ungroundedness of 'all human praxis' (hidden in the instance of *homo sacer*) becomes the foundation for all legal behaviour. This action, which is unspeakable (as with the experience of Voice), 'destines man to community and to tradition' (1991: 105).

It is to this 'ungroundedness' of the human that we can attach the idea of human rights. For although these are commonly thought to be borne by a pre-existing being with qualities and an identity to whom these rights can be attributed to in virtue of these qualities and identity, the 'ungroundedness' of the human implies that it is in the act of invoking human rights that one comes to *assume* the condition of being human. Rather than a prior decision having to be made as to the content of human identity and thus of human rights, rights exist to the extent that they are claimed. The human, as the subject of human rights is, as it were, retroactively constituted through the act of claiming such rights. As a result, we are able to get around the two key problems already mentioned in relation to a defence of human rights, namely:

1. They are ultimately founded on the human as essentially biological (what has been called having human rights in virtue of one's humanity).
2. The issue no longer exists of a non-public sphere as a domain where one is not fully human, because, due to the fact of language (amongst other things), the distinction between public and private, freedom and necessity, civilised and uncivilised ceases to be viable.

The latter point is reinforced in the contemporary world by information technologies such as the internet.[8] Nation-state borders cease to be relevant or at least cease to have the relevance they had a generation ago.[9]

THE UNGROUNDEDNESS OF THE HUMAN AND THE INHUMAN: VIOLENCE, LAW AND GESTURE

Perhaps the strongest supplementary indication that human rights can survive and even benefit from Agamben's critique relates to the fact that even if the human is based in an ungroundedness or 'non-place' (Birmingham 2011: 141), it is still *the human* which is at issue or which is exposed. Or rather, even if the human is the outcome of the ungroundedness of language and the law, it is still the nature of the human which is central. Law and language, it is timely to recall, are essential aspects of human rights discourse. The overriding question which all of Agamben's work fails to answer, however, is whether *homo sacer* could ever be the subject of human rights. In part, this is in keeping with Agamben's intention to illuminate the role of bare life in the foundation of the law. But, on another level, Agamben has effectively valorised an instance of the human which, from the point of view of human rights, is also the non-human (or between the human and the non-human) and thus could never be subject to human rights protection. It is an entity which could never invoke human rights in an act of discourse, because it is totally alone and abandoned and yet it is the foundation of the law. In the condition of 'ban', no possible interlocutor exists as the recipient of any *énonciation*, even though *homo sacer* has been forced into the position of abandonment. It is not a natural condition. The non-human – or the inter-human (*homo sacer*: that which is reduced, hypothetically, to bare life) – thus has the same status as the slave for Arendt: a being between the human and the non-human, outside the province of the law and thus outside of all means of protection. Here it is possible to argue that *homo sacer*, even within Agamben's own interpretation, is less an instance of bare life and more an incarnation of violence: a way that a form is given to violence as action, exemplifying the ungroundedness of the human.

We are saying, then, that *homo sacer* is the incarnation of violence – a violence which is not represented, but is enacted. In short, what identifies *homo sacer* above all else – what makes him bare life – is that he can be killed without this being a crime.[10] Not murder, not homicide, not wickedness, but pure violence is what is evoked here.[11] As an incarnation of violence, the killing of *homo sacer* also gives an insight into what pure violence would be like. Are we not, then, referring to an absolutely arbitrary act? Clearly, *homo sacer*, understood in this sense, brings us towards the limits of what can be represented or expressed. On this basis, there would be no intrinsic meaning in *homo sacer*, only a potential to have meaning or not to have meaning attributed to such an entity. For the latter cannot be grounded in any way, following Agamben's claim about the ungroundedness of the human. In response, it is important to remember that although *homo sacer* may have been rendered speechless, language and significant gestures are part of his being.

Moreover, *homo sacer* is still human, even if this be as the exclusion from the human which is included. Or, to recall the *Muselmann* of the camps, we are dealing with the inhuman part of the human. One must be human to become inhuman. In such circumstances, the smallest gesture can become hugely significant. As Birmingham recounts, citing Agamben:

> Referring to Robert Antelme's account of the young Italian student from Bologna who blushes when he is called out of line just before being shot, Agamben argues that the blush of shame is the embarrassment of having to die. We who live on after him bear witness to this blush: 'It is as if the flush on his cheeks momentarily betrayed a limit that was reached, as if something like a *new ethical material* were touched upon in the living being?' (Agamben 2002: 104) Shame provides the new ethical material for thinking the subject of right; it reveals what is most intimate about us in our subjectivity and yet we can never assume it or adopt it as our own. (Birmingham 2011: 142–3 [emphasis in original])

In a certain sense, shame would be a very human way of living one's sense of being inhuman. For consciousness, it might be unbearable, but in its manifestation, it confirms that one can only be inhuman in so far as one is also fully human and vice versa. If the *Muselmann* is the incarnation of the inhuman, it is also true that: '[s]imply to deny the *Muselmann*'s humanity would be to accept the verdict of the SS and to repeat their gesture' (Agamben 2002: 63). It is gesture that may well be crucial here. For as Birmingham says: 'Agamben links the appearance or taking-place of language to gesture' (2011: 148), and '[g]esture is the opening of the space of the purely human itself' (149).

Under the influence of the theory of gesture of German critic Max Kommerell (see Agamben 1999b: 77–85), where 'poetic verse' would be an instance of gesture, it is possible, as Birmingham shows, to see Agamben uniting gesture with the purely human and thus with bare life as a way of life, however minimal this might seem. To understand how this works, we need only think of the blush, but we can also evoke the apparently almost deathly shuffle of the *Muselmann*. The shuffle does not signify, but it is intelligible. It is the gesture that belongs to the inhuman and gives the purely human its intelligibility. This shuffle, in other words, is not a means of moving from one point to another, but a way of moving; everyone, after all, has a way or style of walking. The point is that there is no biological level in itself, even to the extent that each biological function also has its own way of being. Indeed, it is 'impossible to separate the *bios politicos* from *zoē*' (Birmingham 2011: 145). In another example, albeit a veritable limit case taken from Dostoyevsky, Agamben refers to the episode in *The Brothers Karamazov* where, 'instead of emitting a saintly odor', the corpse of Starets Zosima 'gives off an intolerable stench' (Agamben 2002: 80). But even the stench of putrefying human flesh, so apparently open to being labelled as entirely inhuman, can give rise to the pure human, as even a stench has its unique way of being. It is the taking place, as it were, of odour itself. Agamben's point, then, is that the inability or refusal to recognise the dimension of the human that remains irreducible to utility and quantification – that cannot be objectified as 'bare', biological life, which, as we saw in the last chapter, is how the human tends to be defined in the modern era – is the very basis for the operation of sovereign power.

For Agamben, then, gesture, above all else, confirms life as a '*way-of-life*' (2000: 4 [emphasis in original]). It is the latter which is the embodiment and incarnation of politics, whereas bare life is the concern of the sovereign. Thus, the mistake that many commentators on Agamben make is to refuse to see a separation between sovereign power and the political. Yet the following passage could not make things clearer on this point:

> A political life, that is a life directed toward the idea of happiness and cohesive with a form-of-life, is thinkable only starting from the emancipation from such a division, with the irrevocable exodus from any sovereignty. The question about the possibility of a nonstatist politics necessarily takes this form: Is today something like a form-of-life, a life for which living itself would be at stake in its own living, possible? (Agamben 2000: 7–8)

Power, by contrast, 'always founds itself – in the last instance – on the separation of a sphere of naked life from the context of forms of life' (Agamben 2000: 4). Seen in this light, the Western tradition of political theory has thought that it was studying politics, when, in fact, it was merely studying power. No doubt it is only when the notion of a 'way-of-life' is made explicit that this point becomes clear.[12]

POTENTIALITY, IMPOTENTIALITY AND (THE IMPOSSIBILITY OF) BEARING WITNESS

Important as Birmingham's interpretation of Agamben is, especially on the *Muselmann* and bearing witness, there is one aspect of her account which, if not overlooked, is in need of amplification. This is the aspect that concerns the impossibility of bearing witness and is related to Agamben's notion of potentiality as coupled with contingency. Agamben, as we noted briefly in the previous chapter, had already linked Aristotle's notion of potentiality to the possible suspension of the law in relation to the sovereign exception. Unlike Agamben, many interpreters of Aristotle have viewed potentiality uniquely as the capacity (*dynamis*) to accomplish something in the future and have noted that Aristotle compares this with actuality. What is less often commented on is that Aristotle also refers to a 'want of potentiality' (Aristotle 1995: 1046a29), which Agamben translates as 'impotentiality'. And, our author adds, this 'means that in its own originary structure *dynamis*, potentiality, maintains itself in relation to its own privation, its own *sterēsis*, its own non-Being' (Agamben 1999a: 182). To clarify this, Agamben gives his own translation of the following passage from Book IX of the *Metaphysics*:

> What is potential [*dynamis*] is capable [*endekhatai*] of not being in actuality. What is potential can both be and not be, for the same is potential both to be and not to be [*to auto ara dynaton kai einai kai mē einai*]. (Aristotle 1050b10)[13]

Potential, in light of Aristotle, is thus also the potential 'not to be', which Agamben defines as 'impotentiality' (1999a: 182–3). The latter can be seen to be applicable across a range of domains, but particularly as concerns the notion of bearing witness to what occurred in Nazi concentration camps. In this sense, not only does the *Muselmann* convey his humanness in his gestures; he also embodies witnessing what went on the camps, in so far as he bears witness to the impossibility of bearing witness, or, to put things in terms of (human) potentiality, the potential to bear witness includes the possibility of not bearing witness or of the impossibility of bearing witness.

Thus, as Agamben presents it, the impossibility of bearing witness is part of the process of bearing witness. For just as potentiality includes impotentiality, just as, in other words, impotentiality is integral to potentiality, so the impossibility of bearing witness is part of the potential to bear witness. In this way, the impossibility to bear witness ceases to be a totally lost cause, whereby the erasure of the witness, so to speak, is equivalent to the loss of all contact with those who perished at Auschwitz and elsewhere.

The same principle applies to language, especially when language is understood as discourse in Benveniste's sense. For, then, it becomes a matter of speaking or not speaking, of the taking place or the not taking place of language. Only by way of the latter procedure can silence and the failure of communication be understood as an essential part of language, not language's failure. This is why the enactment of language (*énonciation*), not the statement made (*énoncé*), is crucial to Agamben's analysis of the *Muselmann*'s situation in the camps. To all those who say that we cannot (must not?) speak of Auschwitz (see Adorno), Agamben says that this 'not speaking' is itself a form of speech, that the negative, fundamentally, is not absolute nothingness, but a form of communication, just as the inhuman is part of the human. Birmingham summarises Agamben's position by saying that: 'Contra Aristotle, the space of the political is not the realm of logos; instead, it is the realm of communicability, which is never about something, but rather is the exposure or the taking-place of a "commonality of singularities"' (2011: 150).

Just as it is possible to propose that the unconscious, as recognised by Freud, decentres subjectivity so that the 'it' (*es*) speaks or so the unconscious is exposed through the subject, discourse (the act of language) performs a similar function in Benvensite's semiotics of language. Moreover, the Heideggerian influence is also in evidence in Agamben's approach, in so far as, for Heidegger, communicability is the communicability of language speaking, of language being exposed, as instanced by poetry. The language user is as much in language as he or she is a language user – a notion implying that language is a tool and thus is essentially functional. Heidegger, who influenced Agamben on this point, problematised the idea that the nature of language could be accessed by way of a meta-language – a language *about* language: 'We speak of language, but constantly seem to be speaking merely *about* language, while in fact we are already letting language, *from within* language, speak to us, in language, of itself, saying its nature' (Heidegger 1982: 85 [emphasis in original]); 'Man acts as though he were the shaper and master of language, while in fact language remains the master of man' (Heidegger 1975: 215). To speak *about* language is, in Benveniste's terms, to be at the level of the *énoncé*, not at the level of the enactment of language, which allows the exposure of the human, as Birmingham has shown. Just as reflection for Heidegger gives way to hermeneutics in relation to facticity and reveals the latter to be irreducible to a fact or facts, so, too, the act of discourse becomes the instantiation or exposure of the human as the being whose very being is language, whose being, in other words, is shown in and through language. In sum, then, it is important, Agamben tells us, not to allow the subject–object duality to dominate our appreciation of language as such.

The Image as the Impossibility of an Image of the Human

In keeping with the theme of impotentiality as embedded within witnessing, language and the human, we find a number of images evoked by Agamben in *Remnants of Auschwitz*. The first and most notable of these – in light of Primo Levi's evocation – is the Gorgon. In Greek mythology, of course, the female face of the Gorgon turned anyone who viewed her to stone. For Levi, as we learn from *Remnants*, the *Muselmann* is the one who 'has seen the Gorgon'. 'But what', Agamben asks, 'in the camp is the Gorgon?' (2002: 53) For Agamben, the Gorgon is a 'prohibited face' – such a face which 'cannot be seen because it produces death, is for the Greeks a non-face' (53). It is thus never described in terms of something which is before the eyes (*prosopon*). Yet at the same time, this non-image, as it were, has a fearsome power of attraction, as though the very prospect of death called one to tarry with it, as though there were a seeing of what cannot be seen. A kind of positivity would thus break through the negative shield. Agamben comments: 'The *gorgoneion*, which represents the impossibility of vision, is what cannot *not* be seen' (2002: 53 [emphasis in original]). Here is an invisibility which becomes part of the visible.

On a broader level, the *Muselmann* becomes an integral part of the logic that we have encountered in the Gorgon and in the impotentiality of potentiality. This is part of Agamben's attempt to deliver (if this is the right word) the *Muselmann* from the Nazi project of making the impossible, the inhuman, the unspeakable and the invisible the absolute and total realities of the camp, so as to ensure the complete erasure of all its inmates from history and from the human as such. Not to recognise the possibility of a certain positivisation of the negative in the contexts outlined is, Agamben claims, 'to accept the verdict of the SS and to repeat their gesture' (2002: 63). For a fellow inmate such as Bruno Bettleheim, to lose one's dignity and self-respect in the camp was to lose moral orientation and thus was to lose one's being as human (see Bettleheim, cited by Agamben 2002: 56–7). In terms of what we have presented above, to lose one's humanity is, Agamben shows, also to confirm one's humanity. For only the human can be excluded from the human. Indeed, 'humans bear within themselves the mark of the inhuman' and 'their spirit contains at its very centre the wound of non-spirit, non-human chaos atrociously consigned to its own being capable of everything' (2002: 77). This, as we shall see in the following chapter, is one of Agamben's most hotly contested claims.

Just as the Gorgon evokes the potentiality of an image of the impossibility of the image (of a non-image, so to speak), so the potential of language harbours the impossibility of communication, of not speaking or communicating. Thus, 'the simple acquisition of speech in no way obliges one to speak' (2002: 65). Because language is characterised in this way, the possibility of non-communication and silence can be included in the potentiality of language itself. Linked to witnessing, this means that the impossibility of witnessing has to be included within the very possibility of witnessing itself. In Agamben's words: 'only if language is not always already communication, only if language bears witness to something to which it is impossible to bear witness, can a speaking being experience something like a necessity to speak' (2002: 65).

Poetry and Life

Language can, of course, also be seen in terms of its potentiality to achieve a form of communication. In other words, it can also be viewed positively, just as gesture is viewed positively as an index of the human.

In an essay written in 1991 as a preface to a collection of poems by Giorgio Caproni entitled 'Expropriated Manner' (collected in Agamben 1999b), Agamben explicitly addresses the relation between poetry and life: 'The poet is he who, in the word, produces life' (1999b: 93). Then our author defines the sense in which life is to be understood in Caproni's poetry, as follows: 'Life, which the poet produces in the poem, withdraws from both the lived experience of the psychosomatic individual and the biological unsayability of the species' (93). This is not life as *zoē*, to be sure, but rather, in the broadest sense, it is life as a way of life (*bios*), but presented in a way that adds to the richness of there only ever being a way of life. This presentation is seen in the idea of 'manner', where something occurs in the poem of which the poet is not entirely aware or, in any case, of which the poet is not entirely in control. Manner may be contrasted with style as the more self-conscious use of language and is the actual evidence of the working of language on the life of the poet. Manner compared to style is an 'impropriety' (one is reminded of the Italian Jew's blush), which often occurs (as in the case of Goethe) in late poetical works or, in the case of Melville's last novels, in 'mannerisms and digressions [which] proliferate to the point of breaking the very form of the novel, carrying it away toward other, less legible genres (the philosophical treatise or the erudite notebook)' (1999b: 97).

For our purposes, manner (which no doubt opens out into the realm of 'bad' poetry) evokes, once again, the inexorable exposure of the human. More than style, which is more in keeping with the *énoncé*, manner shows the enactment of language, for it is what is encountered without ever being looked for (as is the case with style). Perhaps, indeed, the ultimate form of manner is obscenity as the negative form that repels, but which cannot but be endured. The human includes this endurance that language often makes its recipient confront. Manner, then, is also gesture and, as such, is essentially another aspect of exposure. But what is exposed, what is revealed, is not an objectification of the human, it is the process of exposure as such. In other words, in this reading, the human is that which never ceases to expose itself in the obscene and improper, as well as in the proper, sense.

'*Inoperativity*'

In *Language and Death* (1991), Agamben, talking about Hegelian negativity, refers to Bataille's concept of '*négativité sans emploi*', often translated as 'unemployed negativity',[14] but in this case as 'disengaged negativity' (1991: 49). Later in *Homo Sacer*, Agamben refers to the 'theme of *désoeuvrement* – inoperativeness' in relation to the debate on sovereignty and the end of history between Kojève and Bataille (1998: 61). Even though it is based on a questionable interpretation of Hegel, Bataille raises the issue as to where human work and praxis (negativity) might be directed, once the era of the 'project' and of achieving things (history) has come to an end. This is, in fact, for Bataille, the end of the era of utility and of what he calls the 'restricted economy', in light of the flowering of the 'general economy' of communication as the ecstasy and intoxication of 'inner experience'. In his recent work, *The Kingdom and the Glory* (2011), Agamben uses the term 'inoperativity', in order, as he sees it, to go to the heart of *oikonomia* or glory. As Agamben explains:

> We can now begin to understand why doxology and ceremonials are essential to power. What is at stake is the capture and inscription in a separate sphere of the *inoperativity* that is central to human life. The *oikonomia* of power places firmly at its heart, in the form of festival and glory, what appears to its eyes as the inoperativity of man and God, which cannot be looked at. (2011: 245–6 [emphasis added])

Clearly, the twist that Agamben performs, vis-à-vis Bataille, is to show that inoperativity, no doubt surprisingly, can be functional to the working of power. The 'inoperativity of the divinity' and the 'glorification in which human inoperativity celebrates its eternal Sabbath' (2011: 245) are not foreign to power, as we might have hoped. Thus:

> Human life is inoperative and without purpose, but precisely this *argia* and this absence of aim make the incomparable operativity [*operosità*] of the human species possible. Man has dedicated himself to production and labor [*lavoro*], because in his essence he is completely devoid of work [*opera*], because he is the Sabbatical animal par excellence. (2011: 245–6)

As glory, as the 'festival and idleness', inoperativity becomes the 'glorious nutrient of all power' (246). Thus Agamben, in defining economy as *oikonomia*, glory and spectacle and not as something that simply refers to utility as conventionally understood, nevertheless links this inoperativity to the governing process as such. For, it might be agreed, the human has no deeper ontological status than an 'ungroundedness', 'openness' and 'purposelessness'.

So it seems that what we have to understand is that power has hitherto taken over inoperativity for its own ends. The questions that we, like Agamben, must ask are:

> Why does power need inoperativity and glory? What is so essential about them that power must inscribe them at all costs in the empty centre of its governmental apparatus? What nourishes power? And finally, is it possible to think inoperativity outside the apparatus of glory? (2011: 247)

In the crossover from the theological to the secular, glory is presented as an essential element to the functioning of power, even though it, at the same time, remains distinct from it. Another way of putting it is to say that politics (as inoperativity) has historically been inextricably bound to the workings of power as governmentality and that, hypothetically, to separate politics from power (which Agamben foreshadows doing in a future investigation) would entail the dismantling of the functioning of power as we know it.

Significantly, in Agamben's recent work, which he also includes in the *Homo Sacer* series, inoperativity begins to overtake the very division between *bios* and *zoē* and perhaps renders them 'inoperative' in the analysis of politics: 'The political order is neither a *bios* nor a *zoē*, but the dimension that the inoperativity of contemplation, by deactivating linguistic and corporeal material and immaterial praxes, ceaselessly opens and assigns to the living' (Agamben 2011: 251). While on the one hand inoperativity seems to liberate the human from its 'biological and social destiny' (251), on the other hand it seems, as we have said, to be implicated in power in the sense that it becomes incarnate in power's glorification. Here it is important, once again, to distinguish between power and politics, for if inoperativity is functional to power, it has yet to be made fully extant in the realm of politics. Thus, Agamben urges: 'nothing is more urgent than to incorporate inoperativity within its own apparatuses' (2011: 251), that is, within the apparatuses of politics. Poetry, as inoperativity *par excellence*, thus does not need to be brought into the political sphere; rather it must be shown to provide the analogy of purposelessness within which politics as praxis works. Thus, poetry, being the 'linguistic operation that renders language inoperative' (251), can illuminate the potentiality of politics.

From Agamben's account, the great difficulty for poetry becoming the model of inoperativity for politics to follow stems from the emergence of 'spectacular society' and the domination of the media. The latter, as the vehicle of public opinion (the modern form of acclamation), provides the modern version of glory for power, so that glory remains at the centre of the political system, because politics is still equated with the workings of power: 'As had always been the case in profane and ecclesiastical liturgies, this supposedly "originary democratic phenomenon" is only once again caught, orientated, and manipulated in the forms and according to the strategies of spectacular power' (2011: 256).

Agamben's claim that the media is a modern version of glory and the conduit of power – the modern form of public opinion as acclamation, which power needs in order to function – is based on the notion of the 'society of the spectacle' in Guy Debord's sense. The media becomes the presence of the people as such in contemporary society. The media, as the quintessential instance of modern technology, are now inseparable from the grip of power – the power that enables inoperativity to be commandeered to act in power's interests. Debord's analysis is linked to Schmitt's on public opinion as the modern form of the acclamation with the result that:

> the entire problem of the contemporary spectacle of the media domination over all areas of social life assumes a new guise. What is in question is nothing less than a new and unheard of concentration, multiplication, and dissemination of the function of glory as the centre of the political system. (Agamben 2011: 256)

Of course, today, human rights discourses and practices cannot be separated from the society of the spectacle – images of humanitarian disasters and atrocities become simply another spectacle, filtered and disseminated through the media. While human rights proponents say that the media and modern communication technologies are essential in bringing to light human rights situations around the world, allowing us to bear witness to human rights violations, we must at the same time be wary of the politically disabling impact of such spectacles and the way that they do not in any sense present a serious challenge to and, indeed, may even contribute to the glorification of, contemporary regimes of spectacular sovereign power.

The key question that Agamben raises – already intimated above – is how can an autonomous and inoperative politics emerge in this scenario, if the media in the grip of power allows almost no scope for alternative strategies to arise? Important as this question is, it is no doubt just scraping the surface of the problem. This is particularly true, given that Agamben, inspired by Heidegger, is seeking an ontological basis for politics. More will be said about this later; it will suffice for now to say that if Agamben admired Debord as a strategist, we might ask whether it is possible to use an ontological approach strategically – one that strives to escape the metaphysics of the *doxa*. The quick answer would seem to be 'no'. On the other hand, it might well be that only an ontological approach is able to evade and resist being incorporated into the current political logic dominated by the *doxa* of 'usefulness' and based on a productivist metaphysic that would link the political with work. This is why Agamben, as we have seen, says that: 'Man [. . .] is the Sabbatical animal par excellence' (2011: 246). Substituting the human for 'Man', we can say that, as an essentially Sabbatical animal (that is, as an animal which defines itself in terms of its essential being in contradistinction to work), the human is also an essentially political being. But this essential being, Agamben implies, has been covered over and hidden to the point where operativity, or what Bataille calls the 'restricted economy' of utility, uses inoperativity for its own ends.

But, no doubt, one should also spend more time reflecting on the precise difference between power and politics not just in Agamben's theory, but also more broadly. For it is at the intersection of these two domains that the greatest ambiguity remains. This is the issue to be addressed in succeeding chapters. For now, let us say that whatever assessment one comes to make about Agamben's audacious trajectory, it is arguable that language is the major focus around which the entire edifice of the *homo sacer* theory pivots, as well as the possible terrain for rethinking the human in ways that allow us to avoid *homo sacer*'s ultimate fate.

Notes

1 For Agamben, the point is to explain the way that separation occurs: 'What is man if he is always the place – and, at the same time, the result – of ceaseless divisions and caesurae? It is more urgent to work on these divisions, to ask in what way – within man – has man been separated from non-man, and the animal from the human, than it is to take positions on the great issues, on so-called human rights and values. And perhaps even the most luminous sphere of our relations with the divine depends, in some way, on that darker one which separates us from the animal' (2004: 16).

2 It might seem that this echoes Derrida's invocation of a performative in his interpretation of the American Declaration of Independence and Declaration of Human Rights. Derrida points out, for example, that the people '*as such* do *not* exist *before* the declaration' (2002: 49–50 [emphasis in original]). And maybe we could say that the case is similar for human rights: human rights effectively do not exist before they are actively invoked. In her interpretation of the relation between Agamben and Derrida on this point, Birmingham believes that the idea that Jefferson's signature can stand for or represent the whole people – that the people are presupposed in Jefferson's signature – is what Agamben finds problematic. For Agamben, says Birmingham: 'the coming community will not be declared on the basis of a presupposition or a representation' (2011: 148). As Birmingham rightly points out, for Agamben, the pure event of language (its taking place), which is the basis of the 'coming community', precedes meaning, 'yet there is intelligibility' (148).

3 The thought of Jacques Rancière in his article 'Who Is the Subject of the Rights of Man?' (2004) begins to move in this direction. The short answer to Rancière's question is that the subject of human rights is one which invokes human rights in a given act of discourse (= an *énonciation*), thus in a given context.

4 For Agamben, contingency, as we shall see, is important for understanding the notion of potentiality as containing the possibility of impotentiality: the possibility that something might not take place. Thus, *énonciation* also contains within it the possibility that 'an act of discourse' might not take place.

5 The distinction between *énonciation* and *énoncé* evokes Heidegger's notion of facticity, as presented in Chapter 3. For in his differentiation of facticity from fact and, we could add, reflection from hermeneutics, Heidegger is attempting to grasp Dasein in its very being, in its very assumption of its 'thereness', as we saw Agamben saying (1998: 150–1). In this sense, Dasein becomes a way or act of being (*énonciation*), not being as objectified in reflection or discourse (*énoncé*).

6 Levinas' quasi-phenomenological approach, which we shall examine in a subsequent chapter (see Chapter 8), provides further clarification of the significance of 'claiming'.

7 'Ungroundedness' means no essence, no prior qualities and no given identity. What is, only in its being instantiated: something akin to facticity, but also to Hegel's nothingness or pure negativity.

8 On a pragmatic level, as Derrida points out, the very existence of the inter net and email 'is on the way to transforming the entire public and private space of humanity' (1998: 17).

9 This perhaps explains why borders are more obsessively controlled today, revealing a certain ambiguity or crisis in nation-state identity.

10 Here, the aspect of violence in Agamben's depiction of *homo sacer* cannot be emphasised strongly enough. Indeed, a transductive (= the meaning of each entity depends on the existence of the other) relation exists between violence and the one killed, such that without violence, *homo sacer* would cease to have any meaning. *Homo sacer* becomes the exemplar of violence, to the extent that its very *raison d'être*, as it were, is to be the victim of violence.

11 Let us not forget that, for Arendt, a key element of the realm of necessity is violence.

12 Here, the act as such will figure most importantly in Agamben's view of the political, giving rise, as we shall see later, to the term 'inoperativity' – a term evoking the need to escape a productivist metaphysic. This, at least, is something of which Arendt's view of political community is not guilty, founded as it is on freedom and creativity.

13 The same passage, plus a preceding one in volume two of the Barnes edition of Aristotle, reads: 'Every potentiality is at one and the same time a potentiality for the opposite; for while that which is not capable of being may possibly not be actual. That, then, which is capable of being may possibly not be actual. That, then, which is capable of being may either be or not be' (1995: 1050b9–10).

14 Or perhaps more prosaically as 'idleness' (see Boldt's translation in Bataille 1988: 48).

Chapter 5

NIHILISM OR POLITICS? AN INTERROGATION OF AGAMBEN

In previous chapters, there has arisen a series of questions concerning Agamben's notion of politics and what sort of alternatives might be conceivable in his rather stark analysis of the seemingly inexorable trajectory of modern biopolitics and sovereign exceptionalism. Even though the tone is more optimistic regarding the human and the political in the latter part of *The Kingdom and the Glory*, *Homo Sacer* and *Remnants of Auschwitz*, by contrast, give the impression that the entire destiny of Western politics lies in the concentration camp and in the reduction of everyone to 'bare life' or, worse, to *homines sacri*. Much of what Agamben says in these key texts would seem to support this bleak outlook. Moreover, many commentators are critical of what they regard as the metaphysical and ahistorical nature of Agamben's thinking, as if the 'biopolitical catastrophe' (1998: 188) that awaits humanity is forged in earliest antiquity, in the initial separation of *zoē* and *bios* in Greek thought, and simply unfolds throughout the course of Western history, entrapping us within the infernal logic of power. Indeed, there is something that seems rigidly deterministic about Agamben's analysis of biopolitics and its intertwining with the sovereign exception. This is not helped by the vagueness and opacity of Agamben's alternative figures of life and community. We know that he makes certain references in different places to 'inoperativity' or 'impotentiality', to life as a 'form-of-life' which escapes or transcends law and sovereignty and even to the 'coming community'. But from a more familiar, not to say every day, standpoint with regard to politics, the precise meaning of such terms, suggestive though they are, is often difficult to grasp. Thus, it is difficult to see how such concepts could serve as positive figures of resistance to the workings of modern biopolitical sovereignty or, indeed, as a model for any sort of meaningful political agency. This has led many to dismiss Agamben's thought as nihilistic or apolitical. For instance, Paolo Virno considers Agamben to be a 'thinker with no political vocation' (Virno 2002).

We disagree with this view and suggest that there is a notion of ethics, politics and action to be found in Agamben's thought. Part of this chapter, and the following one, will be devoted to teasing this out. It is clear that Agamben is gesturing towards a completely different conception of politics – one that cannot be slotted into the predominant categories and frameworks of political theory, a tradition that, for the most part, is still oriented around the problem of sovereignty and its legitimation. Also, as we will show, Agamben's notion of politics departs in interesting ways from that of a number of his contemporaries in continental philosophy, including Ernesto Laclau, Chantal Mouffe and Antonio Negri. Exploring these differences will go a long way towards clarifying what Agamben actually understands as politics. We know that Agamben wants to make some sort of distinction between power and politics, thus invoking lines of resistance, contestation and alterity. Yet, at the same time, this distinction is often unclear or even blurred in his writing. Sharpening these conceptual lines will therefore be crucial to gaining a better understanding of the place of politics in Agamben's thought.

Furthermore, a deeper engagement with these political questions is important for developing an alternative approach to human rights. As we have seen, Agamben is highly critical of existing conceptions of human rights, seeing them as discourses which participate in the reduction of people to 'bare life'. One of the problems highlighted here by both Arendt and Agamben, albeit in different senses, is the depoliticising effect of human rights. One of the aims of this book is, therefore, to rethink the politics of human rights – or better, to think human rights as a politics – while at the same time avoiding the trap of simply resituating rights within the traditional categories of citizenship and the public space. This demands, as we can already see, an alternative conception of politics – one that is no longer localised within the nation-state or built around the traditional problematic of sovereignty. Indeed, it points towards a completely different conception of political agency and community, one that, as we argue and as Agamben himself hints at, is already being prefigured in the phenomenon of statelessness.

As a way of clarifying the contours of the political in Agamben's thought, we will first explore a number of important critiques of his work, many of which, although not all, centre around the charge that his thinking is incompatible with any viable or coherent conception of ethics or politics. Criticisms come from other quarters as well. whether it is to do with, as is alleged, the gratuitous, excessive and even 'pornographic' use of the example of Auschwitz and the *Muselmann*; questions concerning the original distinction in Greek philosophy between *zoē* and *bios*; his inadequate understanding of law and *nomos*; or his reductionist and deterministic reading of sovereignty. The aim here is not necessarily to defend Agamben against these charges, although, certainly, his position is defensible on many of these points, but rather to show how some of these criticisms, even if they might ultimately be wide of the mark, at the same time open up important questions and aporias in Agamben's thought. Moreover, an encounter with these critiques will shed some light on new ways of thinking about the foundations, as well as the enactment, of human rights today.

AUSCHWITZ AND THE *MUSELMANN*: EXPLOITATION? AESTHETICISATION?

Perhaps the most controversial area of Agamben's thinking is his treatment of the Shoah, particularly in his major works, *Homo Sacer* and *Remnants of Auschwitz*. Many object to what they regard as the excessiveness of Agamben's claim that Auschwitz is the 'paradigm' of our biopolitical present. Strikingly, Agamben sees the camp 'not as a historical fact and an anomaly belonging to the past (even if still verifiable) but in some way as the hidden matrix and *nomos* of the political space in which we are still living' (1998: 166). The camp is, he argues, a specific juridical and biopolitical space characterised by an unlimited state of exception, which is somehow still with us. In the same way that the prison, for Foucault, served as a grid of intelligibility for analysing the rest of disciplinary society, the camp, for Agamben, is a matrix for understanding our modern day spaces of exception – everything from the refugee camp to temporary zones of detention for 'illegal' migrants through to Guantánamo Bay. This suggests a certain continuum or commonality between these spaces, as well as between totalitarian and liberal–democratic states.

Many have criticised what they see as the inordinate and hyperbolic nature of such claims. Others have held as offensive the suggestion that there is an equivalency between contemporary sites of detention and the Nazi concentration camp or that, for instance, the refugee or the detainee in Guantánamo has essentially the same status as a victim of Auschwitz. To say this, it is argued, denies the historical uniqueness and singularity of the Shoah, insults the memory of its victims and trivialises it by comparing it with more benign or less dire situations. It also ignores the important differences between the absolute vulnerability and nakedness of the Nazi camp inhabitant and the more legally qualified, although no doubt ambivalent, status of the refugee, who cannot accurately be seen as 'bare life'. As Carl Levy puts it:

> Agamben and his more enthusiastic followers lack any proportionality, when they distastefully lump together varieties of refugee camps, Auschwitz, and even gated communities. Refugees are not cannon fodder for radical metaphysical arguments, and should not be equated to (a historically inaccurate) mass of passive, half-dead inmates of Auschwitz's work camps. (2010: 100–1)

In a similar vein, Philippe Mesnard criticises what he sees as Agamben's oversimplified account of the Nazi camps – one that ignores the variegation of spaces within the camps and the lives they contained. This totalising, impressionistic and historically inaccurate account is an example of Agamben's 'aestheticization of disaster', as Mesnard puts it; it is this lack of attention to the specificity of the camp that allows Agamben to subsume everything within it and to see it as a model or paradigm for the whole of society, history and modernity (Mesnard 2004: 139–57).[1]

Yet for all this consternation over the excessiveness of Agamben's argument about Auschwitz, one cannot help but be struck by the excessiveness of such criticisms themselves. Nowhere does Agamben suggest that there is a moral equivalence between the Nazi camp, the refugee camp or the terrorist detention site; to highlight parallels in their juridico-political structure is very different from saying that one site is as bad as the other. Moreover, if we are to prevent outrages such as the Holocaust from ever occurring again, it is surely important to try to grasp the broader logic of power that made it possible and by exploring potential sites in which something similar could again emerge. On the question of Agamben downplaying the historical uniqueness of the Nazi camp by seeing it as a paradigm for the operation of power at a society-wide level, we need to better understand his particular use of the 'paradigm'. For Agamben, a paradigm is a singular example, which illuminates a broader set of relations or situation to which it also belongs; it is a kind of exhibit which makes a series of relations intelligible. Thus, the paradigm is both different from other relations – it is singular – and, at the same time, reveals something in common about the nature of these other relations. The paradigm is thus neither strictly inside nor outside the set of objects of which it serves as an example.[2] The use of the concentration camp as a paradigm of power relations – in the same way that the Panopticon operated as a paradigm of disciplinary society for Foucault – does not necessarily mean that all these elements are the same or morally equivalent to one another, but rather that they share some underlying logic or potentiality.

We can understand Agamben's point about the 'inner solidarity' shared between totalitarian and democratic regimes in a similar way (see 1998: 10). The argument here is not that one is as oppressive or violent as the other, but rather that they both have to be analysed on the terrain of biopolitics, which means that, at times, their differences can become blurred and indistinct and one can pass imperceptibly into the other. Is it not naïve in the extreme to assure oneself of the absolute sanctity, virtue and superiority of liberal–democracy, while the regimes which bear this name today have securitised themselves in ways that seem to violate their proclaimed liberal–democratic principles?

However, a more serious and worrying objection to Agamben is his use of the figure of the *Muselmänner* in *Remnants of Auschwitz*. The *Muselmann* is, as we have already explained, the absolute figure of bare life, the living dead of Auschwitz, the one who shuffles lifelessly through the camps and who, through malnourishment and deprivation, no longer reacts to external stimuli. These desolate figures – more dead than alive – are an example of the almost complete desubjectification experienced by some in the camps. And yet, according to Agamben, it is precisely because of their dehumanisation – because they occupy the threshold between the human and inhuman – that they are not only the ultimate witness to the unspeakable suffering, cruelty and tragedy of the camps, but they reveal a new understanding of ethics which can no longer be based on the notion of human dignity, but rather must include the inhuman or the inhuman part of the human (2002: 64).

Yet, J. M. Bernstein has expressed repugnance at what he sees as Agamben's exploitation of this tragic figure as grist for his philosophical mill. Bernstein accuses Agamben of an aestheticisation of the *Muselmann* that is akin to pornography – 'pornography of horror', as he puts it (2004: 2–16). His argument is that because the focus of Agamben's lurid philosophical gaze is on the solitary figure of the *Muselmann*, rather than on the wider phenomenon of the camps and the historical conditions that gave rise to them, this is something like the pornographic gaze that isolates, captures and photographs a certain figure, removing it from any contextualisation. This figure becomes the object of our fascination. Just as the *Muselmann* bears witness to an unbearable horror, so Agamben bears witness or, rather, invites *us* to bear witness to the *Muselmann*, drawing our gaze towards this abject figure. The *Muselmann* is that which both repels and fascinates us. Just as with the pornographic image, we cannot help but look; horror and suffering are no less enthralling than images of sex. And just as the pornographic image exploits and does violence to the subject it captures, so, too, does Agamben's portrait exploit the unfortunate figure of the *Muselmann*. As Bernstein says:

> I want to say that there is something pornographic in Agamben's philosophical portrait of the Muselmann, the pure desire to bear witness. That something that in the territory of pornography might be at issue here is indirectly hinted at by Agamben when he contends that in 'certain places and situations, dignity is out of place. The lover, for example, can be anything but 'dignified', just as it impossible to make love while keeping one's dignity.' When this is coupled with the pure desire to bear witness the way a photograph just witnesses, then witnessing begins to sound like an aestheticized looking, and what is looked upon is the body without dignity. Does that not place us in the region of pornography? (2004: 8)

This is a serious charge, but one that, we would argue, is misplaced. For one thing, Bernstein is guilty of a sleight of hand here. It is surely something of a jump to take Agamben's general example of lovemaking as also involving a lack of dignity and then to interpret him as suggesting that there is somehow a link or parallel between lovemaking and the *Muselmann* or, rather, a parallel between witnessing lovemaking (that is, pornography) and witnessing the *Muselmann*. This is simply not what Agamben is getting at. Moreover, rather than Agamben engaging in a lurid aestheticisation of the *Muselmann*, we find instead a much

more philosophical perspective that avoids the temptation of gratui-
tously depicting scenes of horror. It is very different, for instance, from
the works of those like Wolfgang Sofsky (2003) or Adriana Cavarero
(2009), which at times seem to relish lurid descriptions of extreme
violence, brutality, suffering and cruelty. Furthermore, it is important
to make the obvious point that there are no photographs in *Remnants
of Auschwitz*; instead, at the end of the book, there are a series of testi-
monials from camp survivors who found themselves in the position of
Muselmänner. The witnessing that Agamben speaks of does not refer
so much to the visual field as that of testimony, this being the most
emphatic proof of the horrors of the camps.

Nevertheless, is there something repulsive, as Bernstein contends,
in developing a notion of ethics around the *Muselmänner*? Agamben's
point here is that the figure of the *Muselmann* in his extreme degradation forces us to rethink our standard conception of ethics, and
especially the idea of human dignity that they are founded upon. The
Muselmann is emphatically without 'dignity'; he has lost his humanity in any recognisable sense. And yet, Agamben argues, if we are to
simply exclude the *Muselmann* from humanity and therefore from the
field of ethics altogether, we risk repeating the gesture of the SS (2002:
63). Therefore, the ultimate test of ethics must be to recognise the
inhuman in the human. Bernstein, however, objects to this preoccupation with the inhuman as an appropriate terrain of ethics; he finds 'all
but unintelligible' and 'grotesque' Agamben's claim that the fact that
life exists in the 'most extreme degradation' becomes 'the touchstone
by which to judge and measure all morality and all dignity' (2004: 8).
But Agamben's challenge needs to be taken seriously: if we construct
ethics around the recognition of human dignity and moral autonomy,
do we not risk excluding from ethical consideration those whose degradation has robbed them of these qualities? The fact that the *Muselmann*
and those like him do not seem to qualify to be called human because
they have been stripped of everything (dignity, civil identity, capacity to
act, capacity to bear witness) has meant, as we have shown in Chapter
4, that a case in their defence has been all but impossible to mount. As
we have seen, if matters are left there, as Agamben argues, the Nazi
position is confirmed. This is why, in terms of potentiality which must
include impotentiality (the possibility 'not to'), the human has to be
found in the inhuman.

ZOĒ AND *BIOS*, BARE LIFE AND *HOMO SACER*

The figure of the *Muselmänner* in Agamben's analysis might be seen as the most extreme form of 'bare life' – life stripped down to mere biological existence and deprived of any kind of political or symbolic significance. Indeed, in the case of the *Muselmänner*, even his biological existence is constantly in jeopardy, as indeed was the situation with all the inhabitants of the camps. Yet, at the same time, Agamben wants to suggest that 'bare life' is a condition that in one way or another confronts us all; indeed, that under the reign of modern biopolitical government, as Foucault has it: 'what follows is a kind of bestialization of man achieved through the most sophisticated political techniques' (cited in Agamben 1998: 3). Yet, as we have alluded to before, one can detect a certain ambiguity in the idea of 'bare life'. Is it the same as *zoē* – life as mere existence, as the fact of being alive – as distinct from *bios* – as a 'form of life' – defined according to the original division that Agamben identified in ancient Greek thought? Or does 'bare life' only emerge within the field of modern biopolitics and with the intervention of the biopolitical state, which includes it in the form of its exclusion? Does 'bare life' only emerge when *zoē* enters the *polis*? When it becomes the preoccupation of government?

As Jacques Derrida points out, there is often a slippage between these terms (2009: 325–6). At the very least, Agamben suggests that *zoē* and its original separation from *bios* is the ontological field that gives rise to 'bare life'; it is this separation which makes 'bare life' possible, and it is this separation which, as we have suggested, Agamben wants to overcome in his notion of life as 'form-of-life'. Or on another possible reading, bare life is the threshold that mediates between *zoē* and *bios*. It is unclear, then, whether bare life is the same thing as *zoē*, a separate entity or a relation between identities.

A related question might be raised about the originary distinction in ancient Greek philosophy between *zoē* and *bios* – a distinction that so much of Agamben's argument hinges on in *Homo Sacer*. Derrida, for one, has questioned the accuracy of Agamben's reading of Aristotle on this question – a reading which largely follows that of Arendt in its insistence on the strict separation in Greek thought between the qualified, public and political life of *bios* and that of the simple, natural life, whose proper domain is the *oikos* or 'home' (see Agamben 1998: 2). But as Derrida shows, there is a very real ambiguity surrounding this distinction, and it is never clear-cut. What genuinely problematises this division is the notion of *zoon politikon* in Aristotle's *Politics*; man is described here as a 'political animal' – a creature with a unique capacity for political life. According to Derrida, this instantly jeopardises Agamben's conceptual distinction, blurring the lines between *zoē*, *zoon*, the animal (as a being simply alive) and politics – the vocation or form of life proper to man (*bios*). As Derrida puts it, this looks 'like an exception to the rule he [Agamben] has just stated, namely Aristotle's *politikon zoon*: i.e. a *zoē* that is qualified and not bare' (2009: 327). How can 'bare' life be at the same time not bare, but qualified, indeed, political, without disrupting, at least to some extent, the very foundations of Agamben's argument? It would seem to raise questions about the coherence of Agamben's notion of 'bare life'. Perhaps it suggests that life can never be simply life itself in a strictly biological sense, but is already always qualified. Perhaps life can never be absolutely separated from vocation, from politics. Perhaps life is always already political and has some sort of political capacity or potential; indeed, the possibility of life as a form-of-life and therefore as political life is something Agamben himself elsewhere invokes. Moreover, as we have proposed, this is the only way to see life if we are to have any hope of reviving human rights.

LAW AND *NOMOS*

The ambiguity that might be identified in Agamben's notion of 'bare life' also has implications for his understanding of law, because, for Agamben, law has a specific relationship with bare life; the law under the sovereign exception intervenes on the terrain of 'bare life', holding it in thraldom by withdrawing from it or, rather, withdrawing its protections from it. This is the point at which bare life can become *homo sacer*, in the sense of being outside the law. Of course, the functioning of the law and its relation to life, particularly to the lives of those who are denied its protections, is crucial to the question of human rights. On the one hand, the application of human rights depends on some sort of legal protection for those who face violence and oppression, but as we have so often seen, the law can be ineffective in defending human rights or protecting people from sovereign power.

The question that must be posed is whether Agamben has an adequate conception of law; whether, indeed, the law is only pernicious, working hand-in-hand with sovereign power and even suspending itself in order to accommodate the exception, or whether law might operate in a more benign and positive way, whether it is able to limit sovereign power and protect us against its excesses.

For Peter Fitzpatrick, Agamben, in his analysis of sovereignty and bare life, has downplayed the importance of law as that which mediates between these two entities. In other words, we do not have, and especially not in modernity, an absolutely powerful sovereignty and an absolutely vulnerable bare life, apart from in certain unique situations. Rather, we have, as Fitzpatrick puts it, an 'irresolute' law which underpins sovereign power – a law which treats us ambivalently, but at the same time makes sovereignty itself indefinite and not quite as absolute or decisive as Agamben seems to suggest. Moreover, the law has always had this mediating function, even in the original Roman punishment of declaring someone *homo sacer*. For Agamben, this places the individual concerned outside of the law. However, as Fitzpatrick points out, this is still a situation that is legally prescribed, that has the status of a legal punishment for a specific crime (2005: 51–2). While Agamben's characterisation of *homo sacer* in ancient Rome is not entirely accurate, according to Fitzpatrick, it is even less convincing in later historical periods, and we cannot suppose that this figure is somehow a historical constant. Nor is the figure of the refugee today bare in the sense that Agamben wants to suggest; rather than the refugee existing in a state of abandonment by law, 'the refugee is inclusively recognized as part of the "human" community through international and national laws of some effectiveness' (Fitzpatrick 2005: 69).

So, in sum, while Agamben is seen to argue for law becoming indistinguishable from fact, thus giving rise to the complete dominance of biopower, Fitzpatrick, by contrast, argues that there is always an inexorable part to be played by law, albeit to be the defining moment of sovereignty, which at the same time as it constitutes *homo sacer* is constituted by it.

For both Agamben and Fitzpatrick, then, *homo sacer* points to the dilemma of deciding what is inside and outside the law:

> Since it is not permitted to sacrifice this man, the life of *homo sacer* could be seen as outside of divine law, and since it is not homicide to kill him, that life could be seen also as outside of human law. (Fitzpatrick 2005: 51)

The question is to know in what sense there is a sphere external to the law. Is it the sphere external to, or beyond, the 'normal' case? Clearly, Agamben's argument is that bare life, as incarnate in the *homo sacer*, is external to the law. More ironically, as untouched by the law (even if the law needs this figure to define itself), *homo sacer* stands for life as 'situation', as 'fact', as 'the exception' to the normal case. In short, *homo sacer* stands for (*bare* or *mere*) life over and against the law. However, the further question then arises as to the sense in which *homo sacer* is 'included' in the law 'solely through an exclusion' (see Agamben 1998: 11).

As a legal scholar, Fitzpatrick's point is that the law is never entirely captured in the notion of the normal case, because it is always open to contingency. Were it not so, the normal case would become entirely anachronistic and irrelevant. So change is built into the normal case, says Fitzpatrick: 'Instantiations of the norm always entail a transgression of what the norm had been, entail its becoming "other" to what it was. The norm, in short, always subsists along with its own exception. The exceptional, again, is unexceptional' (2005: 60). Agamben does not pay sufficient attention to this, according to Fitzpatrick.[3]

AGAMBEN AND SOVEREIGNTY

The question of law and nomos is directly related to sovereignty; the exception, which is at the heart of Agamben's conception of sovereignty, implies a specific relation to the law – one of *inclusive exclusion*. The sovereign exception is not the simple abrogation of law, but its suspension, and, for Schmitt, from whom Agamben entirely derives his theory of sovereignty, the authority of the juridical order can only be guaranteed insofar as it can be periodically suspended when faced with a national emergency. Furthermore, the law is what binds us to sovereignty, not only in the sense that the legal subject is integrated into the order of the state, but also in the sense that the law's abandonment – the temporary removal of its protections – is what allows sovereignty to operate in a virtually unlimited fashion. The law is what authorises the state of exception (see Agamben 2005a). Moreover, Agamben warns us that the exception is becoming indistinguishable from the norm, from the everyday functioning of law and politics: 'Faced with the unstoppable progression of what has been called a "global civil war", the state of exception tends increasingly to appear

as the dominant paradigm of government in contemporary politics'
(2005a: 2).

Perhaps this is somewhat dramatic, but with the ongoing securitisation of the state since 9/11 – with exceptional practices such as
detention without trial and expanded surveillance becoming virtually normalised – there does seem to be an element of truth in what
Agamben says. Nevertheless, a number of commentators have criticised
Agamben's conception of sovereignty as too rigid, totalising, reductionist and as foreclosing any possibility of resistance or alternative politics.
The structural logic of sovereignty that Agamben presents appears not
only deterministic, but also ahistorical, as if essentially the same juridico-
political mechanism has remained unchanged from its earliest incep-
tion, embodying a logic which simply unfolds to the present moment.
Whether in ancient Roman law, through to the medieval ban and to
our present horizon of biopolitics, the inner core of sovereignty – the
secret contiguity between the sovereign exception and *homo sacer* – is a
constant and simply plays itself out in different guises. Moreover, while
Agamben claims that his analysis in *Homo Sacer* 'completes, even cor-
rects' Foucault by tracing the existence of biopolitics back to antiquity
and by taking the analysis of sovereignty forward to the present day,
one wonders whether Foucault's patient and meticulous genealogical
analyses of practices of power and government, which are sensitive to
historical shifts and mutations, do not give us a fuller and more accurate
account than that offered by Agamben. It is also important to point
out that despite Agamben's claim that he is redressing the 'blindspot'
in Foucault over the continuity of sovereignty, Foucault never actually
abandoned the problematic of sovereignty and never claimed that sovereignty is somehow no longer with us; for Foucault, sovereignty in the
modern period is simply articulated in different ways, through regimes
of security, government and biopolitics, rather than through the classical
juridico-sovereign image of the king.[4]

So is it the case that Agamben's notion of sovereignty is deterministic
and essentialist? This is the position of, for instance, William Connolly,
who argues that Agamben's notion of sovereignty takes insufficient
account of its complexities and is excessively formalistic. This formalism, moreover, entraps Agamben within the structure of sovereignty
that he wants to transcend. Connolly maintains that, instead, we
should seek to pluralise the concept of sovereignty or, rather, to
recognise that it is already pluralised, it is no longer strictly attached

to the totalising identity of the nation, for instance, and this, in itself, makes it possible 'to negotiate a more generous ethos of pluralism that copes in more inclusive ways with the nexus between biology, politics and sovereignty' (Connolly 2007: 30). As Connolly argues, sovereignty is always shaped by a particular ethos, which varies in different cultural contexts, and, indeed, there are conflicting perspectives, ideologies, religions, political persuasions, legal interpretations, sensibilities and cultural identities within contemporary societies which pull sovereignty in different directions, diversifying and variegating it. Therefore, it is impossible to see sovereignty as a totalising, unified and constant structure unaffected by cultural shifts: 'A change in ethos, which forms a critical component in the complexity of sovereignty, alters the course of sovereignty' (Connolly 2007: 35). The myriad ways in which ethos shapes and resonates with sovereignty are simply ignored in the stark juridico-political formalism of Agamben's account, Connolly argues. Nor are the processes of globalisation and the way they restructure, pluralise and fragment nation-state sovereignty really taken into consideration in Agamben's theory.

No doubt Connolly is right to point out that sovereignty is shaped by all sorts of cultural, religious, legal and economic factors. However, it must be borne in mind that what Agamben is interested in is not the institution of the state, whose historical transformations he is surely not blind to, but rather a specific relation between power and bare life, which he sees as the hidden core of the state – the thread connecting all historical forms of political and legal power, from absolutist monarchies, to totalitarian regimes to modern democracies. The ultimate decision over life and the ability to suspend the normal legal order lies at the heart of all regimes of power. This was something that Hobbes understood well when he conceived of the modern state – the Leviathan or '*Mortall God*' – as the accumulation of the natural right to violence, which was wielded over subjects who had relinquished theirs. Do we not get a glimpse – even today in our modern liberal–democratic regimes – of this violent and exceptional core of sovereignty, when, for instance, civil liberties are curtailed in the name of security or when terrorist suspects are covertly rendered and tortured or when an innocent man, mistaken for a terrorist, is slain by police with complete impunity in a crowded subway station?[5] In such moments of exception, we perceive the true visage of sovereignty. Agamben's depiction of sovereignty is deliberately stark and pared back so as to reveal this dimension of violence and domination that is so often obscured in political theory. Unlike the analysis of Claude Lefort (1989), in which the democratic revolutions of the eighteenth century sundered the link between modern power and the *ancien régime*, Agamben brings to light their violent continuity. Democracy only covers over this relation; it does little to limit power, and, at times, it can even intensify it. The democratic sovereignty established in Rousseau's *Social Contract* turned out to be just as absolutist, if not more so, as those monarchies and tyrannies from which it was purported to decisively break. As Esposito shows, the democratic body politic exemplified in Rousseau simply reincorporates and reinstitutes the sovereign relation within the idea of the nation, which becomes much more totalising and potentially totalitarian than any previous regime (2011: 116–17).

Moreover, it is by no means clear that globalisation and the detachment of sovereignty from the nation produce a pluralisation of sovereignty, as Connolly suggests. Indeed, the very contrary seems to be occurring; globalisation seems to be having the paradoxical effect of intensifying measures of border control and surveillance – fuelled by an increasingly xenophobic and anti-immigrant political discourse in most Western societies – and leading to a proliferation of spaces of the sovereign exception. Offshore detention sites such as Guantánamo Bay immediately come to mind. While we might be witnessing the decline of the idea of *national* sovereignty – at least as it has been traditionally understood since the birth of the Westphalian system and the French Revolution – sovereignty itself, detached from the nation, reproduces itself beyond and across national borders. Moreover, as Wendy Brown shows, the proliferation of walls, fences and borders within, at the edges of, and beyond national territories have become the symbol for sovereignty in the global age. This is symptomatic, on the one hand, of the waning of national sovereignty (here, the increasing preoccupation with border control and 'illegal' immigration can be seen as a sort of hysterical reaction to the experience of the loss of national identity) and, on the other, of a re-articulation and projection of sovereignty (see Brown 2010).

A further criticism, along similar lines to Connolly's, comes from Andrew Norris, who points to the ambivalent implications of Agamben's highly abstract and metaphysical understanding of sovereignty and politics. For Norris, one of the problems is the lack of clear ethico–political coordinates in Agamben's analysis: 'far from bringing concepts such as rights, authority, public interest, liberty, or equality, more clearly into view, Agamben operates at a level of abstraction at which such concepts blur into their opposites' (Norris 2005: 263). Clearly, such established coordinates of political philosophy have no purchase in Agamben's thought, and we need to look elsewhere for political tools, as we shall do later. However, Norris' criticism mostly concerns Agamben's preoccupation with the Schmittian logic of the exception, which, Norris argues, not only informs his understanding of sovereignty, but actually structures his general line of thought. This can be seen in the way that the paradigm becomes prominent in Agamben's philosophy, leading to a decisionistic mode of thinking, one that is very different, for instance, from the Kantian mode, where the emphasis is on universal, rational judgement, and which, in a sense, parallels the sovereign decision:

> The clear implication of Agamben's own explanation of what makes something exemplary of paradigmatic is that in claiming a paradigmatic status for the camps he is and can only be making an unregulated decision that cannot be justified to his readers in a nonauthoritarian manner. (Norris 2005: 275)

In other words, in conveying a deterministic, totalising picture of sovereign exceptionalism, one whose inexorable destiny lies in the camp – in taking this as the very paradigm of life under biopolitical sovereignty and, at the same time, refusing the standard normative coordinates upon which we might critically evaluate and judge such power relations – Agamben, it is claimed, imposes his analysis in an absolutist way, without appeal to general validity. His line of thinking actually resembles the sovereign decision itself. Norris goes as far as to say that:

> Unfortunately, Agamben's acceptance of Schmitt's decisionism makes it impossible for his analysis to claim any general validity. Perhaps worse, it puts him in the position of deciding upon the camp victims one more time, thereby repeating the gesture of the SS in precisely the way he says we must avoid. (2005: 278)

However, this is a perplexing and highly dubious claim on the part of Norris. It seems that he has somehow conflated or confused two quite different things, namely, what Agamben says about the nature of sovereignty and his actual mode of thinking, claiming that one follows necessarily from the other. To say that the structure of sovereignty is decisionistic and ultimately leads to the camps surely does not mean that one's own thinking is decisionistic and somehow repeats the gesture of the SS. It is very odd to suggest that describing a relation of power as authoritarian means that one's own thinking must also be authoritarian and somehow imitative of the thing one describes.

One suspects that a misperception of this kind has something to do with Agamben's avoidance of normative criteria of the Kantian kind, which establishes universal norms of moral judgement and validity. The sovereign exception is not morally evaluated in Agamben's analysis, at least not explicitly; rather, its terrible operation is simply described. Nor does Agamben place much faith in normative principles and institutions such as rights, in order to limit this operation. But surely this does not mean that his analysis somehow participates in the gesture of the sovereign exception. It means merely that a politics and ethics of resistance to power must be theorised in a different way. It is interesting to see here how Norris' critique of Agamben parallels commonplace criticisms of Foucault, namely, that his analyses of disciplinary and bio-power, because they, too, avoided explicit normative judgement, were apolitical, nihilistic, ethically vacuous or even complicit in the operation of power they described. Such objections, however, largely miss the point. Like Foucault, Agamben's analysis is clearly a critical and politically engaged one; indeed, like Foucault, he is obviously describing a situation of power and domination that he considers highly pernicious. How could this be in any sense in doubt when he takes the concentration camp as the paradigm of modern power? Yet, what he does not do is set up an explicit normative framework of judgement – a gesture which he regards as futile.

Connolly, too, has highlighted political problems with Agamben's account of sovereignty, although he certainly does not go so far as to suggest that Agamben's thinking is authoritarian. Rather, it is to do with the very impossibility of politics in Agamben's argument. Connolly argues that the starkness of Agamben's concept of sovereignty paralyses any attempt to resist and transcend it. That is to say that because sovereignty for Agamben is so totalising and deterministic, progressive politics can only be conceived as one of total opposition to, and transcendence of, sovereignty. Yet, at the same time, the operation of sovereignty is so absolute in Agamben's account and the gestures towards resistance and political alternatives are so vague, thin and inadequately explained, that the sort of emancipation invoked by Agamben does not seem possible. Agamben is therefore caught at an impasse – a trap that he has made for himself and cannot get out of. As Connolly puts it: 'Nowhere in *Homo Sacer,* however, is a way out of the logic actually disclosed [. . .] Agamben thus carries us through the conjunction of sovereignty, the sacred, and biopolitics to a historical impasse' (2007: 27).

To some extent, Connolly's diagnosis of Agamben is correct – his notion of sovereignty invokes an all-or-nothing politics of opposition to, and transcendence of, sovereignty. There is little in Agamben's account to suggest that sovereignty can be pluralised, renegotiated or democratically ameliorated in the manner Connolly suggests. Agamben, we would argue, works in a very different, ontological register, invoking a politics without sovereignty. This is something we shall explore later.

THE QUESTION OF POLITICS IN AGAMBEN

Connolly's judgement is generally reflective of that of many of Agamben's interlocutors – that he has no politics. In other words, his depiction of power is so totalising, and his ethical and political figures are so ambiguous and problematic, that he leaves us in a political deadlock from which there is no hope of escape. Part of the problem, it is argued, is Agamben's apparent scepticism and pessimism about most forms of emancipatory politics and his inability to propose any concrete alternatives. Ernesto Laclau is one who considers Agamben's account to be politically vacuous. He points first to the reductionism of Agamben's notion of the ban as the relation of exclusion from the law, which reduces its victim, *homo sacer,* to an undifferentiated, bare, politically irrelevant status. However, Laclau suggests an alternative reading of the ban, where those placed outside the laws of the city are not politically meaningless, bare entities, but might actually constitute a collective identity of opposition to the city. Here we have not the relation that Agamben suggests between law and lawlessness, but a relation of opposition between two opposed collective identities and two sets of incompatible laws (Laclau 2007: 11–22). The possibility of this sort of antagonistic relationship, which Laclau sees as being at the core of the political, is discounted and neglected in Agamben's account. Thus Laclau raises the very interesting and vital question of what happens when *homo sacer* fights back; what happens when the bandits go from being amorphous, bare and vulnerable entities – non-subjects – and become an organised force of opposition?; what happens when they go from being a defenceless victim to an active political subject? Laclau gives the example, taken from Fanon, of the lumpen-proletariat who turn in an organised and collective way on the colonial city from which they have been excluded.

Perhaps we could imagine collective political subjectivation amongst even more marginalised and excluded subjects today – stateless people. If they organise themselves into communities, into collective bodies of resistance – as they often have done – do they still remain *homo sacer* or is this term now utterly inadequate? In drawing attention to the potential transformation of the relation of exclusion into one of antagonism, Laclau has touched on something extremely important for any consideration of politics in Agamben's argument. As Laclau points out, unless there is some space for resistance and antagonism, there is no possibility of politics. One of the dangers is, then, that if all we have in Agamben's landscape is the figure of the lonely, isolated, defence-less *homo sacer* caught in the ban and at the mercy of the all-powerful sovereign, then we have no possibility of politics. For Laclau: 'Agamben has clouded the issue, for he has presented as a political moment what actually amounts to a radical elimination of the political: a sovereign power which reduces the social bond to bare life' (2007: 16). Where we disagree with Laclau, however, as we shall expound later, is with his contention that relations of hegemony – which translates into the taking over of the space of the state – is the only way to conceive of politics. For Laclau, the emancipation from sovereignty that Agamben seeks is equivalent to the elimination of politics. We suggest that despite the ambiguities of his account, Agamben allows us to think politics beyond the field of sovereignty.

Nevertheless, the key point that Laclau makes, contra Agamben, is that there is no such thing as bare life. Bare life is always politicised. There is always something which exceeds bare life – and this is where the possibility of politics arises – something with which we, in essence, agree and with which, we suggest, Agamben, at least implicitly, agrees. The problem with Agamben, it is argued, is that the deterministic and teleological nature of his thesis, in which the relationship between sovereignty and bare life unfolds towards biopolitical totalitarianism, neglects sites of politics and subjectivation which elude and resist this logic. The social field is differentiated and heterogeneous and cannot be wholly assimilated into this deterministic, homogeneous logic that Agamben delineates. Even the forms of social regulation and inscription that Agamben sees as part of the totalitarian logic of modernity are never one-sidedly dangerous in this way and can have, Laclau argues, emancipatory possibilities. The main problem with Agamben, according to Laclau, is his anti-politics – his dismissal of all political institutions and discourses as simply part of the totalitarian logic of modernity and as stepping stones to the camp:

> The myth of a fully reconciled society is what governs the (non-) political discourse of Agamben. And it is also what allows him to dismiss all political options in our societies and to unify them in the concentration camps as their secret destiny. Instead of deconstructing the logic of political institutions, showing areas in which forms of resistance are possible, he closes them beforehand through an essentialist unification. Political nihilism is his ultimate message. (Laclau 2007: 22)

On the other hand, as we have already indicated, Laclau, at least to some extent, misses the point of Agamben's analysis. For Agamben, it is not that there is bare life, but rather that through the mechanisms of power (both modern and ancient), a category of bare life (a life outside and disqualified from law and political community) is invented by sovereignty – it is, in fact, a creation of sovereignty. The latter must be seen to include the processes of categorisation that make bare life possible. While one can agree that Agamben provides the starkest version of this disqualification, a weaker version, as we have seen, is to be found in Arendt as a representative, like Laclau, of the orthodox position of political theory – a position which says that freedom (the political) can only be attained once the problem of necessity (the satisfaction of the needs for biological survival) has been solved. So the resistance that is needed must now be seen to be the result of the failure to recognise that the human as such is essentially political. This is why Agamben says that the human is the sabbatical animal par excellence. Thus, if resistance is called for, it is against the kind of categorising inherent in the framework that Laclau, like Arendt, unquestioningly employs; within this frame of reference, only some are worthy of freedom.

The 'political options' that Laclau alludes to in the quote above – which he claims that Agamben neglects – refer to the categories of citizenship and the incorporation of bare life into political institutions, which he believes contains emancipatory possibilities (like the granting of political and social rights, for instance). However, from our point of view, this simply recreates the division between bare life (necessity) and politically qualified life (freedom), which is the root of the exclusion and violent domination of bare life in the first place. What is called for, and what we argue is implicit in Agamben's thought, is a completely different understanding of politics and political action – one that cannot be confined within the existing tradition of political theory.

In contrast to Laclau, Jacques Rancière's axiom of equality, we suggest, takes us closer to the actual movement of Agamben's thought. For in terms of an essential equality, politics can only be inclusive.

RANCIÈRE'S ARGUMENT FOR HUMAN RIGHTS

From Rancière's perspective, however, Agamben is in error in rejecting human rights as an idea inextricably linked to bare life. He points to the importance of the discourse of rights as marking the terrain of political subjectivation and struggle around the very terms of their inscription. Rights are a way, Rancière says, of constructing or giving expression to a *dissensus*, which he understands as 'a dispute about what is given, about the frame within which we see something as given' (2004: 304). Rancière gives the example of the demand by women after the French Revolution for the recognition of their equal rights as citizens – rights which were formally guaranteed to them in the Declaration, but which were denied to them in practice by the political order which claimed to be founded on such principles. In claiming such rights, these women put the consistency of the constitutional order to the test and, in doing so, constituted themselves as subjects of rights:

> Women could make a twofold demonstration. They could demonstrate that they were deprived of the rights that they had, thanks to the Declaration of Rights. And they could demonstrate, through their public action, that they had the rights that the constitution denied to them, that they could enact those rights. (Rancière 2004: 304)

So in contrast to Arendt, on the one hand, who sees the Rights of Man as politically impotent and marking the exclusion of some as bare life or bare humanity from the polis, and in contrast to Agamben on the other, for whom the Rights of Man mark the pernicious *inclusion – included exclusion* – of bare life as sacred within the polis, Rancière proposes that rights signify neither an exclusion nor inclusion. Rather, they mark the gap or disjuncture between these two situations – this is the gap of politics. As Rancière says:

> It appears that man is not the void term opposed to the actual rights of the citizen. It has a positive content that is the dismissal of any difference between those who 'live' in such or such a sphere of existence, between those who are or are not qualified for political life. (2004: 304)

The implication of Rancière's argument is to problematise the central distinction, affirmed by Arendt and analysed by Agamben, between *zoē* and *bios*. From Rancière's perspective, the enactment of human rights by people who are at the same time denied those rights is what cancels out or at least unsettles this distinction, as it forces a relation of equality between those who are politically qualified – for example, citizens of nation-states – and those who are deemed not to be. Rights, then, should not be dismissed, even though they are often treated with utter hypocrisy and disdain by the governments of the world. They can be invoked and used as discursive tools and as ways of staging scenes of dissensus, even by those without any formal status, such as illegal migrants and those in refugee camps: 'These rights are theirs when they can do something with them to construct a dissensus against the denial of rights they suffer' (Rancière 2004: 298–310).[6]

The question that immediately arises here is whether, even within Rancière's admirably subtle framework and possibly against his intention, an a priori distinction might not be activated between those who are inside and those who are outside the political community. For if, as we believe is the case with Agamben, there is no place *essentially* external to politics, the need for a fight for inclusion would cease to exist. What would exist – and Arendt is illuminating here – are people always already acting and thus revealing themselves as a 'who' (subject) and not as a 'what' (object).[7] If we return to Rancière's example of women in the French Revolution, it is clear that, there, women would already be in the position of political activists, even if they had not been formally recognised as subjects in the system and were excluded from formal political practices and workings of power at that precise historical moment. To be human is to be an activist – one who can engage in political action. The problem here is that the term 'activist' is used too narrowly – almost to refer to a profession – so that it largely excludes from the political those who have to fight for a place in the existing formal mechanisms of government, including citizenship. It is clear that one does not only begin to be a true political actor as a citizen. Rancière acknowledges the apparent (and it is only apparent) depoliticisation that rights seem to be undergoing today under our regimes of post-political consensus in the West – something which can also be seen in the reduction of human rights to *humanitarian* rights and their parcelling out by the West to the figures of bare humanity in more deprived parts of the world. This is something which, as we have seen, prompts Agamben's scepticism concerning rights. However, Rancière says that:

> For all this, they [rights] are not void [. . .] The Rights of Man do not become void by becoming the rights of those who cannot actualize them. If they are not truly 'their rights', they become the rights of others. (2004: 307)

We would like to suggest, in partial agreement with Rancière, that human rights are not null and void today, that they have a radical political potential which is worth salvaging. However, it is crucial to be clear here about the meaning and significance of the term 'politics'. In this light, we also want to take into account Agamben's powerful insights about sovereignty and biopolitics (or biopower) – insights which others, like Laclau and Rancière, say condemn him to political nihilism. There is no doubt that Agamben throws a spanner in the works, making it challenging to think about human rights in politically valid terms. In order to create a space in his analysis for a politics of human rights, we need to overcome a major area of ambiguity in his work: can a coherent distinction be made between politics and power? This will be the focus of the next chapter.

Notes

1 A similar point is made by Dominick LaCapra (2003: 262–304).
2 For a more detailed explanation of paradigms in Agamben's work, see Durantaye (2009: 223–6).

3 An additional criticism made by Fitzpatrick is that it is impossible to know from what position Agamben is mounting his critique: 'one must wonder, as with the pervasion of bare life, from what omniscient position Agamben can discern such things – discern these entities as being utterly and ever beyond the human' (Fitzpatrick 2005: 66). This criticism, however, seems to lack substance, as it would apply to any effort that seeks to adopt an ontological perspective on the world.

4 Indeed, in his lecture series *Society Must be Defended*, Foucault shows how the ancient sovereign right to kill is still part of modernity, working, as it did, in conjunction with Nazi biopolitics – an analysis which is uncannily close to Agamben's, yet which Agamben nowhere acknowledges (see Foucault 2003).

5 We are referring, of course, to the tragic killing of Jean Charles de Menezes in 2005 in a London tube station.

6 Todd May has used Rancière's argument here to explore the struggles of Algerian sans-status or 'illegal' migrants without regular status in Montreal (see May 2008: 121–34).

7 For a discussion of this aspect of Arendt's theory, see Lechte (2007).

Chapter 6

POLITICS, POWER AND VIOLENCE IN AGAMBEN

When we come to explore the question of politics in Agamben's thought, everything hinges, it seems, on whether we can make a clear distinction between politics and power (sovereignty), and yet, on the surface of things, it appears that this distinction is fraught with complexity. The problem here is actually twofold. First, Agamben, in many places, seems to conflate these two terms. Indeed, almost everything he says in *Homo Sacer* appears to point to the whole of politics becoming entirely subsumed within biopolitics and the sovereign exception, that is, within the order of power. Indeed, biopolitics and sovereign exceptionalism appear to constitute the very field of politics. Under biopolitics, life and politics become indistinct: *'The novelty of modern biopolitics lies in the fact that the biological given is as such immediately political, and the political is as such immediately the biological given'* (Agamben 1998: 148 [emphasis in original]). Similarly, the sovereign moment of the exception and, particularly, the relation of the ban become the key figures of politics. We have to remember, also, that the camp is described as the very *nomos* of our modern political space. Second, as we have seen, any gestures towards an alternative conception of politics remain just that – *gestures*. They are vague, enigmatic and lack concreteness. So arriving at a clear conceptual distinction between the order of power and politics, particularly some form of political subjectivity and action, is very difficult at the outset. However, it is also apparent that Agamben does want to formulate a notion of politics and ethics that is different from power – that, indeed, resists and escapes it. Therefore, if such a distinction cannot be made, not only are Agamben's critics correct, but we have no means of escaping the depressing conclusion that *homo sacer* is the true founder of the polis and our destiny does, indeed, lie in the camps.

At the same time, we could say that it is precisely because Agamben opposes and seeks to transcend the logic of the sovereignty – the regime of the state and the constituted politico–legal order – that a radical distinction between power and politics is genuinely conceivable, perhaps more so than in most mainstream political theory, which tends to see the practice of politics as the exercise of power. In other words, it is the sovereign tradition of political theory, where politics is seen in terms of statecraft or as the problem of legitimating political authority, which is unable to make any sort of distinction between politics and power; for this tradition, politics *is* power. Indeed, we recall here the complaint of both Connolly and Laclau in the previous chapter concerning Agamben's absolute opposition to sovereignty: his unwillingness to think how sovereignty might be pluralised and negotiated or how we might construct hegemonic relations of opposition within the order of the state leaves no space for politics. Here we take a somewhat heretical line and propose that it is precisely *because* of this radical opposition to sovereignty and political power and the desire to think outside it that Agamben is a political thinker *par excellence*. This is to suggest that Agamben opens up the possibility of an alternative, ontological conception of politics that is outside the state and its laws and that transcends the problematic of sovereignty. Most of the established ways of thinking about politics – whether in terms of the different types of regime that we find in Aristotle, as the instituting of sovereignty through the contract or as the normative evaluation of politics through frameworks of law, justice, procedure or rational deliberation – would, from Agamben's perspective, refer to the order of *power*. Politics is something different.

Politics and the political

While it is clear that Agamben's view of politics is different from that of normative political theory – he could not be any further, for instance, from Rawls or Habermas – he also departs from much of continental political thought as well. One of the recent preoccupations of continental political theory has been to distinguish between categories of 'politics' and 'the political'. This distinction is most clearly formulated by Chantal Mouffe:

> By 'the political', I refer to the dimension of antagonism that is inherent in human relations, antagonism that can take many

forms and emerge in different types of social relations. 'Politics', on the other side, indicates an ensemble of practices, discourses and institutions which seek to establish a certain order and organize human coexistence in conditions that are potentially conflictual because they are affected by the dimension of 'the political'. (2000: 101)

So, here, *politics* refers to the general political order of things, the world of institutions, laws, governmental practices and rationalities – what might be called the constituted order. By contrast, *the political* is the dimension of antagonism which, at times, erupts within this order and which has the potential to reconstitute the political space, to produce a different order. A parallel might be drawn here with Rancière's distinction between the orders of politics (*la politique*) and police (*la police*). The latter can be seen as the settled socio-political order of established norms, laws, discourses, practices and identities, while *politics* is the moment of disruption created by the staging of the dissensus of the uncounted, invisible part of society, the part which has no part[1] – as we saw with the case of women demanding rights from the post-revolutionary political order in France. So in Rancière's terms, *the police* is roughly the same as what Mouffe understands as *politics*, and *politics*, while not exactly equivalent, has some parallels with what she takes as *the political*.

Now the question is whether Agamben can be situated within this framework. Does the distinction between power and politics – which we hold as crucial to his thinking – parallel the distinction between politics and the political? One side of the equation seems, at least on the surface of things, to fit: what Agamben would see as power – the biopolitical regime of government and state power – seems to be similar to the order of politics in Mouffe's binary. But things become tricky if we try to assimilate the conception of politics in Agamben into Mouffe's category of 'the political'. This is because Mouffe takes her understanding of the political in large part from Carl Schmitt, especially from his friend/enemy opposition, which he sees as being at the heart of the political relationship (see Schmitt 2007; Mouffe 1999). The problem here is that the friend/enemy opposition is, for Schmitt – as it is ultimately for Mouffe as well – a way of shoring up the identity of the sovereign state by defining its limits; differentiating itself from an external enemy is a way of constituting the demos as a unified identity that rallies around the political order. In this sense, the friend/enemy distinction has a similar function and, indeed, is very closely related to the sovereign moment of exception. It is clear that there is a very close relationship between sovereignty and the political: the moment of the political, for Schmitt, is precisely the moment of the constitution and affirmation of sovereign power and, for Mouffe, it is the dimension around which hegemonic struggles and projects of state formation are constructed. All politics, in this sense, are hegemonic politics – the proper site of political decision-making is the sovereign state – and there is no 'beyond hegemony' (Mouffe 2005: 118). In many ways, then, Mouffe is part of the political theory tradition centred on the problem of sovereignty. The political, while it is the unruly underside of the social–political order, always at the same time works within, or is projected towards, the paradigm of the sovereign state and refers to new political projects that aim to hegemonise the state.

So from Agamben's point of view, the notion of the political, as put forward by Mouffe, cannot be separated from sovereignty. Indeed, for Agamben, what Mouffe terms the political (and which, for Agamben, would be inseparable from power) manifests itself precisely at the moment of the sovereign exception in the Schmittian sense. The political decision, which Mouffe sees as constituting the *demos*, is, from Agamben's perspective, inextricable from the sovereign decision. Furthermore, as with the political, the state of exception is a sort of rupture in the normal order of things – the order of law – which temporarily suspends everything, but this is simply the expression of power at its purest, even though or, rather, because it bears an uncanny proximity to lawlessness. Put simply, then – and this is where the problem lies – the dimension of the political, which Mouffe sees as being different from the order of power, is, for Agamben, inseparable from it. In Agamben's terms, what Mouffe calls the political is the point at which power transgresses norm and law, yet, in doing so, it is also what nourishes and affirms this order that it exceeds. The distinction that Mouffe tries to make between politics and power breaks down or, as Agamben would put it, becomes a zone of indistinction.

CONSTITUTING/CONSTITUTED POWER

By contrast, Antonio Negri tries to disentangle the moment of the political, which he calls *constituent* power, from the order of power or what he calls *constituted* power. He suggests that while democracy is usually thought in terms of both constituent and constituted power – as both the expansive moment of production that founds a new order *and* as the order itself – democracy contains an insurgent dimension that at the same time resists its incorporation into a new order: 'Constituent power resists being constitutionalized' (Negri 1999: 1). Every constitution, every established order of power has a founding moment which exceeds it and which it cannot entirely regulate or contain. If we think, for instance, of a revolution as the founding moment of new order of law and power: the revolution is a qualitatively different form of power to the system of power it founds; it is about movement, creativity, rupture and becoming, as opposed to stasis, law and authority. As Negri says: 'the paradigm of constituent power is that of a force which bursts apart, breaks, interrupts, unhinges any pre-existing equilibrium and any possible continuity' (1999: 10.1). If the revolution is not eventually contained, incorporated and put a stop to, it becomes a threat to the new order, which is why every post-revolutionary order has its Thermidorean moment of reaction. So what Negri wants to arrive at is an understanding of pure constituent or counter – power, without the constituted order that usually follows from it: an immanent power of constant creation and becoming (a translation of *potenza*²) – without its crystallising into an established order of power and law, without its becoming sovereignty. Indeed, for Negri: 'the concept of sovereignty and that of constituent power stand in absolute opposition [. . .] if an independent way of developing the concept of constituent power exists, it has excluded any reference to the concept of sovereignty' (1999: 21.2). Rather than having as its trajectory the completion of sovereignty, constituent power desires constant revolution.

Constituent power, for Negri – in his Spinozian ontology of immanence and totality – is the terrain of the immanent productivity and materiality of life. It is from this domain of the abundant materiality of life that revolutions emerge and that even human rights have to be thought, in contrast to liberal ideology, which sees the origin of rights in contractualism. On the contrary, only 'worldly absoluteness' can be the guarantee of rights (1999: 27.8). This notion of immanent life as the grounding of rights, rather than the social contract, is a suggestive and important idea that will be taken up later. However, from the point of view of Agamben's argument, might there not be something problematic about Negri's attempt to develop a positive biopolitics – a project of revolutionary emancipation that takes place on the biopolitical terrain? We know that Agamben sees biopower/biopolitics as a totalising field of governmental regulation that works on and reproduces bare life, interacting with the sovereign state of exception with catastrophic consequences. There does not seem to be anything redemptive about biopolitics in Agamben's analysis. Negri, by contrast, wants to distinguish between biopower and biopolitics – the former referring to the regimes of control, regulation and the exploitation of life, characteristic of the global system of power that he and Michael Hardt refer to as Empire (see Hardt and Negri 2000). Biopolitics, on the other hand, is the fertile field of social life forged by 'immaterial labour' and communication, in which new forms of commonality, as well as positive figures of resistance and emancipation – that is, the multitude – emerge.

We shall argue that there is, indeed, a positive politics – even a kind of positive biopolitics – present, at least implicitly, in Agamben's philosophy. However, this is quite different from that proposed by Negri (and Hardt). It is not based around notions of work, production, immaterial labour or a particular programme of revolutionary emancipation,[3] and it is here that Negri's analysis of the emergence of the multitude through the forms of production and labour performed under Empire so closely parallels the Marxist narrative of the developing revolutionary capacities of the proletariat. Rather, if there is a positive biopolitics to be found in Agamben – and we say there is – it is to be thought through the notions of 'impotentiality' and 'inoperativity'.

Inoperativeness and Exodus: Positive Biopolitics

Here, we shall explore two interrelated figures in Agamben's thought – figures which, we argue, are ethical and political. We have already discussed *inoperativeness* (or, in French, '*désoeuvrement*') at some length in a previous chapter (see Chapter 4), but we want to propose this as a distinctly political concept. Inoperativity is closely related to the idea of *potentiality* – a potentiality that is not exhausted or expended in becoming actual, just as constituent power is not exhausted in the act of constitution. If we are to retain an autonomous understanding of potentiality, then it is important that we also think about *impotentiality* or the potential to not act. As Aristotle – from whom Agamben derives this notion of potentiality – proposes, the potential to be or to act is also the potential or capacity to not act or not be. Now, as Agamben points

out, this potential to not be is a way of thinking about the sovereign
ban, 'which applies to the exception in no longer applying' (1998: 46).
What defines sovereignty is its self-activating potential – the potential
to act or to not act – the indistinction between which is evident in
the indeterminacy of the state of exception, which, after all, is always
decided by the sovereign. So what is needed, according to Agamben, is
another form of potentiality which is 'entirely freed from the principle
of sovereignty and a constituting power that has definitively broken
the ban binding it to constituted power' (47). This implies, as Agamben
says: 'nothing less than thinking ontology and politics beyond every
figure of relation, beyond even the limit of the relation that is the sovereign ban' (47).

Another way of thinking about a form of being which escapes sovereignty is through the curious figure of Bartleby from Melville's short
story, *Bartleby the Scrivener*. Bartleby's refrain 'I would prefer not to'
whenever he is asked by his employer to perform a task, Agamben
sees as the ultimate gesture of impotentiality, which 'resists every possibility of deciding between potentiality and the potentiality not to'
(48). To think about this gesture of refusal in political terms, we might
invoke the problem of voluntary servitude, which is perhaps the central
enigma of politics itself. Sixteenth-century thinker Étienne La Boétie's
radical claim was that power in itself is nothing, an illusion – one that
we constitute through our voluntary obedience to it (see La Boétie
1983). Therefore, to free ourselves from power does not require an
act of revolution so much as simply turning our backs on power and
refusing to give ourselves to it any longer. We destroy power simply by
saying 'I would prefer not to' – in other words, refusing to participate
in the rituals and practices by which power is created and sustained. 'I
would prefer not to' is a rebellion against the ways in which we have
been subjectified or in which we have subjectified ourselves – it is a
working of ourselves out of power, as Max Stirner proposed with his
notion of the insurrection, as opposed to revolution.[4] Here, unlike
Negri, the destruction of power is not achieved through revolutionary
activity, but through a kind of radical *inactivity*.

Bartleby's gesture is one of inoperativeness and exodus. Bartleby
withdraws from the world of work and activity, which has no meaning
for him; he simply refuses to operate and cooperate. However, this
withdrawal is not simply passive. In Bartleby's insistent refusal to
participate, he threatens the destruction of the system of power

(and capitalism), whose survival depends on continual regulated activity.

This is close, in some ways, to the idea of exodus, which comes from Italian autonomist thought – a tradition which has had an influence, albeit an ambivalent one, on Agamben. Paolo Virno defines exodus in the following terms: 'I use the term Exodus here to define mass defection from the State, the alliance between general intellect and political Action, and a movement toward the public sphere of Intellect'. Exodus is characterised, furthermore, as an *active and engaged withdrawal* – one that, moreover, founds a new kind of autonomous public space, what Virno calls a Republic (1996: 196). This notion of a new, autonomous Republic as the sphere of general intellect and political action is theorised against the context of Arendt's notion of the public sphere of action, which she distinguishes from the sphere of intellect, on the one hand, and work, on the other. For Virno, in the post-Fordist era of capitalist production, work, intellect and action have combined to form a new kind of commonality and a new mode of politics. From Agamben's point of view, in contrast to this, the coming community and the new forms of being that he is interested in cannot be based around work – here he is closer to Arendt – but around the notion of inoperativeness, which is not inactivity or inertia as such, but rather a new form of life and way of living that is singular. As he puts it in *The Coming Community*, inoperativeness is 'the paradigm of the coming politics' (Agamben 1993: 93).[5]

DIVINE VIOLENCE: BENJAMIN'S AND AGAMBEN'S ANARCHIC APPROACH TO POLITICS

Leaving this matter aside for the moment, is there, nevertheless, any purchase in Negri's distinction (discussed above) between constituent and constituted power and in his contention that the former can be thought and realised without, and against, the latter? Is this how we should think about the notion of politics as distinct from power in Agamben? It is interesting that Agamben remains sceptical of Negri's attempt to formulate an autonomous notion of constituent power in opposition to sovereignty: the fact that constituent power neither emerges from, nor is limited to instituting, the constituted order does not necessarily free it from sovereign power (see Agamben 1998: 43). The problem here is to do with potentiality, and Agamben highlights the link between the notion of constituent power in its potential for constant revolutionising, and the logic of sovereignty, which embodies the potential to suspend the law and declare a state of exception at any moment. Can we not say that the situation of revolution bears a paradoxical resemblance, and even parallel, to the sovereign state of exception? Both are situations in which the normal order is suspended and in which anything could happen. Perhaps, then, the constituent power embodied in a revolution is inextricably linked with sovereignty through the dimension of exception common to both of them. For this reason, Agamben would remain sceptical about revolutionary politics in the classical sense, seeing it as still caught within the logic of sovereignty. However, according to Agamben, Negri's analysis has value in highlighting the ontological dimension, rather than the strictly political dimension, of constituent power. The key question here relates to the 'constitution of potentiality' and the way that a new possibility is opened up for rethinking the relationship between potentiality and actuality. However, for Agamben, this does not resolve the issue, but simply shifts its ground to one of ontology. Rather, as he puts it: 'Only an entirely new conjunction of the possibility and reality, contingency and necessity [. . .] will make it possible to cut the knot that binds sovereignty to constituting power' (1998: 43). But what might this new conjunction be?

To answer this question, we need to understand more precisely how constituent power is bound to sovereignty. Only then can we explore possible ways of undoing this relationship. Indeed, this is a crucial problem for any radical politics and particularly those based around human rights. The historical experience of revolutions has been the reinvention of state power, and this perhaps points to a sovereignising tendency that is immanent within the very logic of revolutionary politics itself. Thus, the French Revolution, based on the Rights of Man, produced the Jacobin Terror. Similarly, the Bolshevik Revolution, based on the communist ideal of the liberation of humanity, eventually led to the Stalinist state. To investigate this paradoxical tendency in revolutionary politics to reproduce state power, we turn to Walter Benjamin, particularly to his 'Critique of Violence' ('Zur Kritik de Gewalt'), an essay which, alongside Schmitt's *Political Theology* – there is an interesting subterranean correspondence between these two works – had the most decisive influence on Agamben's understanding of law and sovereignty, particularly in its exploration of the intimate relationship between law, violence and power.

The ethical problem that Benjamin addresses in this essay is how to develop a critique of violence that does not simply reproduce it. His point is that we cannot critique violence simply on the basis of law and legal authority, because this is itself inextricably bound to violence in a number of ways. Nor can we make any coherent distinction between legal and illegal, legitimate and illegitimate violence. The law always articulates itself through a violence which both preserves its boundaries and exceeds them, and violence always establishes a new law. Violence is always present in the very founding of a new legal system. He gives the example of military violence, which establishes a new legal system in place of the old through the signing of a peace treaty following a conquest; as well as the death penalty, which signifies law's ultimate sovereign power over life and whose purpose is not so much the punishment of those who transgress the law, but the establishment of new law. We could also point to revolutionary violence – the domain of constituent power – which abolishes one system of law and power only to found a new one in its place. Law and violence are not opposed, at least not in a straightforward sense; violence is at the very origins and foundations of the law. Violence brings the law into being, breathes life into it and gives it vitality: 'violence, violence crowned by fate, is the origin of the law . . .' (Benjamin 1996: 242).[6]

The main conceptual distinction that Benjamin introduces to explain this relationship is between 'lawmaking' (*rechtsetzend*) violence and 'law-preserving' (*rechtserhaltend*) violence: the violence that establishes a new law and the violence that enforces the existing law. This is the same distinction that Agamben is concerned with – *constituting* and *constituted* power (see 1998: 40). Like Agamben, Benjamin sees these two forms of violence as collapsing into one another, so that there is a continual oscillation between the two. The key example he gives is that of the police, in which is combined 'in a kind of spectral mixture' (Benjamin 1996: 242) these two forms of violence. The use of police violence for the purpose of law enforcement is obviously law-preserving. Yet, it is also lawmaking, because the police act at the very limits of the law and have the authority to determine how the law is applied in certain situations. The police, at times, act outside the law or at its margins, in order to enforce it. The legal violence of the police is felt throughout the civil space, determining the law in those spaces of exception where its limits are unclear:

[T]he police intervene "for security reasons" in countless situations where no clear legal situation exists, when they are not merely, without the slightest relation to legal ends, accompanying the citizen as a brutal encumbrance through a life regulated by ordinances, or simply supervising him. (1996: 243)

We are reminded of the deployment of the discourse of 'security' to authorise exceptional police powers of detention, surveillance and violence against terrorist suspects. However, what is also evident is the mundaneness, the everydayness of police violence. Police violence is neither entirely inside nor entirely outside the law, but rather inhabits a no-man's land in which one blurs into the other. The law articulates itself through a violent enforcement that it cannot control and which exceeds its limits; a violent excess, which both disturbs and constitutes the limits of the law. This continual blurring of the line, this legal ambiguity which is at the very core of police power, is why Benjamin describes it as: 'formless, like its nowhere-tangible, all-pervasive, ghostly presence in the life of civilized states' (1996: 243).[7]

Moreover, if the law is to be understood through its connection to violence, at the same time, violence is to be understood through its connection to law. Benjamin's critical claim is that violence is violent precisely *through its relation to law*, whether it is the violence that preserves the legal system or the violence that overthrows the legal system, only to found a new one in its place. This makes radical politics and questions of opposition, resistance and revolution deeply problematic and ambiguous. We need to come to terms with this mysterious core that unites law and violence and generates the continual oscillation between them.

This is where, perhaps, a certain anarchism might be detected in Benjamin's and, as we shall see later on, Agamben's argument, as well. Benjamin invokes Georges Sorel's distinction between the *political* general strike and the *proletarian* general strike. For Sorel, whose thought is inspired by anarcho-syndicalism, the political strike seeks to put pressure on the capitalists to grant the workers better conditions, whereas the proletarian strike seeks to directly transform relations of production. Furthermore, while the political strike works through the mechanism of the state and is therefore prone to the manipulations of socialist politicians, the proletarian strike turns away from the state and fosters the development of autonomous relations amongst workers themselves. In doing so, it presupposes the abolition or radical transcendence of state power. While the former mode of action seeks only to reform society, the proletarian strike is a radical rupturing of existing society (see Sorel 1961). The former is social democratic and, ultimately, reformist, whereas the latter is anarchistic.[8]

Importantly, for Sorel, while violence is intrinsic to this revolutionary rupturing – indeed, Sorel sees the proletarian struggle with bourgeois society as taking place on a mythical 'battlefield' – violence should be understood as symbolic and ethical, rather than as actual physical violence against persons. Indeed, Sorel makes an important distinction between what he calls bourgeois 'force', which refers to the legal violence of the state and involves the imposition of a certain social order – exemplary here is the Jacobin Terror following the French Revolution – and proletarian 'violence', a term which Sorel reserves for revolutionary violence, which declares war on state power itself and on all imposed social orders and yet which is, *for this reason*, ultimately bloodless (1961: 171–2). For Sorel, what makes violence *violent* in a physical sense, what turns violence into 'force', is its legalisation and state-ification. Violence against the state, by contrast, precisely because it is genuinely revolutionary, will be considerably less violent.

In Sorel, the distinction between the political and proletarian strikes and between force and violence highlights two alternative paths in radical politics. We would suggest that this is not simply, or not even, the alternative between reformism and revolution, but rather the alternative between a sovereign-centred politics and a non-sovereign or anti-sovereign politics. We might say that this is a distinction between different modes of constituent power. Here, sovereign politics refers not only to the social democratic or reformist strategy of working within the state capitalist system, but also to the revolutionary vanguardist strategy of the violent seizure of the state and the ruthless use of state power to consolidate the revolution. Looking at things in this way, Lenin and Bernstein, for instance, are on the same side; they both operate within the same sovereignist or statist paradigm. Sorel has identified the problems with the statist strategy: not only does it fail to radically transform social relations – something which can only be achieved through direct autonomous action – but it also, at least in the vanguard case, involves the worst forms of violence (force) in the suppression of counter-revolution and in the imposition from above of a new social order. The problem here, as reiterated by Benjamin, is that this sort of instrumentalist, means-ends, strategic politics only founds a new authority, a new law and a new sovereign, and it does so through violence.

The question here is whether there can be a radical politics which escapes this dialectic of violence and law. This is a key question in our exploration of Agamben, and, here, some consideration of anarchist political theory might be illuminating. Anarchism works within a paradigm of non-statist politics that is certainly much closer to Sorel's proletarian strike. Moreover, its revolutionary politics is very different from that of the Marxist tradition in the sense that anarchism always remained suspicious of state power, believing that a so-called workers' state would be just as oppressive in its own way as the bourgeois state. Indeed, this went to the heart of the dispute – at once conceptual, political and strategic – between anarchism and Marxism, a dispute that goes back to the nineteenth century, where the First International was fiercely divided between Marxian revolutionaries and statist socialists, on the one hand, and libertarian socialists on the other. This concerned a complex debate about the use of state power in revolutionary politics and whether the state was simply a reflection of economic relations and class interests, as the followers of Marx argued, and could therefore be used by the proletariat, or whether it constituted an autonomous sphere of domination, which therefore needed to be destroyed rather than captured, as anarchists like Mikhail Bakunin and Pyotr Kropotkin contended.[9] Furthermore, the anarchists argued that the vanguardist strategy of the Marxists – later to be embodied in Leninism – in which the revolution was led by the Party, would only perpetuate state power and establish new post-capitalist relations of domination and exploitation. Rather, a genuine social transformation, characterised by Bakunin as a 'social revolution', as opposed to merely a 'political revolution', would involve the overthrow of state power (1953: 372–9).

Anarchism might be seen as the ethical and political horizon of Benjamin's critique of legal violence, and, indeed, Benjamin's enigmatic notion of 'divine violence' – violence not bound to the law – should be understood as a kind of anarchic moment that strikes at the law, embodying a transformative rupture, but which does not spill blood. Divine violence is to be distinguished from 'mythic violence', which is the violence that founds the law, which brings the law into being and fixes the subject as perpetually enthralled before it. Mythic violence is the founding violence of the state and the legal order, something which also applies to the strategic and statist violence of revolutionary politics. By contrast, divine violence destroys the law, disrupting its boundaries. Divine violence is the only way to break out of the interminable oscillation of law and violence and to destroy the power that generates it:

> On the breaking of this cycle maintained by mythic forms of law, on the suspension of law with all the forces on which it depends, finally therefore on the abolition of state power, a new historical epoch is founded. (Benjamin 1996: 252–3)

The abolition of state power which founds this new historical epoch suggests something like an *anarchy-to-come*. Moreover, Benjamin suggests that the possibilities for non-violence might be found in the world of private relationships and agreements based on 'courtesy, sympathy, peaceableness and trust' (244) – in other words, in the autonomous, voluntary and consensual relationships that are found, anarchists argue, in everyday social relations and which point to the possibility of life beyond law and state power.

Apart from this anarchic dimension – which we shall say more about later – there are two elements in Benjamin's discussion of violence that we want to emphasise and which have an immediate bearing on Agamben: first, the ambiguous relationship between divine violence and the state of exception. As Agamben sees it, divine violence in Benjamin cannot be reduced to sovereign violence. If it could, Benjamin's notion of the abolition of state power would be simply incoherent.[10] However, Agamben says that divine violence should nevertheless be understood in relation to the state of exception, as it 'is situated in a zone in which it is no longer possible to distinguish between exception and rule' (1998: 65). However, if divine violence is to be understood in terms of the state of exception, as it involves, as Benjamin puts it: 'a suspension of law with all the forces on which it depends', then this is surely different from the *sovereign* state of exception which regenerates the system of law and violence, which Benjamin and, indeed, Agamben want to free us from. We are surely not talking about a situation of extreme power beyond law that typifies the sovereign state of exception, but something different, perhaps a *real* state of exception as opposed to a fictional one,[11] which implies the dissolution of sovereignty itself and, as Agamben himself puts it, the deposing of violence.

Second, we find in Benjamin a notion of bare or 'mere' life. The operation of 'mythic violence' – the violence which reinstates the law – consigns mere life to guilt, like the violence that transfixed Niobe into a perpetual testimony to her own transgression against the gods. Divine violence, by contrast: '"expiates" the guilt of mere life' and, moreover, purifies the guilty not of guilt, but of law (Benjamin 1996: 250). This helps us to clarify how Agamben understands bare life in relation to law; what makes bare life vulnerable to power is not its bareness as such, but the imprint of law – the law which, in Benjamin's case, imbues it with guilt and, in Agamben's case, incorporates it in the form of excluded inclusion into the clasp of sovereign power. Bare or mere life beyond law, or in a different relationship with law, would be free. This points to the possibility, in Agamben, of a different understanding of bare life: this is not the life of *homo sacer* caught in the loneliness of law's abandonment, something which makes the law evermore oppressively and ubiquitously present, but a life which is freed from the law altogether, freed from even its absence; a situation where, as Agamben puts it: 'One day humanity will play with law just as children play with disused objects, not in order to restore them to their canonical use but to free them from it for good' (2005a: 64). This also implies the closing, or rather the complete transcendence, of the original *zoē/bios* distinction.

We want to suggest that these notions that we find in Benjamin of divine violence, the abolition of state power and the anarchic life beyond law and sovereignty also reveal something important about Agamben's own notion of politics and provide some clues as to how the unbinding of constituent power from sovereignty might be achieved. At the same time, we have to be cautious about categorising Agamben's politics as anarchist in any simplistic sense – there are virtually no references to anarchist political theory in his work, apart from a brief and dismissive remark in the introduction to *Homo Sacer*.[12] Nevertheless, Agamben's proximity with anarchism might be seen in a more oblique way in his call for new ethical and political forms, indeed, forms of belonging or community which transcend, or are no longer bound to, sovereignty and law, something which clearly prefigures a kind of anarchism, or in his enigmatic prediction of a central conflict between the state and humanity, something that was foreshadowed in the Tiananmen Square uprising and its bloody aftermath:

> *The novelty of the coming politics is that it will no longer be a struggle for the conquest or control of the State* [something which would be

characteristic of Marxist–Leninist vanguard politics, for instance],
but a struggle between the State and the non-State (humanity), an
insurmountable disjunction between whatever singularity and the State
organization. (Agamben 1993: 84.5 [emphasis in original])

The resonances with anarchism in this scenario are striking, although
what is invoked here is a *different sort of anarchism*: the coming politics,
he goes on to say, is not about the uprising of already existing social
forces and identities against the state, but about the emergence of an
entirely new form of relations between people – a form of community
of *singularities* that eludes any identity or representation; a situation
which the state finds intolerably threatening. Such notions of the
coming politics and coming community are crucial for thinking about
a new way of understanding politics of human rights today. However,
what is apparent is that if Agamben's notion of politics is not anarchist
as such – or not unproblematically so – then at least it may be understood through some idea of *autonomy*: it seems clear that he is pointing
towards the possibility of forms of autonomous life, being, community
and politics which are no longer constituted around the state and
which refuse the imprint of sovereign power.

Moreover, in Agamben's more recent work on government and *oiko-*
nomia, he suggests that government, which might be said to constitute
the administrative element of the structure of sovereignty, the other
being Glory, is itself 'anarchic'. By this, he means that it is without
foundation: at the centre of the 'governmental machine' is an empty
throne. This is the secret of government: hidden behind its veils is an
empty centre of power. Government is a nihilistic machine whose blind
operations are, for that very reason – and here Agamben cites the case
of 'collateral damage' – all the more devastating. It is this empty throne
that Agamben says we must 'profane' if we are to liberate life from law
and power and reveal the inoperativity proper to it (2011: xiii). That
government is anarchic in this way – and here we should take note of
the ambiguity of this term – means, as La Boétie (1983) recognised long
ago, our servitude to power is entirely voluntary and that all we have to
do is stop giving ourselves to power for the nakedness, emptiness and
impotence of power itself to be exposed.

The challenge, then, is to conceive of being – forms of life and
existence – which exceed defined identities and relations and in which
it is impossible to distinguish between potentiality and actuality. This

seems to parallel the task of thinking life always as a form of life – in other words, a life in which it is impossible to isolate and separate bare life from vocation. What could this involve? Agamben has alluded, as we have seen above, to new forms of community, new forms of singularities being in common, which at the same time avoid defining a fixed identity for themselves – a sort of *post-identity* politics that Agamben recognised in the Tiananmen Square uprising, but which we might also catch glimpses of in, for instance, more recent forms of emergence, such as Occupy. The way in which many contemporary forms of activism – anti-capitalist occupations, No Borders networks or even hacktivism – adopt the gesture of anonymity and resist assimilation into the representative structures and practices of statist politics embodies something like the anti-political, anti-sovereign politics that Agamben is getting at here. It is surely wrong to dismiss such phenomena as non-political (rather they are *anti*-political, which is something different) simply because they work autonomously from the state and from statist and representative modes of politics and do not propose a particular agenda. In doing so, they refuse to play the usual game of 'politics' – a game whose rules are already determined in advance by sovereign power. Instead, in their gestural politics, where they emerge and behave in unexpected and unpredictable ways, they might be seen as something like a more politically relevant form of 'flash-mobbing', and their effect is much more disturbing to the regime of power than standard forms of protest. This is politics of a different kind, what might be termed a *politics of anti-politics*.

CONCLUSION

These figures we have invoked to give shape to Agamben's politics – notions such as inoperativeness, exodus and the community to come – might still seem somewhat enigmatic and, moreover, appear to leave us still with some distance to travel if we are to formulate an alternative politics of human rights, although here it is telling that one of the key figures of the Exodus, for Virno, is the rather antiquated notion of the *right to resistance* (see 1996: 203–6). Maybe the language of rights has a role to play after all in defining these new forms of community and being-in-common. But what is valuable here is the possibility of constituting a different form of community and a new autonomous political space, which is no longer defined by the sovereign state. While we have some reservations over Virno's use of the word 'Republic' to characterise this space – something which still seems to invoke the traditional notion of the public sphere, which we see as one of the main impediments to renewing human rights – such notions are nevertheless important for decentring or decoupling politics from the sovereign state and for imagining new human rights practices and communities. In response, then, to the many, like Paulina Tambakaki, who are critical of what they see as the anti-politics of human rights, we want to say that the tension she explores – human rights or citizenship? (see Tambakaki 2010) – means not that citizenship should be privileged as the properly political status, as she suggests, but rather that human rights directs us towards new forms of community and belonging that transcend the state.

The main aim of this chapter, however, was to demonstrate, in opposition to many of his critics, that Agamben's thinking is not apolitical. Rather, we have tried to show that Agamben gives us new ways of thinking about politics which are no longer tied to the principle of sovereignty and which, instead, are designed to jam the infernal machine of power.

Notes

1 For a full elaboration of this, see Rancière (1999).
2 '*Potenza*' is often translated as 'power' or 'ability' (to act or to do). In the latter sense, *potenza* has also been translated as 'potential', which is how Agamben would want to see it, for this carries within it the notion of 'impotentiality' (*impotenza*) (see Agamben 1998: 45).
3 Such notions imply work, operativity, projects and deliberate activity with a specific goal, whereas for Agamben, as we have seen, and this is confirmed by his notion of inoperativity: 'Man [. . .] is the Sabbatical animal par excellence' (2011: 246).
4 In *The Ego and Its Own*, Stirner says: 'Revolution and insurrection must not be looked upon as synonymous. The former consists in an overturning of conditions, of the established condition or *status*, the state or society, and is accordingly a *political* or *social* act; the latter has indeed for its unavoidable consequence a transformation of circumstances, yet does not start from it but from men's discontent with themselves, is not an armed rising but a rising of individuals, a getting up without regard to the *arrangements* that spring from it. The Revolution aimed at new arrangements; insurrection leads us no longer to *let* ourselves be arranged, but to arrange ourselves,

and sets no glittering hopes on "institutions". It is not a fight against the established, since, if it prospers, the established collapses of itself; it is only a working forth of me out of the established' (1995: 279–80 [emphasis in original]). Stirner's notion of insurrection or 'revolt' (*Empörung*) – which might be another way of understanding a politics of inoperativity – is also directly referred to in Agamben's *The Time that Remains* (2005b: 31–2), where he sees it as one possible interpretation, which he calls 'ethical–anarchic', of the Pauline *as not* or *hōs mē*. The 'as not' is understood here as a refusal of vocation or, to be more precise, a vocation or calling which is at the same time a negation or the bringing to the end (in the sense of messianic time) or a rendering inoperative of all vocations and all juridical–factical conditions: '*The messianic vocation is the revocation of every vocation* . . . What is vocation, but the revocation of each and every concrete factical vocation?' (Agamben 2005b: 23 [emphasis in original]). Stirner, as we can see, is not proposing a direct overthrow of conditions and institutions, but rather a more radical, ontological transformation of our relationship with them, a sort of internalised revolt such that power is rendered inoperative; the insurrection is an acting and living through the *as not*, in other words, as though such external conditions *did not* exist.

5 Here the allusion to Nancy's (1991) *Inoperative Community* should not be lost.

6 This does not mean that, in certain circumstances, the law cannot be used against violence, even against state violence and the violence of securitization, but rather that its relationship with violence is always ambivalent.

7 Also, Agamben, in his more recent work on governmentality or *oikonomia*, shifts the focus from sovereignty to the daily administrative functioning of government and the police (see Agamben 2011).

8 In Benjamin's articulation of Sorel's distinction: 'the first of these undertakings is lawmaking but the second anarchistic' (1996: 246).

9 Bakunin explains this differing understanding of state power: 'They [Marxists] do not know that despotism resides not so much in the form of the State but in the very principle of the State and political power' (1953: 221).

10 Confusingly, Benjamin writes that: 'Divine violence, which is sign and seal but never the means of sacred dispatch, may be called "sovereign" violence' (1996: 252). But 'sovereign', which is in quotation marks, surely means something different here than state or political sovereignty. Perhaps an approximation might be made with Bataille's notion of sovereignty (which is also an *anti-sovereignty*), which is explored in the final chapter.

11 Agamben says that: 'It [divine violence] stands in the same relation to sovereign violence as the state of actual exception [. . .] does in relation to the state of virtual exception' (1998: 65), as if to imply that the state of excep-

tion associated with sovereignty is not a real, but a fictional or 'virtual' state of exception.

12 He says (1998: 12): 'The weakness of anarchist and Marxian critiques of the State was precisely to have not caught sight of this structure and thus to have quickly left the *arcanum imperii* aside, as if it had no substance outside of the simulacra and the ideologies invoked to justify it. But one ends up identifying with an enemy whose structure one does not understand, and the theory of the State (and in particular of the state of exception, which is to say of the dictatorship of the proletariat as the transitional phase leading to the stateless society) is the reef on which the revolutions of our century have been shipwrecked'. As we have shown, there are important differences between anarchist and Marxist theories of the state, particularly over the question of the 'transitional' period in the revolution – differences which Agamben simply ignores here – and, indeed, Agamben's criticism is more pertinent to Marxist theory. Is there nevertheless something important in what he says about the classical revolutionary tradition in general? Perhaps the problem is that when a revolutionary project is fixated on a particular goal or object – the capture or overthrow of the state – then it remains somehow caught within the logic of sovereignty. The key, perhaps, is to relinquish the classical idea of grand emancipatory projects based on a means-ends strategic way of thinking and to think politics in an ontological sense (*ontological anarchy*) as the *realisation of the freedom that we already have*. This idea will be developed further in Chapter 8.

Chapter 7

AGAMBEN, THE IMAGE AND THE HUMAN

INTRODUCTION

In a strikingly apposite statement of aspects of what is to follow in this chapter, the American cultural critic Henry Giroux writes that: 'Audio-visual representations have transformed not only the landscape of cultural production and reception, but the very nature of politics itself, particularly the relationships among nationalism, spectacular violence, and a new global politics' (2006: 17). And our author adds that: 'It is impossible to comprehend the political nature of the existing age without recognizing the centrality of the new visual media' (2006: 17). We are thus drawn to ask how visual media and the image as its key component form the basis of the political in the contemporary society of the twenty-first century. An important aspect of Agamben's thinking on politics is precisely concerned with the image, especially with regard to Guy Debord's notion of the 'society of the spectacle'. As we shall see, what Agamben eventually considers the primary element of Debord's theory and film practice is its capacity to reveal the medium or 'mediality' as such. Whether or not one accepts this view of the image as mediality, if the image is complicit with power in contemporary society, it is important to understand what we are dealing with when we encounter the image.

With this in mind, let us first consider aspects of Giroux's reading of Debord, for the latter locates the spectacle at the heart of politics. Then we shall analyse the nature of the image, both in its everyday sense and also in a more ontological sense. For perhaps if we are able to establish what is essential to the image, we will be better equipped to grasp the link between politics and the image in Agamben's thought.

Here, it is important to recall that the objectified image is always an image captured after the event, after the image has had an impact and done its work as an image. To speak only about the image as object (as presented in the media, for example) would be equivalent to saying that the nature of language is entirely encompassed in the *énoncé*, whereas we have seen that the enactment of language (its existential aspect as an *énonciation*) is crucial for an appreciation of language as such. Therefore, we could say that before any analysis can take place, we are already impregnated, as it were, with an image of statelessness. In order to establish what this image might be, it is important to understand how the image works. Can it be seen in terms of a pure mediality, as Agamben claims? This is one question that we shall keep at the forefront of our inquiry.

To turn again to Giroux, we see that in his reading, Debord certainly links the spectacle and the media images that constitute it to the capitalist market and consumerism (the image replaces the commodity), but that crucially, we suggest, he links visual media to the workings of power. Communication technologies work for corporate capital and map new forms of control (Giroux 2006: 26). Most of all, the spectacle confirms: 'the pedagogical as a crucial element of the political' (25). Being saturated by the media, in short, leads to changes in behaviour – behaviour that harmonises with the interests of power. Thus, if the media, in the interests of power, promotes fear and uncertainty in a climate where 'shock becomes the structuring principle in creating certain conditions of reception for the images and discourses of terrorism and fear' (17), this will mould an audience's perception of the world. Thus, advertisements encouraging people to report 'unusual' behaviour to the authorities can be seen as an example of the way in which media images promote securitisation over the values of privacy, freedom of association and speech and the like. If this is so, the media image participates (and there is no doubt a certain irony here)[1] in the production of bare life in society to the extent that the mass of recipients seamlessly absorb the content of the media message without question. To adapt Agamben's phrase, the media would be in force without significance[2] and, as such, would become equivalent to fact or life. Our intention is to move beyond this interpretation of the image as the handmaiden to power and to see it in an essentially political guise.

Pragmatically, or in an everyday sense, images play a role in human rights situations. Thus, with Rwanda, Guantánamo Bay and the 'Children Overboard' video in Australia, as well as with the recent

example of Syria, the presence of images has had a crucial impact on the
way that these situations have been perceived and understood. This is
so on several levels. On one level, images are conceived of as vehicles of
evidence. Why and how an image can constitute evidence remains to be
established. We will distinguish between the evidential aspect, for which
the image is a vehicle, from the image as such. The evidential aspect is
composed of indexical signs. Let us call the latter the image's forensic
level.[3] Revealed here will be the marks of violence (as in torture and
death – see Abu Ghraib prison torture in Iraq in 2004) against individuals and groups, as well as evidence relating to the treatment of asylum
seekers, refugees and terrorist suspects (see images of inmates in the
Guantánamo Bay detention centre, the detention centres in Australia
and refugee camps throughout the world). Perhaps a special case of the
use of images is found in the 'Children Overboard' affair in Australia,
October 2001, where the Australian Government and supporters of the
refugees interpreted the video images of children in the sea very differently. Publicly, the Australian Government claimed that the children
were thrown into the sea by asylum-seeker parents in order to draw
attention in spectacular fashion to their plight and to ensure that an
Australian Naval vessel would pick them up. In effect, the claim was that
the adults used the children for political purposes. However, in October
2002, an Australian Senate inquiry found that senior members of the
Government were aware of the falsity of these claims and knew that the
photographic evidence was, to say the least, entirely inconclusive.

The second way in which images are important pragmatically is
through their iconic status. This corresponds to the rhetorical figure of
synecdoche or the part standing for the whole. The face, for instance,
can function as a synecdoche. When images of people are shown, such
as the haunting image of the Afghan refugee girl which appeared on
the cover of *National Geographic* in 2005, it is the face that stands for
the whole – a whole which cannot appear as such. This is so, even if it
is often supposed that the icon is a single instance of a multiplicity of
identical instances, which is the basis of stereotyping. A true evocation,
on the other hand, avoids the stereotype. Sartre defines evocation in
the image as quite distinct from perception. Thus, he says, with regard
to a line drawing, we must not:

> believe that the lines are given to me first, in perception, as lines
> pure and simple, to be given afterwards, in the imaged attitude, as

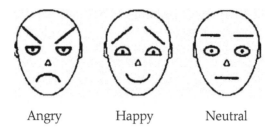

Angry   Happy   Neutral

Figure 1 Evocation (Source: Windows clip art)

the element of a *representation*. In the perception itself, the lines are given as representative. (Sartre 2004: 35 [emphasis in original])

We have, for example, lines evoking moods.

Thus, as seen in Figure 1, a line can immediately evoke a face, a dot, an eye; as with, for example, a jack-o'-lantern, triangles are eyes, the oval shape is a head and the line and the point together are the face – the part for the whole. In a sense, there is no 'pure' line any more than there is 'bare life'. For a line is always an evocation; bare life – to turn to this for a moment – is always, in fact, a way of life. Perhaps this is also reinforced by the principle of phenomenology – an image is always an 'image of'. For an image is the presence of the thing in its absence.

The third pragmatic aspect is the image as metonymy. An example of this would be the image of a celebrity linked to refugees by association or to stateless people through images depicting good works or signs of solidarity. The process is to bring the image of the celebrity into conjunction with those whose cause is supposedly being defended. Advertising uses a similar strategy, where a product evokes good qualities simply by virtue of continual association.

Examples of the pragmatic conception of the image need to be analysed, in order to establish the significance of Agamben's approach for human rights. But to do this, it is necessary to probe more deeply into the nature of the image, in order to remain within the spirit of Agamben's more ontological, if not Heideggerian, approach to the image and politics. We say 'in the spirit of' and not 'in the fact of' Agamben's approach, because in his very appreciative appropriation of Guy Debord's notion of the 'society of the spectacle', it appears that a more pragmatic or 'ontic' take on the image is in evidence.

AGAMBEN, THE IMAGE AND THE HUMAN

When Agamben engages with Debord's cinema, he makes a clear statement regarding his own conception of the image, so we must seriously ponder this. For Debord, we recall, the centrality of images in the society of the spectacle entails the image as the mediator of all relations in society (Debord 1994: Section 4). Indeed, a society has come into being which valorises the image above all else. What was directly lived is now mediated through images. In effect, a picture of someone or an internet contact now serves, Debord claims, as a substitute for direct contact. This implies that Debord's ontology of the image (as opposed to his sociology) is one where the image is a second, weaker form of the real or is even a simulacrum, which has become entirely detached from the real. Because the image is a weaker form of the real and because it has become dominant in a given form of society, social relations are diminished.

Here, we note that there is the additional point that the society of the spectacle also evokes the centrality of the spectator who views a scene at a distance or, at least, who is not, as such, part of the spectacle made available for mass consumption. The consumer of spectacles is thus part of the affirmation of the subject–object relation that dominates the metaphysics of modernity. The consumer of spectacles is not in the world, so much as he or she is fundamentally an observer of the world that has become an object for delectation. If spectacles are essentially images, this, indeed, implies that images have become – or it is believed that they have become – simulacra or objects in their own right. On this, many commentators simply follow Debord and assume that an image is: 'first and foremost an object in the world, with physical characteristics, just like any other object' (Aumont 1994: 102).

The possible attraction of Debord is not contained in his conception of the image, but rather in the fact that he distils the *doxa* of the image as the object that it is possible to 'know', like any other object – a conception rampant in modernity and capitalist social and political forms. The *doxa* form of the image is based on a fundamental misrecognition – a misrecognition, we argue, that is crucial to the maintenance of sovereign power. The latter has an interest in keeping the image as object on the side of bare life and thus separate from a way of life – life as it is lived. The image as object, then, refers us to the way that the image currently functions in social and political life.

Consumers of spectacles thus do not conceive of themselves as being 'in' the spectacle. To do so would contradict the very notion of the image as an object and, by implication, would also undermine the consumer as a subject who views spectacles. If, by contrast, one is already in the world and therefore already in images, just as one is in language, the image takes on a very different hue – one that means that images, like the enactment of language (= *énonciation*), are not in any sense an objectification. Thus, they are not equivalent to an *énoncé* or completed statement, which is also an objectification (for example, as is illustrated in the sentence (*énoncé*) 'Peter hit Paul' (that is, subject, verb, object), which is much analysed in linguistics). By contrast, we say that the image is precisely something which cannot be objectified, because it becomes that entity which reveals or exposes the world as such and is not itself the thing exposed.

Gesture and Mediality

Of major significance regarding the image in Debord's cinema and gesture, as Agamben presents it, is that both are supposed to make mediality visible. Neither image nor gesture remain entirely transparent; they are no longer reducible to invisible means enabling a visible end to appear in the form of meaning, representation and so on. Similarly, with the face (Agamben 2000: 91–100), appearance appears as such; it does not disappear into a deeper reality. The face thus enables a thwarted appearance to claim its rights: appearance can appear *as* appearance or, rather, as that which appears. In sum, Agamben is intent on demonstrating that forms of mediality (of which the image is an instance) can appear as such: the invisible can be rendered visible or, rather, the invisibility of the image can be rendered visible; appearance can become extant; gesture can enable gesturality to appear. While gesture is intimately linked to language, it is not, as such, linguistic. Here, again, the point is to appreciate the extent to which gesture, like the face, like the *énonciation*, like appearance and facticity, is a mode of exposure and revelation, not an object (*res*).[4] Like Heidegger, perhaps, Agamben sees appearance in terms of the actual appearing of a certain reality or truth. Appearing is not cut off from what appears, as is implied by the classic difference between appearance and reality.

Be this as it may, there is a question as to whether in his haste to counter what he sees as the transparency of the medium in Hegel, Agamben – maybe against his intention – ends up objectifying mediality and thus the image with it. Indeed, just as Brecht wanted theatre to make its mediations visible and as Godard wanted cinema to do the same, so Agamben also wants the image to be opaque, as it were. A question arises as to whether the image and gesture fall in with the *énoncé* (or the objectification of the word), rather than with the *énonciation* or act of language, as Benveniste outlined it. We will consider this issue again in relation to Agamben's approach to Debord's cinema. For our part, at least, there is an enactment of the image – the image that makes present the imaged in its absence – before there is the image as object, as opaque. Such a conception also links up with an understanding of the image as bound up with religious themes, where, for example, the image of Christ can evoke his divinity.[5]

Mediality and Indexicality

We know, then, that Agamben wants to push this point about exposure and revelation with respect to Debord's cinema, arguing that Debord's achievement is to render visible the invisibility of the image. As Agamben explains:

> The current conception of expression is dominated by the Hegelian model according to which all expression is realised through a medium [in English in the text], whether this be an image, a word, or a colour which, in the end, must disappear in the completed expression. The expressive act is completed once the means (*moyen*), the medium, is no longer perceived as such. The medium must disappear in what it gives us to see, in the absolute which shows itself, which is reflected in it. By contrast, the image which is subject to repetition and stoppage [in Debord's strategy] is a means, a medium, which does not disappear in what is given to be seen. This is what I would call a 'pure means' which shows itself as such. The image is itself given to be seen in place of disappearing in what it gives us to see. (1995: 4)

Clearly, from this passage, if a pure means 'shows itself as such' – that is, shows itself as a means – it would seem that it is not a matter of the image becoming an object to be analysed. The image here would not be equivalent to an *énoncé* (for this is the level of the 'end' of language) – the level at which the analysis of language can take place. Rather, we have to conclude that matters are much more complex. Something reveals itself, without becoming an object. Mediality, the image, reveals itself *in its very transparency*, without thereby becoming an object. Sartre's criticism of the 'illusion of immanence', where an image–object appears in parallel with the thing itself, thus ceases to be pertinent.

Mediality, *énonciation* (act of language) and the image can no doubt be added to a significant list of domains which cannot be rendered accessible through analysis and objectification. Indeed, objectification would be equivalent to a falsification. These domains would include: thought, context, experience, the sacred, the human and political action as freedom.

Consequently, our view is that before being able to fully assess the importance or otherwise of human rights, it is necessary to come to grips with the meaning and significance of the human that is not an objectification, but a revelation of pure means.

However, despite the potential subtlety of his notion of the image as mediality, Agamben's approach in general shows a lack of attention to the historical context and etymology of the term, image. For his part, Jean-Luc Nancy suggests that, in Christianity, the image is the 'real presence' (2003: 27). Moreover, he adds: 'It is always sacred' (11). As the 'distinct', it is also 'invisible', like the sacred (30), and yet functions as the evidence of the invisible. It is a *'monstrance'*, which evokes the Catholic *ostensory*: 'the receptacle for displaying the host to the congregation' (OED). As Nancy puts it, the image is: 'a prodigious sign which warns of a divine menace' (47). But a question quickly arises here: can an image be a sign?

Moreover, Nancy is not entirely illuminating or convincing in the points that he makes. For in asserting that it is the distinct and the separated (like the sacred), the image risks becoming an object in its own right, despite Nancy's intention to the contrary. On the other hand, in claiming that the image is present in the marks left by the torturer (2003: 45), we are reminded of the key issue of human rights with which we are concerned, even if the idea of an indexical sign as image would need more extended consideration than we can offer here. Suffice to say that the mark as sign is of a different order to that of an image of a mark or marks on a human body, for example. Marks on the body – stigmata, scars, tattoos, blemishes, cuts, scratches, wounds of all kinds, insignia – are signs that exist by way of an image. The image would be the *presence* of the marks, not the marks as such. An image, then, is not itself a sign, but can be the vehicle for signs (marks).

THE IMAGE, VIOLENCE AND THE INDEXICAL SIGN

For Nancy, then, the image and violence go together: 'Violence is always implicated in an image' – at least this is so the moment we leave the *doxa* of the image, which presents it uniquely in its mimetic character (2003: 44). Such a claim is enigmatic to say the least, but appears to be possible when one mistakes an indexical sign for an image. As we saw earlier, this could mean that the marks of violence on a body could be equated with the image. It emerges, then, that the forensic aspect of the image is, in fact, the indexical sign as borne by the image. This distinction, closely linked to that of the difference between the image and what is imaged, can be clarified by taking the example of a painting – for example, a self-portrait by van Gogh.

In his self-portrait of 1889, completed in the year before his death, all the indices are there to evoke a true van Gogh work: the swirling brushstrokes – not to say, the characteristic swirling lines *in* paint – the clarity of colour, the unadorned face, the saturated orange of the beard, the dominance of blue and so on.[6] In the most literal sense, such a work has the *stamp* of van Gogh all over it. This is its indexical aspect. Its image aspect is a different matter. As an image, the painting makes van Gogh present, much as Sartre's friend, Pierre, is made present by a portrait (see Sartre 2004: 6). This is why we can say, pointing to the above work: 'This *is* van Gogh'. With an image, we are thus unaware of the indexical side of the painting. The presence of van Gogh himself blots this out. When we say that van Gogh is the artist of this portrait, we speak indexically. When we are no longer in the mode of inference characteristic of an indexical sign and instead say that this is van Gogh, inference gives way to presence, transparence and to the image.[7]

On this basis, if we take as an example the case of Abu Ghraib prison torture in Iraq in 2004 which was mentioned earlier, we say of the photographic image of Lynndie England holding a leash attached to a prisoner lying on the floor: 'this *is* Lynndie England'; 'this *is* a prisoner lying on the floor'; 'this *is* a leash'. This is the work of the image. When we conclude that being attached to a leash and lying on the floor implies torture, we are then in the realm of the indexical sign. What is clear is that there can be no indexical sign without the image, but that an image is not reducible to an indexical sign.

Consequently, it would be necessary to take issue with Nancy and say that violence is not reducible to an image – that the image and violence are not inextricably linked, even if images frequently provide the raw material of violence. Blood on the floor in the Abu Ghraib images thus implies violence. Blood thus becomes an indexical sign. It might be said, however, that certain images are intrinsically violent by the very fact that they make the imaged visible, such as might occur in obscene images or in images revealing a harsh truth of one kind or another. This seems to be what Nancy is alluding to when he links the image to truth and says: 'violence has its truth as truth has its violence' (2003: 45) – a neat formulation, but is it illuminating? Is it illuminating especially when the meaning and significance of terms such as 'violence', 'truth' and 'image' are so difficult to pin down? If truth is revealing – *alētheia* in the Greek/Heideggerian sense – what are the implications of this? As one astute commentator on Heidegger has said: 'This dis-closedness of Being to Dasein is, according to Heidegger, what truth means in the most primordial sense' (Suvák 2000: 6). Again: 'For Heidegger truth is something that happens, and so it is an event of being (*Ereignis*) which is only revealed to us' (Suvák 2000: 7). To show how complex the issue is here, Heidegger also links freedom as 'letting beings be' with the 'essence of truth' (Heidegger 1993: 127). On this basis, were the image to be connected to truth in the Heideggerian sense, it could be understood in terms of showing, hence Nancy's emphasis on the link between image and *monstrance*. The image, no doubt, is a showing or a revealing. We could thus say that where there is a showing – where there is an appearing of something – there is an image. Indeed, the image would be the appearing as such.

At first glance, none of this concern with ontology is evident in Agamben's take on the image. He seems to accept that the image in its spectacular guise is an object cut off from any authentic origin. Recall: 'Everything that was directly lived has moved away into a representation'; 'The images detached from every aspect of life fuse in a common stream in which the unity of this life can no longer be reestablished' (Debord 1994: Sections 1 and 2).

However, Marie-José Mondzain (cited in Agamben 2011: 2) has analysed the image in relation to the Trinity in the Byzantine era, particularly in the era of iconoclasm, invoking in the process a key term in Agamben's later work – *oikonomia* or economy – which Mondzain argues is important in Christian theology, evoking as it does the discourse on the notion of relation (*skhésis*) (2005: 29). The image, on this basis, is not simply a visual object.

This theological approach to the image, while evoking much more sympathy from our author in *The Kingdom and the Glory* – concerned as it is with matters theological – is very different from the approach of Agamben as supporter of Debord. For the image here becomes an object – if it is a medium, then the medium itself becomes an object. Transparency gives way to pure opacity. This is what Sartre would call the 'illusion of immanence', where there is both the real (thing, reality, object and so on) and an image, perhaps an image of the object, but one that constitutes a kind of second reality (see Sartre 2004: 4–7).

Analogon, *Schema and 'Inoperativity'*

But what of that which cannot appear? Would an *analogon*, which supposedly operates when it is impossible for something to be represented, presented, symbolised or signified, need to be called upon? God or divinity, death, nothingness, chaos, infinity or time could be instances of this impossibility. The analogon approximates what Kant called the *schema*, where he argued that indeterminate entities such as triangulation, magnitude, substance, time or number could not be rendered by any determinate image (= representation) whatsoever. According to Kant, therefore, the schema comes into play when there is no available image to do justice to the thing or where a specific actual image would mis-present the thing, such as when a single number is used to stand for all numbers.[8]

The schema is necessary, said Kant, because the image itself is effectively a determinate object. Due to this quality of the image, therefore, it is inadequate for the task set, which is to bring indeterminacy into view. Kant – and, as we have seen, today he is not alone – treats the image as a determinate object in its own right, thus committing the error that Sartre came to call the 'illusion of immanence' (Sartre 2004), by which he meant the treatment of the image as an object separate from what is imaged. The problem, as Kant perceived it, was that the specific quality of determinateness of the image put a limit on what could be imaged. But if one adopts the view that the image cannot be separated from the imaged – that it is the imaged that gives rise to the image and not the reverse (see Lechte 2012) – Kant's problem evaporates, and there is no longer any need for the schema or for an analogon. Furthermore, if indeterminacy thus becomes the focus of thought, any image of indeterminacy will consequently be coterminous with thought as such.

Consequently, we see that Kant inaugurates an error that has been pervasive in modernity when it comes to comprehending the image. It is that the nature of image determines what can be imaged. In Kant's case, the determined nature of the image renders it incapable of presenting indeterminacy. A similar problem exists with regard to the photographic image and movement. Because the photographic image itself is deemed to be the incarnation of stillness, a photograph cannot present movement. Bergson and, after him, Deleuze have no doubt been the most eminent purveyors of this idea.[9] Analogously, the nature of language is frequently seen to be an obstacle to what can be said (for example, the fact that it is made up of words). This is the basis of the idea of the inexpressible – 'what cannot be put into words'. Agamben clearly takes a very different approach here. For, he argues, language is precisely what enables the inexpressible to be presented. This, indeed, is the essential task of language. Were it not so, linguistic, symbolic and image forms would risk becoming a mass of clichés and maybe this is what is now occurring. The most crucial context in which such an insight has real significance is in relation to the claimed impossibility of the Shoah ever appearing in linguistic, imagistic or symbolic form. To claim that it can do so is often deemed to be equivalent to sacrilege; for what appears or is presented, it is said, must always fall short of the horrendous reality, which may even risk falling into banality. In a now well-known response, Agamben replies to the argument that Auschwitz is 'unsayable' and asks: 'But why unsayable? Why confer on extermination the prestige of the mystical' (2002: 32). He concludes his point by arguing that the 'speech of language' takes place 'where language is no longer in the beginning, where language falls away from it simply to bear witness' (39). Indeed, it is within the very potential of language to fall into silence or into non-language. This can happen in face of the impossible. The contingent possibility of the collapse of language is part of language's potentiality.

Were an analogon to be invoked in the context of human rights, this might occur with regard to the notion of an inclusion that is not based upon exclusion or, indeed, in relation to the notion of the human as such. But, equally, an image understood as not being an object might be necessary in Agamben's terms, in order to evoke the exposure of the human in the 'taking place' of language. Thus, in Mallarmé's poetry, Agamben discovers an 'inoperativity'[10] that evokes nothing more nor less than the taking place of language – an inoperativity that, Agamben says, opens the way to a new mode of the political: 'In this inoperativity, the life that we live is only the life through which we live; only our power of acting and living, our act-*ability* and our live-*ability*. Here the *bios* coincides with the *zoē* without remainder' (2011: 251 [emphasis in original]). In sum, the political: 'is neither a *bios* nor a *zoē*, but the dimension that the inoperativity of contemplation, by deactivating linguistic and corporeal, material and immaterial praxes, ceaselessly opens and assigns to the living' (2011: 251). More than anything, inoperativity exposes the human, in so far as the human is the life as it is lived in the coincidence of *zoē* and *bios*. We would say that the image emerges as the appearance of living that is an inoperativity.

Consequently, it is a mistake to think of the political as the sphere within which the good society is to be realised. Rather, politics is praxis without outcome (an inoperativity), so that praxis would be the taking place of the political as such. In Arendt's terms, what is created in politics is subordinated to the act of creation itself. The image – albeit in its mass media version – thus comes into play as the exposure of the inoperativity of political praxis. Through the image, Agamben argues, the glory of politics (what used to be embodied in ritual, liturgies and ceremonies) is now found in public opinion as acclamation (2011: 256). The only problem is that the latter has also been appropriated by sovereign power, without there being any clear mode of extrication. There is, thus, still more to be considered here.

THE IMAGE, DECEPTION AND THE POLITICAL

Let us now return to Agamben's approach to the image and consider what the implications for politics might be. Does Agamben's position ultimately amount to subscribing to a phenomenal form of the image? In this context, the text of interest is a lecture in French by Agamben on the occasion of a retrospective in 1995 of Guy Debord's six films. We shall quote from this particular French text (Agamben 1995). Agamben makes two key points concerning the image: first, that the image is something of interest quintessentially to humans and not to animals.

Second, what Debord's cinema makes visible, as we have seen, is the invisibility of the image, its mediality. This is an insight that Agamben does not manage to hold consistently. Agamben, then, has this to say about the human and animal attitude towards cinema:

> Man is the only being who is interested in images as such. Animals are greatly interested in images, but to the extent that they are duped by them. Show a fish the image of a female and he will ejaculate, or, to trap it, you can show a bird the image of another bird; it is deceived by it. When an animal realises that an image is involved it become entirely uninterested in it. Now man is an animal who is interested in images once he recognises them as such. This is why he is interested in painting and goes to the cinema. A definition of man from our specific view point could be that man is an animal who goes to the cinema. He is interested in images once he has recognised that these are not true beings. (1995: 1)[11]

In light of the fake image of Osama Bin Laden's body circulating on the internet in May 2011, it is as well to return to the issue of the image as object; for, once again, it might be claimed that unless an image were an object in its own right, fake images would be impossible and being deceived by images would also be impossible. This, of course, refers us back to the examples given by Agamben, where animals can be deceived by mistaking, as he claimed, an image for reality. How is it possible to mistake an image for reality if an image is always the presentation of the imaged in its absence? We have said that an image *qua* image fulfils its task when it recalls the imaged, whatever this may be. In a certain sense, therefore, the fake image still recalls Bin Laden – no one will dispute that – and to this extent, the image is confirmed as an image. However, as mentioned at the outset of this chapter, there is also what we have called the 'forensic' mode of the image, where the image is the vehicle of indexical signs that are evidence of something – of the existence of asylum seekers and detention camps, violations of human rights, poverty and so on. Things then become more complicated. For although there is no image without the imaged and the image is the inexorable evocation of the imaged, the image is not the same as the imaged. The image is not a thing or object and yet it is not identical to the thing imaged. Indeed, it is invisible – a characteristic known at least since Byzantine times. Thus, an image can deceive.

Deception, then, via the image would seemingly occur because the image as such can present something that passes for an imaged, whereas, in fact, it can be a pure simulacrum: an image removed from any actual imaged whatsoever. For the human, a *trompe-l'oeil* would have similar features to that of the simulacrum. Here, clearly, a distinction is operating between the image and what is imaged, so that it appears undeniable that the image is an autonomous object in its own right, that it has qualities specific to it as an image, as Kant said in referring to the determinate aspect of every image. This is the basis upon which Agamben can say that, for the human, painting and cinema – *qua* autonomous images – can have an attraction for the human in their own right. Is the idea that the image is not an object thereby refuted? Are we indeed not confronted with another ontology of image, which is that it is an object? Must we not concede that the *doxa* of the image is, in fact, correct? At minimum, we need to explain again how a deception is possible.

Here we are reminded of Lacan's invocation of the Greek story about Zeuxis and Parrhasios (1973: 95). Zeuxis painted grapes so well that birds began to peck at them. The painter then challenged Parrhasios to better the accomplishment, whereupon Parrhasios, sometime later, brought Zeuxis to his studio, where his masterpiece was apparently covered by a veil. When Zeuxis asked to see what was behind the veil, Parrhasios revealed that the veil was not real, only an image. The human being, says Lacan, is the one predisposed to want to look behind the veil. The look, here, will often differ from what one sees, because it is driven by (the object of) desire (*objet petit a*).

Lacan continues by saying that in deceiving an animal with an image, it is not a matter of a perfect representation of an object, but the fact that the 'eye of the birds was deceived'. The look triumphs over the eye or over what one sees. Later, Lacan emphasises the point that the deception of an animal by an image does not in any way imply realism (1973: 102). Lacan continues by explaining how, with *trompe-l'oeil*, jubilation arises when it is realised that the thing is only an image. This is when seeing and the look merge with one another (1973: 102–3).

We would say, however, that despite appearances, the image still does not become an object. For, in a sense, the fish cited by Agamben and the birds pecking at the grapes cited by Lacan both behave in a way that suggests an appreciation of the image as an image, which is the equivalent of the thing in its absence (the fish) or even the presence of the thing as such (the birds). To say that the grapes become real to birds is to say that the brushstrokes that produced it and the surface on which it was painted do not in any way figure in the birds' field of attention, which these would have to do if the image were an object. Even for the birds, as for the fish, an image is not an object or a thing, but is the imaged as such.

Although Lacan prefers to emphasise the jubilation in recognising that the *trompe-l'oeil* is a *trompe-l'oeil*, thus implying that there is a real thing on one side and a false thing on the other, it is more pertinent to note that what is imaged will remain and endure beyond the difference between the real and the imaginary. A *trompe-l'oeil*, even after the discovery of the deception, will evoke something other than what it is as an object of perception (coloured paint on canvas). It is this insight that we need to bear in mind when considering the relation between the image and the human.

THE IMAGE AGAINST THE SPECTACLE

The problem now is that it is difficult not to conceive of the society of the spectacle as a form of life independently of bare life. But no doubt the notion of secularisation also needs to be addressed, despite Debord's references to the sacred (1994: Section 25). Debord's sacred is, in fact, a pseudo-sacred, within which, along with myth, power shrouds itself in order to govern the spectacle. Debord does say, however: 'The spectacle in general, as the concrete inversion of life, is the autonomous movement of the non-living' (1994: Section 2. See Agamben's characterisation of the *Muselmann*). Ultimately, as we have seen, the image for Debord, at the level of ontology, is unreality (but not in the sense of the *irreality* of the image in Sartre, which is closer to the virtual and which brings what is imaged into presence in its absence). This implies that it does have an autonomous existence. However, we need to ask: if the image is not a simulacrum, how can it have an autonomous existence?

The further question is: how can an image be a pure commodity and, at the same time, 'a representation' necessarily referring to a 'represented'? Here, the issue is one of receptivity in the society of the spectacle. We suggest that it is only because the image is not constituted by the subject that we can speak about 'adoption' in Bernard Stiegler's sense (2001: 138–46). Audience/spectatorship theory tends to go in the other direction and propose that an image is what is projected into it.

This position is thus 'subjectivist'. A whole range of issues centre round receptivity.

Digital technology is often thought to change the image. Indeed, technology and the image are often conflated. We know, for instance, that the digital image has the capacity to eliminate difference without leaving a trace – a factor which can only add to the capacity of authorities to erase identities. This latter point has implications for human rights in the sense that the digital image is integral to the police identikit portrait, which is constructed without any trace of its construction. A key example is the entirely homogenous 'Face of Sydney', morphed from 1,400 images of a diverse range of people, from a baby at two weeks' old to people in their nineties.[12] It is also hardly necessary to mention the human rights implications of the seemingly endless proliferation of digital surveillance technologies, from CCTV cameras in public places to the use of biometrics and facial recognition technology in airports and other contexts. For instance, the use of full body scans in security zones in airports produces, in a similar manner to the 'Face of Sydney' image, a shadowy outline of the human body which is utterly homogenous. Could there be a better symbol of the way that surveillance technologies work to produce this anonymous, non-descript figure of bare life, stripped of any individuality or even subjectivity?

Ultimately, however, the image (understood as a revealing) and the spectacle are two different things. For the spectacle only works to the extent that it sustains the idea that an image is an object (equivalent to an *énoncé*) that is entirely immaterial and superficial, whereas true reality is material and profound. This is another version of the old metaphysic of the appearance–reality opposition. This is the metaphysic that Debord has no qualms in asserting. However, we suggest that the putative opposition between the immaterial image and concrete reality thus needs to be rethought, lest this supposed insight into the way that capitalism and sovereign power work should turn out to be a point of extreme blindness as to the way things really are.

AGAMBEN AND THE *MUSELMANN* AS IMAGE OR PERSONIFICATION

Does Agamben not need the magic of the image, according to Sartre and Barthes, to truly do anything like justice to the presentation of the *Muselmann*? What is the real link between bare life and its image? This requires a fuller elaboration of the Gorgon in light of Robert Buch's reading of Agamben's *Remnants of Auschwitz*. We suggest that this is fundamental. Regarding its iconic and imagistic status, Buch is absolutely unambiguous in stating that the *Muselmann* is located in the tradition of the Christian *'vera icon'* (true icon) and is, for Agamben, the 'true image of man' (Buch 2007: 179, 181 and *passim*). Buch is, in particular, critical of the logic of politics that Agamben puts forth, saying that, in revealing our blindness as to the significance of the *Muselmann*, Agamben reveals his own blindness to the connotations that his work gives rise to and to the tension between the *Muselmann* as bare life and the same notion in *Homo Sacer*, where bare life is defined clearly in opposition to the (true) sacred.

For Buch, Agamben's goal in *Remnants of Auschwitz* is to point not only to the actual blindness of the *Muselmann*, but also to the ignorance of commentators on the death camps – that is, to the 'blindness of those who think themselves seeing' (2007: 184). In Buch's reading, the *Muselmann* is 'a haunting figure' that 'conjures up a long-standing iconographic tradition' (185), particularly Christ's face as the *vera icon*, so that the *Muselmann* would become, like Christ on the cross, the 'epitome' of suffering (185). Furthermore, Buch argues that the *Muselmann*'s extreme passivity and powerlessness is also evocative of the Christian *gloria passionis* (glorious suffering). Buch comments: 'In this example of extreme suffering a reversal seems to be imminent: it seems to contain a special kind of knowledge, perhaps a revelation' (186).

The irony is that something sacred in the transcendent sense begins to emerge precisely in the place where Agamben would like to refuse any connection to it. Buch puts it well when he states: 'in his non-humanity [. . .] the human appears'; 'The sacral seems to return in the somatic' (2007: 185). This implies that it is impossible to see the *Muselmann* uniquely as bare life (if this was, indeed, Agamben's intention), because the closer he approaches the status of bare life, the more sacred becomes his bearing.

Buch shows, then, the extent to which Agamben's work, perhaps despite itself, evokes the sacred and the Christian tradition of the icon/image that, politically, Agamben opposes. Buch does not offer any real commentary on the *vera icon*, and so it is impossible on this basis to link the *Muselmann* conclusively to this tradition. However, it is worth noting, in light of the work of Mondzain (2005), that in Christian (and Orthodox Christian, in particular) theology, the image emerges independently of any given material context. On this basis, Christ becomes the image of God independently of his earthly body. This is to say that the incarnation of the image is independent of its materiality, even if the latter could be an index of its presence. On this basis, the possibility of the *Muselmann* becoming the incarnation of the image of humanity is not ruled out by his status as 'bare life', even if Agamben might want to block this association. Would he also want to block the idea that the *Muselmann* is the personification of the human as such?

The upshot is, then, that any engagement with the image will inevitably evoke its theological history. This is the lesson that Debord (along with most post-war thinking) refuses. Indeed, in his almost violent denunciation of the image as commodity (= secular object *par excellence*) under capitalism, Debord evokes a time of the true image – one where there was no clear separation between image and imaged. This history is inevitably and inexorably contained in the image, despite the secularist push to the contrary, in what is called modernity. This is to imply, too, that with regard to the essential being of the human, the past inevitably inheres in the present – modernity as an essential present is not all there is. For not only does the past inhere in the present, but so, too, do the transcendent aspects of the past. Perhaps Derrida's notion of 'haunting' goes part of the way towards illuminating just what is at stake here, and is no doubt the reason why Derrida opposed the claim that religious sentiment was no longer an essential part of social and political life in our own day (see Derrida 1994).

What would an image be that is haunted by something? Let us say, with regard to the haunted image, that the ostensible imaged (subject) contains an evocation of something else – something other, something that goes beyond indexicality, because it is an integral part of the image as such. Thus, Hans Holbein's *The Ambassadors* (1533) is famously 'haunted' by an anamorphic (distorted) skull as a *momento mori*. Photographs which appear to have unidentified objects in them could also be said to be similarly haunted. With regard to the human and to human rights, we would be interested in images which contain elements that are not conceived as being part of the subject matter.

In the image of the detainees at Guantánamo Bay,[13] light appears to be reflected off an object to the right of the upper portion of the picture. Just what this device is cannot easily be determined, but it is not part of the presumed subject matter of the photograph. Something indeterminate, in addition to what Barthes called the *studium* or narrative aspect of the image, is there. Or we could say that the image, like so many, is 'haunted' by an indeterminate otherness, and this element must be taken into account when confronting images.

THE IMAGE AS ICON

The iconic form of the image – understood here in terms of the *doxa* as synecdoche, rather than in Peirce's sense of the image having the qualities of the imaged – comes into play, as is known when a single element stands for the whole or a multiplicity. Agamben refers to the face of the Rwandan child standing for the suffering of all Rwandan children (1998: 133). Similarly, there is the haunting face of the Afghan refugee girl – now known to be Shabat Gula – taken by photographer Steve McCurry and featured on the front cover of *National Geographic* in 1985.[14]

The girl, then aged 12, was simply called 'the Afghan refugee' until 2002. When she was photographed, Gula was in the Nasir Bagh refugee camp in Pakistan, escaping from the Russian invasion. As such, she came to represent all refugees. After the photo was published, Sharbat Gula disappeared for seventeen years, even if, subsequently, the magazine engaged in a successful quest to find her again in 2002. The story of the search prompted people to donate to the cause of all refugees, once again reinforcing the girl's synecdochic status.

CELEBRITIES AND REFUGEES

With regard to refugees and the image of celebrities, the usual form of presentation is for the celebrity to be dominant and glamorous in the foreground (as in the web-linked image of actress Angelina Jolie[15]), with the decidedly less glamorous, darkened refugee figures in the background. The only real link between refugee and celebrity tends to be that of metonymy created by the image itself. The question we could ask is whether glamour can ever be convincingly intertwined with those members of the human who are in the most precarious and unglamorous of situations.

CONCLUSION

Undeniably, the majority of this chapter has been concerned with the ontological status of the image in relation to Agamben's perhaps more pragmatic treatment, which links the image to the spectacle. The everyday (the *doxa*) encounter with the image in the media is pragmatic in that it accepts the metaphysical notion that the image is an object. Celebrities thus become associated with the refugee underclass purely by a juxtaposition of images, and, moreover, a single image can take on iconic status by standing for the whole, thereby obliterating difference.

The question we are now left with is whether or not an ontological approach to the image can have immediate political effects. As we have suggested, the political itself is not, for Agamben, a realm for achieving specific goals, because inoperativity is the essential quality of the political; therefore, the ontology of the image takes on a more strategic importance. For just as the metaphysics of community as embodied in the nation-state is driven by the metaphysical division of 'inclusion–exclusion' and the idea of the community to be constructed, so the metaphysical notion of the image as object reinforces a pragmatic notion of the image as a spectacle/object to be consumed. Digital technology, which allows the image to be manipulated with ease, only serves to reinforce the view of the image as object. For images can be produced – created – by the human hand. They are objects produced by subjects – something that thus confirms the dominance of the metaphysics of the image. This is the basis upon which the image is reduced, pragmatically, to its media version. It is largely this media version of the image as object which governs the forensic, synecdochic and metonymic modes of the image. Significantly, it becomes clear that it is no longer a matter of what the image brings to presence, but rather a matter of whom or what produces the image. In this regard, the identity of the image is tied to the technology through which it becomes incarnate.

An alternative approach to the (political) ontology of the image may be highlighted by returning to the distinction between *énonciation* as the event of language, of the human, of mediality and the *énoncé* as the completed event, action, statement. Agamben, we recall, makes this distinction key to his approach to politics, language, gesture and the human. Each of these aspects of *énonciation* opens the way to the exposure, revelation or disclosure of the entity in question. Although

Agamben is often ambiguous regarding the image, we can also link the image to the process of exposure, for it is not an object. Every objectification, we have demonstrated, is, as it were, after the event. The trajectory of Agamben's work clearly leads to an appreciation of this insight.

All of Agamben's work, then, moves in the direction of gesturing towards the significance of *énonciation* in philosophy, literature, politics and economics. When the question of the relevance of Agamben's thought is posed in relation to contemporary politics and society, it should be recalled that relevance, like usefulness, is a misleading term, for it places us on the trajectory of the *énoncé*, not that of the *énonciation*. A pragmatic position equally places us at the level of the *énoncé*, not the *énonciation*.

To return to the image in relation to the human and human rights, we should now be able to intuit what it means to encounter images of torture and violence at the level of the *énonciation*. On this level, we experience the violence taking place, not its representation or objectification. Again, to see the 'Children Overboard' video is to experience the event of children in the water after the sinking of their vessel. Of course, an objector might say that it could all be fiction. And this cannot be denied. However, the designation of fiction occurs after the event, not in its taking place. In terms of what is important to us with respect to human rights, the image works to expose the situation of the asylum seeker, of the stateless person, of those on the brink of the abyss.

Notes

1 The irony hinges on the fact that the media, at least within the *doxa*, are seen to promote a 'lifestyle' or way of life and not just the defence of life in its most minimal biological form. However, it is the latter that securitisation, as we see it, is all about, not the former.

2 The original formulation is *law* being in force without significance (see Agamben 1998: 59).

3 See, in this context, Eyal Weizman's recent work on 'forensic architecture', whereby, as he shows, the forensic analysis of destroyed cities and urban landscapes captured in photographs, satellite images and collections of objects (rubble, spent ammunition, medical and autopsy reports) increasingly stands in for the human witness in international legal investigations of war crimes and crimes against humanity. This reveals, Weizman sug-

gests, not only something about the forensic age we live in – characterised by the epistemological and evidentiary importance attributed to objects, rather than subjective testimony – but, more worryingly from our point of view, a certain forensic fetishism shared by both human rights organisations and the military, both of whom are increasingly preoccupied with estimating collateral damage from military strikes. In this nexus of humanitarianism and violence, the fate of civilians is determined by mere algorithms (see Weizman 2011).

4 An interesting commentary on the relation between gesture, thought and politics in Agamben is given by ten Bos (see 2005).

5 The whole issue of iconoclasm and iconophilia in the Byzantine era – from which we have not entirely escaped today – centres on whether, and in what sense, Christ is present (or absent) in his image (see Lechte 2012: 32–46).

6 See the portrait at the Musée d'Orsay in Paris. http://www.musee-orsay.fr/en/collections/works-in-focus/painting.html?no_cache=1&zoom=1&tx_damzoom_pi1%5BshowUid%5D=2401

7 It is perhaps worth recalling Lévi-Strauss' description of Caduveo art, particularly facial painting, which, the anthropologist says, reminds one of: 'Spanish baroque, with its wrought-iron work and stuccoes' (1974: 189). The implication is that this art was originally influenced by the Spanish colonial conquest – it bears the mark of this conquest. The art is thus seen as indexical, rather than as imagistic. In a further move, Lévi-Strauss says that: 'facial paintings confer human dignity on the individual; they ensure the transition from nature to culture' (195). In other words, as the human for the Caduveo is essentially cultural, there is no human face in nature. The facial painting thus constitutes the face itself, so that the face becomes an image or the image constitutes the face, even if there is no mimetic relation between image and face.

8 See Kant (1970: 180–7). For an analysis of the schema and the image in Kant, see Lechte (2012: 78–82).

9 For an elaboration of this, see Lechte (2012: 96–5).

10 'Inoperativity', as we noted in Chapter 6, evokes the French *'désoeuvrement'*, as seen in Bataille's response to Hegel's notion of history at its end as 'unemployed negativity' – the energy force that still remains at the end of history when there is nothing more to achieve. This is when action becomes acts done purely for their own sake, outside of any utilitarian rationale. Jean-Luc Nancy used the term in the phrase 'la communauté désoeuvrée' (see Nancy 1991). The idea that 'community' can be, and needs to be, created is a myth. For the human is, as it were, always already given in community. Thus, there is no work to do to produce community any more than humanity needs to create the means of communication. Communication is also always already given.

11 The French text reads: 'L'homme est le seul être qui s'intéresse aux images
    en tant que telles. Les animaux s'intéressent beaucoup aux images, mais
    dans la mesure où ils en sont dupes. On peut montrer à un poisson l'image
    d'une femelle, et il va éjecter son sperme, ou montrer à un oiseau l'image
    d'un autre oiseau pour le piéger, il en sera dupe. Mais quand l'animal se
    rend compte qu'il s'agit d'une image, il s'en désintéresse totalement. Or
    l'homme est un animal qui s'intéresse aux images une fois qu'il les a recon-
    nues en tant que telles. C'est pour cela qu'il s'intéresse à la peinture et va
    au cinéma. Une définition de l'homme de notre point de vue spécifique
    pourrait être que l'homme est l'animal qui va au cinéma. Il s'intéresse aux
    images une fois qu'il a reconnu que ce ne sont pas des êtres véritables.'
12 See: http://www.smh.com.au/news/national/revealed-the-face-of-sydney
    /2006/10/05/1159641464886.html [accessed 18 February 2013].
13 Link to Guantánamo Bay Detention Centre, Cuba: Pepper Spraying
    http://narwhaler.com/img/3q/v/cop-pepper-spraying-guantanamo-bay-
    inmates-3QVTmb.jpg [accessed 26 November 2012].
14 Link to Afghan refugee image in National Geographic http://hogue
    news.com/wp-content/uploads//2009/07/afghan-girl-615.jpg [accessed 26
    November 2012].
15 Link to Angelina Jolie, 'No one has to be a refugee' http://i.ytimg.com/vi/
    yJr0e18Jqx4/0.jpg [accessed 26 November 2012].

Chapter 8

LIVING HUMAN RIGHTS

Man [the human] cannot at any price, be said to coincide with the mere life in him.

Divine violence [. . .] may be called sovereign violence.

(Walter Benjamin)

The alterity of the Other (Autrui) is in this Other and not in relation to an ego.

(Emmanuel Levinas)

Nguyen Van Thanh, now in his nineties and living in France, is one of 20,000 Indochinese workers who were requisitioned by force to work in France during the Second World War. As Doan Bui points out: 'Nguyen Van Thanh was not considered a citizen. He was an indigenous person' (2012: 50). Nguyen's status, and that of so many others like him during the Second World War, goes to the heart of the situation described by Arendt, namely, that those not inducted as citizens into a political community cannot hope to be the beneficiaries of human rights. The colonial nations' policy in this regard is very clear: only some (and these are obviously not those who are subjected to colonial rule) can be included in the domain that Arendt also calls the realm of freedom. Previously, we have also pointed out that those still deemed to be mired in necessity cannot be said to be free. At best, they might eventually become free, but this is in no way guaranteed, as Arendt's references to the lives of 'savages' clearly indicates. What Arendt says here runs deep in the European tradition of political thought, balanced as it is on the coordinates of necessity and freedom.

Let us not deny, though, that in linking the political realm with freedom, Arendt is on the right track – a track that is taken up by Agamben in his equating of inoperativity with the act done for its own sake and not in the name of a project; an act which, at the same time, exposes the essential condition of the human as one of freedom.

SOVEREIGNTY REVISITED

Sovereign power, however, would seem – at least as understood in its Hobbesian incarnation – to give the lie to any talk about freedom as being the exposure of the human. For as we have seen in Agamben's rendition, sovereign power constitutes bare life (what exists, we have said, without any transcendence – mere aliveness) as that which can be controlled without question. Bare life is the fact of life which signals power's absolute supremacy over it. Bare life is produced by sovereign power; sovereign power needs bare life to confirm its autonomy. If one accepts the link that Agamben makes between power and life in this way, it implies that what is not bare life – that what is, indeed, a way or 'form' of life – at the same time reveals sovereign power's actual vulnerability. A form of life, we saw, was described by Agamben as a life that can 'never be separated from its form'. Form of life, then:

> defines a life – human life – in which the simple ways, acts, and processes of living are never simply *facts* but always and above all *possibilities* of life, always and above all power. Each behaviour and each form of human living is never prescribed by a specific biological vocation, nor is it assigned by whatever necessity; instead no matter how customary, repeated, and socially compulsory, it always retains the character of a possibility; that is, it always puts at stake living itself. (Agamben 2000: 4 [emphasis in original])

This, then, is to understand human life as essentially marked by transcendence – a transcendence that is inextricably linked to the essential freedom of the human. In Agamben's view, sovereign power is always trying to erase the notion of transcendence and freedom by defining the human as nothing more than a fact – a fact of life.

From another perspective, when we think of sovereignty, we have to consider its relationship to law. As the tradition stemming from the Magna Carta reminds us, the law is sovereign. No one is above the law. However, the sovereignty of the law is made entirely ambiguous when we consider the logic of the exception, as defined by Carl Schmitt, where the law is seen to anticipate its own suspension in the interest of maintaining order. With Schmitt, the normal case anticipated by the existing form of the law is overtaken by the exception, so that it becomes impossible, as Agamben has indicated, to know whether the law anticipates its own suspension in order that conditions conducive to its perpetuation can be re-established or whether the law is instituted to ensure the perpetuation of sovereign power. In other words, current political thought cannot answer the question as to whether the law exists to ensure the survival of sovereign power or whether sovereign power exists to ensure that the enforcement of the law. We shall return to this issue later in our reflection on violence.

For its part, the image is also linked to sovereign power as a 'fact' without transcendence. This is why Debord can plausibly draw a parallel between the image and the commodity. The image, however, puts us in touch with the essentially human to the extent that, through the image, a way of life is captured in similar fashion to the way that Christ's divinity is deemed to be accessed via the image of Christ. The human as a form of life is only accessible as an image of life (the form of life made present in its absence). Emmanuel Levinas' thought, which we shall also touch upon later, takes us to a new level here. For Levinas argues that objectification (for example, as practised by the social sciences) entails that the image, like the other, becomes an object. The order of the Same blots out difference or the absolute Other (*Autrui*), as we shall see. But first, it is necessary to further deepen our understanding of sovereignty, in order to appreciate more fully how sovereign power operates. Only then will we be in a position to work out how sovereign power might be countered in the interests of human rights.

Bataille's Vision of Sovereignty

Clearly, the issue to be addressed is the extent of sovereign power's hold over politics, especially as this is reflected in processes of securitisation. What is the sovereign exactly? And how does sovereignty manifest itself? What kinds of relations are involved?

Sovereign power – the highest or supreme power, as Hobbes defined it – is absolute rule retained from the state of nature and incarnated in the civil state. The sovereign is that force which keeps the populace in awe and may only be opposed if it threatens the lives of the populace; for then, the point of moving out of a condition of nature ceases to make any sense. In effect, the sovereign can be absolute, but only in as far as he or it ensures the security of the populace; security being the marker of the difference between the state of society and the state of nature.

In a consideration of sovereignty that could be said to be more psychological in orientation than that of Agamben, Bataille, influenced by Kojève's reading of Hegel, shows that the question of sovereignty cannot be separated from the question of servitude or submission. The latter implies a loss of freedom. It is pertinent to think about exactly what kind of freedom exists under conditions of securitisation. For it might be thought, indeed, that the loss of freedom is the price to be paid for security. Bataille's response is to point out that all conditions of servitude are only ever contingent, for the human *qua* human is the incarnation of freedom or, as Bataille puts it, the human is always 'a being in revolt', for freedom is the essence of the human's being (1988a: 195). What is more, even complete submission can only be pretence of submission, for no act of submission can be absolute.

Opposing the sovereign, then, can only show that revolt (freedom) is sovereign. For, logically speaking, if the sovereign who keeps the populace in awe were truly sovereign, there could never be revolt; there could never be insubordination. The refusal to submit is to reveal that the sovereign is nothing more than a 'so-called' sovereign and that true 'sovereignty' arises out of the challenge to every contingent form of sovereignty. Here, the human in revolt comes to be realised as the freedom that it always already is.

Bataille takes things further in his Kojèvian reading of Hegel's Master/Slave dialectic. In the first place, the Master or Lordship is equated with sovereignty. Thus, the Slave who works does so at the behest of the Master, for he prefers life and servitude – work as servitude – to death. Moreover, the Slave is the incarnation of utility, that is, of everything that sustains biological life, in whatever form this might take. The Slave, moreover, is the principle of work as action (negativity) that transforms what is worked on. The Slave, then, is what he does – his being is in doing – whereas the Master's being is in what he already is. This, says Bataille, is similar to a religious approach, where sovereignty is defined in terms of what one is. Thus, Bataille says, sovereignty has two parts: 'one absolutely sovereign and the other active, in the service of animal ends. Slaves allow him [the sovereign] to be liberated from the active part' (1988b: 352).

The Hegelian idea, as we have already noted (see Chapter 2), is, of course, that eventually the terms are reversed: that not only will the Master come to recognise his dependence on the Slave in enabling him to satisfy, as Bataille says, his 'animal needs' (1988b: 357), but that in directing the Slave in what to do, the Master also becomes implicated in utility, when his identity should be that of one who shuns utility in the interest of military prowess and sacred time – the Slave being the one mired in history as the unfolding of profane time. Profane time, separated from sacred time, is also the time of history as the time of reaching the end of needs satisfaction, the end of utility as the lot of the human, the end of work and the arrival of death as the undermining of every project. Even though history and work repress it, death, above all, is what characterises the being of the Master. Such is the case not only because one became Master by choosing the possibility of death over servitude, but also because the Master is essentially a warrior, a soldier, a military power; he is the one whose life is based on war and the possibility of death at every turn. But more significant, from our point of view, is the fact that work, which would enable the satisfaction of 'animal needs' and thereby ensure the maintenance of minimal biological life, cannot but evoke the death that it seeks to put out of play. In other words, the domain of necessity and the satisfaction of needs, which in the European tradition is deemed to be the inevitable precursor to the domain of freedom, cannot but evoke its other, in so far as death – human finitude – is what can never but be evoked by life. On this basis, necessity may be equated with the animal in the human, so that by implication, it is only when the human has transcended the condition of animality that politics as freedom can take place. The slave, although human, thus becomes the mechanism for satisfying the animal needs of the human.

In his other text on sovereignty (1976), Bataille is even more explicit about the link between necessity, work, utility and subservience. No one who works can live a sovereign life. Here, work may be broadly defined as any activity which produces something for future consumption, so that the future dominates the present. It is only in the break from work – in the intoxicating state of leisure in the present – that sovereignty becomes a possibility. Thus, Bataille writes that the worker drinks a glass of wine 'to escape the necessity which is the principle of work' (1976: 249).

At the level of work as such (the active part), we know that there can be no full sovereignty. Moreover, it is thought that not to stake one's life, to work to provide the necessities of life because one wanted to avoid or at least postpone death is to relinquish sovereignty. But death is postponed on the basis of the very fact of human finitude. It is only because the human is finite (not infinite) that work is necessary. Work therefore evokes death at every turn, and we reach the point where the very separation between necessity and freedom in relation to the human again breaks down. Perhaps this is not entirely in keeping with Bataille's position, for he is quite content to retain the necessity–freedom opposition. But it is also through Bataille that the opposition begins to break down.

Ironically, then, for the human, it is death as such which is sovereign. Every life becomes a form of life in relation to death. In the absence of human finitude, in other words, there would be no forms of life, only life as such – life as God lives it.

Here, it is also interesting to note that, in Bataille's terms, sovereignty is on a par with all those things which render life a form of life, such as art, the festival, love, the sacred, play and war. Each is the stimulus to unproductive expenditure – expenditure in freedom. However, this is to suggest that true sovereignty is freedom, not an obstacle to freedom, as seems to be the case for those (especially the stateless) on the receiving end, when sovereign power acts in the name of the security of society.[1] Security falls within the category of necessity and the maintenance of biological life. For, as the Hobbesian argument would have it, if the need for security is not satisfied, freedom is not possible. What is clear is that if necessity is separated from freedom, only some can be free. Freedom can never be universal, for someone has to do the work. And work, as such, can never give rise to a form of life – life as freedom. This is in keeping, too, with Arendt's notion of political community as only being truly open to those who do not labour. Only when labour (necessity) is overcome can freedom (the political) be realised. Bataille's approach is not radically different from this.

Where Bataille is perhaps different, however, is in the inclusion of religion in the discussion of sovereignty, because religious practices are also a mark of the human. Perhaps, he implies, only God is truly sovereign, for only with God has necessity been totally overcome. God is the absolute, who does not live a form of life, but who is at the origin of all forms of life. So, unlike Agamben, Bataille's sacred does not appear in the interest of secular sovereignty, but in terms of divine sovereignty. Secular sovereignty must always be limited in comparison with divine sovereignty, just as finitude is 'the limited' in relation to infinity. As Bataille says in a number of places, the divine is absolutely unproductive. War, too, is unproductive, albeit *relatively* unproductive, compared to divinity (1988b: 369). On this, we should recall, too, that every form of life *qua* form is also unproductive, for a form of life just *is*.

In what sense, then, does Bataille's approach to sovereignty throw light on the nature of sovereign power in the contemporary situation? The answer is that a sovereign power that constitutes itself in opposition to universal sovereignty is based on an illusion and that, as soon as the sovereign, despite all historical incarnations, is subjected to the scrutiny of critique, it begins to crumble from within.

VIOLENCE

If Bataille opens the way to the possibility of a positive view of sovereignty, it is still necessary to deal with Walter Benjamin's idea of divine violence. As we have seen in Chapter 6, divine violence is to be distinguished from both mythic violence, which establishes the law, and the violence which maintains the law. Divine violence is the violence that is absolutely sovereign in relation to all other violence. There are many complicating factors in relation to Benjamin's ideas here, not the least being the meaning of the term *Gewalt* in Benjamin's 'notoriously difficult'[2] essay '*Zur Kritik der Gewalt*'. For as is known, *Gewalt* can also refer to authority, force and power, not just naked violence, if there is such a thing. More specifically, though, it is clear that Benjamin is concerned with origins, including the origin of the law – an origin which he sees as traumatic and occurring all at once. Violence is the means that brings law into being. An existing form of the law – or the law as such – does not evolve slowly, but comes into being in a manner similar, perhaps, to that of language, which must exist as a complete system or not exist at all. We might, however, still speculate about what existed, if anything, before the law came into being. While Benjamin clearly has in mind particular historical instances where violence has been used to bring about new conditions (the French Revolution, for example), it is the implications of his essay for a theory and ontology of violence that is more interesting today.

For his part, Derrida, in pointing to the broader meaning of *Gewalt* in

German, is able to link the law intrinsically to force, so that there is no pure force or violence on one side and pacific law on the other. The law implies force. But the law is also, Derrida agrees with Benjamin, originally instituted by force or violence. The following passage highlights these points:

> *Gewalt* also signifies, for Germans, legitimate power, authority, public force. *Gesetzgebende Gewalt* is legislative power, *geistliche Gewalt* the spiritual power of the church, *Staatsgewalt* the authority or power of the state. *Gewalt*, then, is both violence and legitimate power, justified authority. How are we to distinguish between the force of law of a legitimate power and the supposedly originary violence that must have established this authority and that could not itself have been authorized by any anterior legitimacy, so that, in this initial moment, it is neither legal nor illegal – or, others would quickly say, neither just nor unjust? (Derrida 1990: 927)

There is, then, 'originary violence', and we will need to address the implications of this at greater length below. But also in need of elaboration is the link between law, justice and force or violence. There is no law, no justice that does not imply force. Historically, this would seem to explain why there is no law without a law-enforcing agency – what is today equivalent to the police. However, Derrida's interest is not, in the first instance, either historical or empirical, but philosophical, so that included in the very meaning of 'law' is the notion of force. Force is what makes the law the law, so to speak – force that is applied in a just way. Reading Pascal as the thinker who best captures what is at stake in the relation between law and force, justice and force, Derrida concludes that: 'justice demands, as justice, recourse to force. The necessity of force is implied, then, in the *"juste"* in *"justice"*' (1990: 937).

Derrida's reading of Benjamin opens up a number of issues concerning the relation between violence and the law. These will be examined below.

Violence, Law and Sovereignty

The first issue concerns the notion, proposed by Benjamin and accepted by Derrida, that the law is based on founding (originary) and conserving violence. Here Derrida summarises the point that the: 'foundation of all states [therefore of all reigning sovereignty?] occurs in a situation that we can thus call revolutionary. It inaugurates a new law, it always does so in violence' (1990: 991). Again, paraphrasing Benjamin, we read:

> The State is afraid of fundamental, founding violence, that is, violence able to justify, to legitimate (*begründen*, 'to found,' [. . .] or to transform the relations of law (*Rechtsverhdltnisse*, 'legal conditions'), and so to present itself as having a right to law. (1990: 989)[3]

Nevertheless, if law and violence are inextricably entwined, one wonders how violence (not law) could truly be originary. Derrida attempts to get around this by implying that violence is always connected to a given system of law and (for example, in a revolutionary situation, as we have seen above) one system of law overturns and replaces another. But then one would have to acknowledge that law is equally originary and that violence is not prior to the law, as Benjamin clearly believes it is. For Derrida, as for Benjamin,[4] founding violence is prior to the (existing form of the) law (this is why there is no law to judge any founding violence; looked at from one system of law, another system is illegal). Moreover, while historically it might appear that violence has played a key constituting role in ushering in new systems of law, it still remains to be proven that violence is an essential ingredient in changing a legal system. Could it not be envisaged that a legal system is self-transformative? Furthermore, is it not naive in the extreme to think that at a single stroke as it were, violence can bring change to the entire socio-cultural and political complex? This is precisely what Gramsci showed when he developed his concept of hegemony. The violent overthrow of a given state is only the beginning – if it is even that – of the revolution, not the end. These lines of thought at least have to be contemplated, lest one be forced to conclude that violence alone is the motor of history. The issue of the nature of violence – considered below – and the possibility of unintended consequences must be taken into account here.

For its part, sovereignty enters the picture when a particular legal system invokes force to maintain itself. The very fact that the sovereign has always felt under threat implies that sovereignty has never been absolute – that the entity claiming to be sovereign is never absolutely sovereign. Benjamin's parting shot at the end of his essay, that only divine violence is truly sovereign, thus makes sense in this context (1996: 252). If historically there is nothing other than regional sovereignty, sovereignty will always be under threat. It will always be concerned with its very survival. Historically, too, sovereignty has not perceived the threat to its existence as simply being external – as deriving from other sovereignties – but also as being internal.[5] Every form of sovereignty, then, is based on the opposition between inclusion and exclusion. Schmitt, of course, sought to radicalise and intensify this opposition through the friend/enemy relation. Consequently, statelessness (the excluded) and sovereignty (the sphere of inclusion) stand at opposite ends of the spectrum in this regard.

Political communities in the Arendtian sense are also regional and are, thus, entities of inclusion and exclusion, even if Arendt herself is ambivalent about sovereignty. In other words, political community and sovereignty would seem to go together. However, if, as this implies, violence and sovereignty are essentially inseparable, as instanced in the exception, are we not returning to the problem of the founding act of sovereignty as one of violence? We thus return to the well-worn path of Hobbes and the social contract, which emphasises the originary violence of the state of nature, as well that of Freud and many others who speculate about the time before the law, the time before the killing of the father and, in Lacanian terms, the birth of the symbolic order. European thinking on the political is thus hampered by founding myths that emphasise the creative power of violence. Benjamin and Derrida do not seem to be any different in this regard. And with his emphasis on the founding nature of violence perpetrated on *homo sacer* in the establishment of sovereignty, Agamben, too, could be included in this category.

An Ontology of Violence?

If there is no sovereign power without violence – if, indeed, violence 'founds the state' and if it is the state which polices the boundaries of inclusion–exclusion – the exact nature of violence as such needs to be identified.[6] In this regard, neither Benjamin nor Derrida (apart from pointing to the multiple German meanings of *Gewalt*) are very illuminating. Could violence ever be grasped as anything other than a pure contingency? Those who talk about violence (especially in terms of its effects) being anticipated thereby weaken their case, for it would have to be asked whether what they are really talking about is violence. But, also, can there really be, as we have seen, such a thing as 'symbolic violence'? Certainly, Derrida thinks so: 'The concept of violence belongs to the symbolic order of law, politics and morals. And it is only to this extent that it can give rise to a critique' (1990: 983). Such a notion of violence, we note, fits more readily into a deconstructionist frame, where the 'purity' of the terms in an opposition is always in question. There is always contamination. Law is thus inevitably contaminated by violence. It is never free from violence. Being enforced (calling on violence) is part of law's nature. Thus, in the example of the general strike: 'Violence is not exterior to the order of *droit*. It threatens it from within' (1990: 989).

Is it possible to speak about violence in general here? Surely it is clear that violence never takes a single form. While the physical violence of the police, military, revolutionary, terrorist and counter-terrorist and of organised crime seems clear-cut, we know that psychological violence, symbolic violence, sexual violence, pedagogical violence and even the violence of road trauma are often referred to. But precisely what happens when violence occurs? Is this not a question that calls out to be addressed, when violence as an experience appears to be so prevalent? Violence is lived as the 'what goes without saying', as the 'self-evident' *par excellence*. Violence is the unspeakable, indefinable and un-analysable. Any phenomenology of violence is thus faced with the difficulty of finding symbolic forms within which violence may be rendered. The fact that there can also be symbolic violence only heightens the difficulty here.

Arendt on Violence

Hannah Arendt's essay *On Violence* focuses on, amongst other things, the nature of modern warfare and the nuclear technology that means now that warfare: 'has lost much of its effectiveness and nearly all its glamour' (1970: 3), with national sovereignty being the main reason that war still exists as a means of resolving disputes. Significantly in terms of the ideas presented in this book, Arendt refers to the folly of the United States in not separating freedom from sovereignty and of following European states in what she calls: 'the bankruptcy of the nation-state and its concept of sovereignty' (6).[7]

Clearly prompted by the political events of the 1960s, including independence movements (in the Vietnam and Algerian wars) and the student movement in the United States, Arendt attempts to draw distinctions between what she sees as the key terms of the debate – terms such as 'power', 'strength', 'force', 'authority' and 'violence' (1970: 43). For its part, violence, phenomenologically speaking: 'is close to strength, since the implements of violence, like all other tools, are designed and used for the purpose of multiplying natural strength until, in the last stage of their development, they can substitute for it' (46). In a way, despite it being invoked repeatedly, we really never find out what violence actually is, apart from being a means (but there are numerous kinds of means). Sentences such as the following are typical: 'Violence is by nature instrumental; like all means, it always stands in need of guidance and justification through the end it pursues' (51). What *kind* of a means is violence? Certainly, it is, itself, administered by other means. In this regard, violence does not depend on 'numbers or opinions, but on implements, and the implements of violence [. . .] like all other tools, increase and multiply human strength' (53). Violence as such is not a technology, but it is administered by technical means. However, we suggest that this is not the full story. For violence may depend on different kinds of technical means for increased potency and, indeed, if the human is itself technical, violence, no doubt, is always implicated in the technical. This, however, does not bring home to us the true nature of its effects.

Violence as Trauma

Violence has an immediate and traumatic aspect. There may be a warning that violence will strike, but no one can be prepared for the strike of violence. It is the impossibility of being prepared that is essential to violence. Does this imply that every event, as unpredictable, is essentially violent? Our answer would be in the affirmative, making the link between violence and weaponry but one form of violence, not the key to understanding violence, as Arendt believes.[8] Arendt does not in any way prepare us for grasping violence as related to the event and truth. This is because, like most thinkers on this subject, she only sees violence as injury to persons and property within conventional political or military activity. A broader consideration of violence is not really within her purview. And it is only our concern to the extent that grasping the full extent of violence, which may include a positive aspect, is of assistance in throwing light on the negative effects of violence, as when, for example, violence is used by sovereign power against stateless people. Only by more deeply understanding violence, can its trajectory be, where necessary, thwarted and controlled.

It is now beginning to look as though everything that comes out of the blue without warning has a violent aspect. We can say that this is violence as trauma. In Freud, trauma is what bypasses the secondary system of reason and the symbolic. Something intrudes into the psyche, which often triggers symptoms, as is the case, Freud found, with war neuroses of the First World War. Trauma, then, is always violent. It never follows a predictable pattern. It is intrusive and unwanted and is closely linked to violation, which we will consider shortly. By way of illustration, we can refer to road trauma. The violence of the traffic accident relates to its completely random and unpredictable nature. No one knows where and when a traffic accident is going to occur.

Violence as Violation

In arguing that violence is essentially an unwanted, not to say illegal, violation of borders, Bataille particularly has in mind the realm of discontinuous beings, where: 'between one being and another there is an abyss, a discontinuity' (1957: 19). Once this discontinuity is penetrated, violated, as in eroticism and what Bataille calls states of communication as states of fusion, things are quite different: borders cease to be of any consequence. Thus, the possibility of unwanted intrusion can only take place for those not in a state of continuity.[9] This implies that violence is a more or less mortal issue for those in a state of discontinuity – the state of individual beings engaged in reproduction. Civil life is the life of borders; erotic life is one of continuity and the evaporation of borders. It is life, essentially, which calls for the institution of borders, while a fluidity of borders constitutes the movement towards death that is characteristic of eroticism. Death, not life: 'has the sense of the continuity of being' (1957: 22). Bataille is not saying that one can do away with borders, but he is saying that there is space in human existence where borders are of no consequence. The point here is to show that what: 'is always in question is to substitute for the being's isolatedness – for its discontinuity – a feeling of profound continuity' (1957: 22). 'Without the violation of the constituted being – who is constituted in discontinuity',

Bataille confirms, 'we are unable to represent the passage from one to another essentially distinct state' (23–4).

With regard to the nation-state and various forms of community, the well-known ritual of hospitality for strangers is geared to render border crossings non-violent. Here, the other (stranger) is made one (part of the community), albeit for a limited time. What we have been exploring is the possibility of making the opposition between inclusion and exclusion redundant, so that all of the human can experience the freedom and community that it already is. The question is: will it be necessary to continue violent and unwanted incursions through borders, in order to render all borders fluid and porous? In other words, will a violation of borders eventually lead to no more violations, because inviolate borders will no longer exist? Only, it will be replied, if the legitimacy of borders as such is challenged, as happened with the fall of the Berlin Wall. This, in part, is what we seek to do in light of thinkers like Agamben.

In regard to the question of statelessness, what is needed more than ever today is a problematisation of borders, border politics and the logic of securitisation and national sovereignty which informs them. This is something that many activist networks and organisations which disrupt border practices or support the rights of refugees and 'illegal' migrants are seeking to do. Yet what must also be recognised is what Étienne Balibar calls the 'polysemic nature' of borders (see 2002: 81) – the way they have, in a sense, become detached from distinct geographical territories and are increasingly shifting, mobile and more difficult to identify. Borders might now be found outside the traditional territories of nation-states – as in, for instance, offshore processing zones for 'illegal' migrants – as well as internally – as in police blockades at protests and even gated communities. Borders might be intensified or relaxed, enforced or temporarily removed, according to the needs of the economy or for matters of political expediency, as we have seen in recent times, for instance, with the temporary enforcement of border controls between several EU countries to stem the flow of 'illegal' migration from North Africa into Western Europe.[10]

Indeed, the whole question of borders and their enforcement and violation – and the violence implied in both – goes to the heart of our discussion here. We are concerned not only with the borders which define, and which are, in turn, defined by, nation-state sovereignty, but also with the borders of any identity and their disruption.

Levinas and the Other

For Levinas, the encounter with the Other is what disrupts and violates the borders of the sovereign self, making the autarchy and ipseity of the self impossible by introducing an element of radical heterogeneity, which cannot be assimilated into the ego's identity. This encounter is thus a form of violence – it necessarily involves a form of 'persecution', in which the self becomes a hostage through the ethical relationship to the Other. Because the borders of the sovereign self are thus unsettled, Levinas characterises this encounter as one of 'anarchy' – it is anarchic because it dislodges the very foundations of essence. The anarchy that Levinas invokes here is quite different from the Hobbesian anarchy of the state of nature (and not quite the same as anarchism as a revolutionary political project); indeed, it is something that resists the totalising tendency of any sovereign politics. He says: 'Anarchy cannot be sovereign like an *arche*. It can only disturb the State – but in a radical way, making possible moments of negation *without* any affirmation' (Levinas 1998: 194 [emphasis in original]). Anarchy, then, is also prior to all sovereignty, just as the Other is prior to the conscious self.

Furthermore, the ethical relationship that Levinas describes points towards new understandings of both freedom and community. For Levinas: 'Substitution frees the subject from ennui, that is, from the enchainment to itself, where the ego suffocates in itself due to the tautological way of identity . . .' (1989: 114). What is being proposed here is not so much the individualist freedom that we are more familiar with – the freedom of one sovereign identity, measured and secured against that of another – but rather, a freedom from the strict borders of sovereign identity altogether, an unchaining from the claustrophobic tautology – and sovereignty is always a tautology – of fixed, bordered identities. Moreover, this getting away from sovereign identities implies the possibility of different forms of belonging, togetherness and community, outside and beyond those currently defined by national polity and citizenship. As Levinas says: 'The unconditionality of being hostage is not the limit case of solidarity, but the condition for all solidarity' (114). It is not too difficult, then, to see how in providing a different view of the human from that currently in vogue, this might be applied to the question of nation-state borders and the threat of disruption to sovereignty posed – or seen to be posed – by the very existence of stateless people. Whether an ethical relationship on the part of sovereign states with regard to stateless people is possible is perhaps doubtful. But what is important here is the way that the very appearance of stateless people somehow throws the consistency and self-identity of national sovereignty into disequilibrium by imposing upon it an ethical demand that opens it up to something beyond itself. In this sense, statelessness presupposes sovereignty's ultimate impossibility or least illuminates its limits and incoherency – something we have alluded to above. It also points to the possibility of alternative forms of community and solidarity beyond the nation-state.

'Collateral Damage'

No doubt, it is never possible to get to the bottom of violence. The best we can hope for is to open it up to thought in the hope of deepening insights and understanding. In this regard, one final aspect of violence is worthy of mention. It is the notion that there can be no use of violence without unintended consequences. As others have said, starting with Max Weber, violence is a train that one cannot get off at will. Violence, then, is not a means like any other, but a means that is sui generis. Sovereign violence – the violence that forms part of the attempt by the sovereign to confirm sovereignty – thus often has unintended consequences, whether this be in the theatre of war in Afghanistan or Iraq or whether it be in controlling opposition forces on the street, in universities or elsewhere. Unintended deaths and injuries can, and often have, occurred to participants on both sides. Indeed, as Agamben claims, 'collateral damage' is a structural, rather than accidental, element of governmental activity: 'When the US strategists speak of collateral damage they have to be taken literally: government always has this schema of a general economy, with collateral effects on the particulars, on the subjects'.[11] For this reason, it is difficult to see how any claim that violence can be done for just or for unjust ends can be supported. For unintended consequences, precisely are, more often as not, entirely unjust. If the alleged war criminal executed in the name of justice was found to be the victim of mistaken identity, if children die in bombing raids in the just war, if the elderly suffer – if all this happens, this putative justice then turns into the worst injustice. Such is the risk with all forms of violence against the person.

LEVINAS AND HUMAN RIGHTS

What, no doubt, is missing from many accounts of violence, including the one enunciated above, is that the human as such calls out for consideration. To make the point, we need to remind ourselves that this consideration pertains for the other even more than for the self. Here, to be sure, the political and moral spheres intersect. We begin to hear ringing in our ears: do unto others . . .; always treat the other person as an end, never as a means; and, in a Levinasian sense, one is originarily responsible for the Other (*Autrui*). Levinas says: 'The order that orders me to the other does not show itself to me, save through the trace of its reclusion, as a face of a neighbour (1998: 140). Previously, Levinas had reiterated that: 'to thematize this relation is already to lose it' (121). Clearly, were we to take Levinas' principles as our guide, we would need to acknowledge that to 'thematise' the nature of human rights and the human is to lose them. Or to put it another way: to produce a concept of the human as the bearer of rights is to do violence to the true or absolute Other. The Other, in Levinas' sense, is not open to objectification, phenomenality, totalisation – to being encompassed in a whole. This Other is always already there before me (in the sense of both time and space); my responsibility to this Other is prior to my being. It is in this context that Levinas opts for the infinite that perpetually challenges totality against the finite, which is constitutive of totality. State sovereignty would obviously be an instance of an instrument which reinforces totality.

Levinas again brings home to us the importance of not thinking of human rights in the patronising terms of 'victim' and 'saviour', which is something that reaffirms the hegemony of the self over the other. Rather, for Levinas, we should think of rights in terms of the non-ontological primacy of the Other (the Other beyond essence), and thus rights become the rights of the other. This opens up a different sort of relationship between the self and other – not one of power and identity, but inter-relatedness based on the '*for-the-other* of the social, of the for-the-stranger' (Levinas 1999: 149 [emphasis in original]; see also Levinas 1993: 116–25). In this regard, there is an echo of Rancière's insight about those who are marginalised, excluded and deprived claiming and enacting rights in a positive self-determining way, rather than simply being bestowed with rights or inheriting them from the West (2004). To some, however, the risk is that we do nothing, that we remain passive before all the horrors of human degradation. Even Agamben's notion of the act as inoperativity holds out this prospect, it might be argued. On the other hand, in terms of Derrida's reading: 'in a world where the face is fully respected (as what is not of the world) there would be no more war' (1967: 158). In other words, the wager is that in a Levinasian sense, once 'egology' has been displaced and the Other appears *as* Other (= the face as full ethical presence), the risk of wholesale violence evaporates.[12]

Sovereign power, we would argue, is heavily implicated in these processes of objectification that makes the Other part of the order of the Same and part of the social world over which sovereign power presides, often ruthlessly. Although he comes at the issue via a completely different route, Agamben is united with Levinas in being alive to the negative effect for the human of sovereign power. Like Levinas, Agamben is equally thoroughgoing, philosophically speaking, in his rejection of the current practice of politics in its entirety. Thus the nation-state must be dismantled, and politics must cease to be about the realisation of a project. Like Levinas, too, Agamben sees the human as that which cannot be objectified in any concept or in terms of any given content. If the human is a being with language, the key aspect is the enactment of this language (the *énonciation*), not language as objectified (the *énoncé*). Like Levinas, Agamben, as we have seen, never reduces the human to its spatial and biological condition (bare life) – to what Levinas would call finitude – but rather sees it as potentiality, which includes the possibility of not acting. Saying, for Levinas, is: 'prior to all objectification; it does not consist in giving signs' (1998: 48). And again, in a manner reminiscent of Agamben, Levinas writes: 'Saying is communication, to be sure, but as a condition for all communication, as exposure' (48).

A fundamental difference between Agamben and Levinas concerns the status of the act. For while Agamben sees the act for its own sake as central to inoperativity and thus part of a different approach to the political, Levinas argues that the absolute Other, who is not part of the order of the Same, is prior to any act.

Another fundamental difference is that whereas Agamben is ambiguous with regard to the image as object and society as a spectacle, Levinas leaves no room for doubt that if the image is objectifying, it participates in the order of the Same that effaces the Other. For our part, though, the image is not of the order of the Same. It is not an objectification, but the presence of the imaged in its absence. It is in this role that it touches on the infinite and the divine.

Ontological Politics: Living the Freedom that we Already Have

In brief, the world of politics, as it is currently structured, cannot accommodate either Agamben or Levinas. This is a sign that things are not right with the world. But this is not to say that things need to change in the sense of an overturning of existing structures, although this might well be a consequence of a more fundamental ontological transformation, whereby the world of the human *becomes truly what it already is*, especially in terms of freedom and justice. Rancière's axiom of equality is an important reference point here; for in it, we have the presentation of equality prior to any empirical realisation of it. In other words, political action involves, indeed, it presupposes the equality that it then seeks to verify. Equality is not the goal of political action so much as its starting point; the presupposition of equality, for Ranciére, is the point of departure for politics, particularly democratic politics:

> Politics only occurs when these mechanisms are stopped in their tracks by the effect of a presupposition that is totally foreign to them yet without which none of them could ultimately function: the presupposition of the equality of anyone and everyone, or the paradoxical effectiveness of the sheer contingency of any order. (1999: 17)

In demanding or making claims for equality or rights, people *act as though they are already equal, already have those rights*; equality thus becomes the precondition of acting.[13] Perhaps in the same way, we could speak of an axiom of liberty; freedom should not be thought of in terms of a project of emancipation, as the goal that awaits us on the other side of the revolution. Rather, it is a question of realising the freedom that we already have, expressing and living what we already are; acting and living, in other words, as though we are already liberated in the here and now.

Living and enacting the freedom that we already have would be the antidote to the problem of our voluntary servitude. For La Boétie, this referred to our unwillingness or inability to acknowledge that we are already free and always were free and that the power that bears down on us and which seems so formidable and insurmountable is simply an illusion created by our own self-abdication. Just as we can will our own servitude, so we can will our own freedom (see La Boétie 1983). So perhaps we can say that liberty, equality and, indeed, justice are not to be understood as the outcome of a project, but reflect the potentiality of the human itself. Once again, this should not be taken as a call for apathy or political inaction; it is not a matter of living our freedom by simply doing nothing. On the contrary, the realisation of our already existing freedom and equality is precisely what makes political action possible.

In the struggle for rights, which is taking place everywhere, albeit in different forms and through different discourses and practices, when people enact the rights they already have, even in unimaginable conditions of oppression and violence, even when they are not part of any established political community, they are revealing what is fundamentally human. They are revealing, in other words, that element of the human that transcends the degradations of power.

CONCLUSION

Traditional approaches to politics, rather than expanding the possibilities for bringing justice to stateless people, confirm that they are, in fact, the objects of an irrevocable exclusion. It is in this sense that any consideration of the human *qua* human and of everything that human rights evokes appears to be confronting an impossible future. This is the case (we hope to have shown) for the following reasons:

1. Political community in Western culture is deemed to be essentially finite: maybe 'many (but can we even be sure of this?) are called' to ascend to it, but, certainly, relatively 'few are chosen', as relations between rich Western and poor non-Western nations, as well as between established political communities and stateless people, demonstrate. Such exclusions will remain, unless we can radically rethink the notion of community in a non-totalising, non-sovereign way.
2. Bare life as the prime empirical instance of necessity is made the yardstick of what must be overcome, before it is possible for humanity to qualify for admission into a political com-

munity that can truly be the home of freedom. Here, to be indigenous – as Nguyen Van Thanh was classified as being by France during the Second World War – is still to be in a position where it is deemed that necessity actually remains to be overcome before citizenship can be bestowed. As we have suggested, it is not simply a question of excluding bare life from our conception of politics, as this simply reinforces the division that is the source of these exclusions in the first place. Rather, it is a question of transcending this division altogether, through the notion of life as always already a form-of-life, thus as always already political.

3. Sovereign power takes absolute priority over all other members of society in the interests of its own survival, just as Hobbes foreshadowed in the seventeenth century. Politics becomes the enactment of the social contract, with all its attendant violence and domination. In Agamben's terms, as we know, sovereign power has contaminated the legal system with the state of exception, so that it is no longer possible to be sure about whether the sovereign exists to enforce the law or whether the law exists to preserve sovereign power. Statelessness and human rights, we have seen, come a very poor second to the necessity of ensuring the absolutism of sovereign power. Avoiding this problem requires, as we have suggested, not only the fostering of non-sovereign communities and autonomous forms of political life, but the rethinking of human rights in terms other than law and legal institutionalisation. Not that these conditions are unimportant, but if we see them as determining our understanding of human rights – as most human rights literature seems to do – then we are limiting ourselves to a very narrow and circumscribed concept, which, once again, begs the question of the rights of the rightless or the rights of those without the right to have rights. Instead, what we have proposed here is to see human rights as revealing what is fundamentally human – outside of both natural and legal rights articulations – and thus, as something which we always already have. This allows a much broader conception of human rights discourses and practices, opening the way to unconventional and unpredictable expressions of human rights.

4. The media and the objectification of the image – an objectification

which one only has to read Levinas to appreciate – wrenches
the human from anything like its sacred or religious heritage.
For Agamben, this is, at the same time, the appropriation of
religious ritual and the Sabbatical festivals by sovereign power
in the interest of its own acclamation. The visibility of the
human *qua* human is, perhaps paradoxically, effaced. For his
part, Levinas points out that the drive for objectification and
obscuring of the infinite by finitude means that the absolute
Other is also obscured by what Levinas describes as 'egology'.
By this, he means that the Other is blotted out by the dominance of the Same. If we transpose (no doubt against Levinas'
intention) this idea onto nation-state power relations, we see
that sovereign power, in invoking media strategies, blots out
statelessness. For nation-states, statelessness does not exist as
a condition to be addressed and as a challenge to the very via-
bility of the nation-state as an entity founded on borders – that
is, in spatiality, which Levinas says is constitutive of the order of
the Same. The stateless are thus blotted out through an objectification (for example, in media images, which also become
objects to be surveyed, scrutinised and controlled) in the interests of the imperialism of the Same. This is an objectification
that is rendered all the more difficult to counter, in that the
stateless are also objectified as 'bare life'. Bare life is nothing if
it is not open to objectification.

5. It is clear that the founding of any nation-state and the formation of sovereign power is thought, by tradition, to be an
essentially violent act. Because the essential basis of sovereign
power is violence, only violence, it is said, can overturn it.
Law, if it is not clearly secondary here, is at least implicated
in violence (both founding and conserving), because there is,
as we saw Derrida argue, no law without the enforcement of
the law. Profound change in the political sphere can only be
revolutionary (that is, violent) change. In response to this, we
have explored a different conception of politics through the
notion of inoperativity. Rather than political action being part
of an overall project of emancipation – which always risks a
new form of sovereignty, a new founding violence – it is an
affirmation of our ever-present humanity, an affirmation of the
freedom, equality and justice that we already live.

Thinking Otherwise

The example of Agamben and, to a lesser extent, Levinas shows that it is possible in politics to think otherwise than in the terms laid down by the order of the Same. But what does thinking otherwise accomplish here? Surely it will be objected that to resort to thinking in such dire circumstances as those exemplified by human rights violations is the worst of all possible strategies. Here, once again, we find ourselves forced onto the terrain of the Procrustean bed of existing oppositions, such as theory and practice; thinking and action; idealism and realism; freedom and necessity. It is the task of this book to have endeavoured to think otherwise than these pre-existing frameworks of thought, including the idea that thinking only has meaning in its being distinguished from practice. What we have written stands for the act itself. It stands for the fact that thinking is the act. This idea is outside existing political categories. But this is the very point where we wish to be – outside, irrevocably outside the existing state of affairs.

When it comes to addressing human rights, Agamben's thinking, we suggest, indicates that the debate is entirely wrong-headed. Far from being an argument about bringing Western freedom to the other, Agamben inspires the recognition that it is this very strategy that is part of the problem. We should now see that in the most profound sense, the other, as the human, *is* already free. Were we not blinded by the order of the Same, nothing would be clearer. Moreover, it is imperative that necessity and freedom, as the key terms of the traditional debate, be displaced from centre stage, where they have served as the basis for Western cultural and political hegemony. The human *qua* human does not, for essential reasons, exist in necessity. The Other is not 'indigenous', in a state of deficit or subsistence, 'savage' (Arendt) or the West's other any more than the Other is 'my other'. It is not, therefore, imperative to bring this other into the human community or to stage his/her liberation through the current modes of implementing human rights.

When the United Nations High Commissioner for Refugees (UNHCR) solicits funds urgently from potential donors, when it describes the horror of the circumstances in which many people throughout the world find themselves and tells us that the consequences will be dire if something is not done in time, it is this implication that there is no time for thought which contributes to the problem at hand.[14] For, above all, the UNHCR has 'victim' emblazoned on its escutcheon. It symbolises the fact that such an organisation can never think otherwise than in terms of the fact that it is *we* (the Same) who must help *them* (object). It is clear that they 'know not what they do', for thinking is not part of the agenda. Our claim is, finally, that it is only thinking which will make any real difference.

Notes

1 The situation with regard to freedom is no doubt complex; the question being whether some can be free or whether freedom has to exist universally or not at all. Like Bataille, we would argue that freedom is the essential quality of the human, and the freedom or sovereignty of the Master against the rest is an illusion.

2 On this, see Judith Butler (2006: 202).

3 This notion of founding violence has clear implications for accepted understandings of rights: if rights are seen to only have force if they are established in law, if they are part of the constitutional order – in the tradition of the rights declarations emanating from the American and French Revolutions, for instance – then are they not inextricably bound up with the founding violence of law and, thus, with sovereign power itself? This is reflected in Agamben's critique of the Rights of Man. As we suggested, to see human rights primarily in the form of declarations and constitutional-legal systems is to see them only in their narrowest and most impoverished sense. Rather, we have been proposing an alternative grounding for human rights in an ontology of the human; their insistence revealed in language, gesture and life experienced as a 'form of life'.

4 Judith Butler captures succinctly what is at issue: 'Violence brings a system of law into being and this law-founding violence is precisely one that operates without justification' (2006: 207). Such violence, in other words, is a pure contingency, thus purely historical – the result of 'fate'. Clearly, if this is how an existing form of sovereign power comes into being, then only counter-violence will change it. The form of sovereignty might change, but what will never change is the cycle of violence founding law.

5 Hobbes refers to the dangers of internal dissent as various infirmities which might afflict and weaken the body politic of Leviathan from within, like 'worms in the entrayles of a naturall man' (1968: Chapter 29, Part 2, 375).

6 How one approaches the question of violence will have implications for the way sovereign power is viewed. We have highlighted the ambivalence of violence: it is central to the foundational operation of sovereignty, rein-

forcing its borders and confirming its autonomy, and, at the same time, it implies – as we see below – the violation of all borders and thus the possibility, as Bataille would propose, of a different understanding of sovereignty, invoking the excess and fluidity of a life that can never be entirely subordinated to power.

7 Even though Arendt saw the nation-state as the only available avenue for defending human rights, the rank opportunism and self-interest dominating nation-state policy towards stateless people appalled her. Nation-states set up after the First World War did not protect minority nationalities.

8 As demonstrated in particular by Derrida, the thought of Levinas radically extends the notion of violence. Thus, violence, for Levinas, would include 'predication' (from the verb 'to be' designating 'what is'), the objectification of the other in a concept to make the other a reflection of the ego-self, but also all objectification, all finitude characteristic of history (see Derrida 1967: 218–19). Horowitz amplifies the issue: 'There is no human violence without thought, without the projection of a totality in which the Same has placed every other in its relations. To Levinas, violence is not so much in the injuries brought to bear upon others, or at least not alone in such injuries. Violence means injuries inflicted on others through 'interrupting their continuity, making them play roles in which they no longer recognize themselves, making them betray not only commitments, but their own substance, making them carry out actions that will destroy every possibility for action' (2002: 217). The most well-known Levinasian summary of this, however, is that Western philosophy is an 'egology': it reduces the absolute Other – the other of the face – to the other as the symmetrical counterpart of the self, characteristic of the self–other cliché.

9 Although Bataille says that: 'the domain of eroticism is the domain of violence, the domain of violation' (1957: 23), this is so in the movement from discontinuity to continuity.

10 In 2011, the French authorities stopped trains travelling from Italy to France, in order to prevent the internal migration of Tunisians who had been granted temporary residence permits by the Italian government, but whose right to move freely within the EU – as stipulated under the Schengen Agreement – was not recognised by the French Government.

11 Giorgio Agamben, 'Metropolis', transcribed and translated by Arianna Bove: http://www.generation-online.org/p/fpagamben4.htm. For a fuller discussion of 'collateral effects' as part of the operation of divine government, see *The Kingdom and the Glory* (2011).

12 The radical nature of this cannot be over-emphasised, for it effectively implies a complete overturning of Western secular culture as a culture of the order of the Same, as it has evolved since the time of the Greeks. When

we are most confident of doing justice to the other, to difference, through existing modes of thought and action, we are, in fact, turning the Other into another version of the self, making difference the Same. What is exterior and infinite is interiorised within the logic of finitude. This is exactly what conceptualisation, objectification and representation does.

13 For instance, in his discussion of the claim for equal rights and political representation made by women in post-revolutionary France: 'they could demonstrate, through their public action, that they had the rights that the constitution denied to them, that they could enact those rights' (Rancière 2004: 304).

14 This is similar to a point made by Slavoj Žižek in his book *Violence*, where he is critical of this moral injunction to jump to the act rather than take the time to think, arguing that this is part of a liberal–humanitarian ideology that, in many ways, obscures, and is even complicit in, the very violence it denounces (see 2008).

BIBLIOGRAPHY

Agamben, Giorgio (1991), *Language and Death: The Place of Negativity*, trans. Karen E. Pinkus, Minneapolis, MN: University of Minnesota Press.

Agamben, Giorgio (1993), *The Coming Community*, trans. M. Hardt, Minneapolis, MN: University of Minnesota Press.

Agamben, Giorgio (1995), 'Le cinéma de Guy Debord: image et mémoire', online article, accessed 21 August 2012. http://espace.freud.pagesperso-orange.fr/topos/psycha/psysem/cinedebo.htm

Agamben, Giorgio (1996), 'Beyond human rights', in Paolo Virno and Michael (eds), *Radical Thought in Italy*, Minneapolis, MN: University of Minnesota Press, 158–64.

Agamben, Giorgio (1998), *Homo Sacer: Sovereign Power and Bare Life*, trans. Daniel Heller-Roazen, Stanford, CA: Stanford University Press.

Agamben, Giorgio (1999a), *Potentialities: Collected Essays in Philosophy*, trans. Daniel Heller-Roazen (ed.), Stanford, CA: Stanford University Press.

Agamben, Giorgio (1999b), *The End of the Poem: Studies in Poetics*, trans. Daniel Heller-Roazen, Stanford, CA: Stanford University Press.

Agamben, Giorgio (2000), *Means Without End: Notes on Politics*, trans. Vincenzo Binetti and Cesare Casarino, Minneapolis, MN: University of Minnesota Press.

Agamben, Giorgio (2002), *Remnants of Auschwitz: The Witness and the Archive*, trans. Daniel Heller-Roazen, New York, NY: Zone Books.

Agamben, Giorgio (2004), *The Open: Man and Animal*, Stanford, CA: Stanford University Press.

Agamben, Giorgio (2005a), *State of Exception*, trans. Kevin Atell, Chicago, IL: University of Chicago Press.

Agamben, Giorgio (2005b), *The Time that Remains: A Commentary on the Letter to the Romans*, trans. Patricia Dailey, Stanford, CA: Stanford University Press.

Agamben, Giorgio (2011), *The Kingdom and the Glory: For a Theological*

Genealogy of Economy and Government. Homo Sacer II, 2, trans. Lorenzo Chiesa, Stanford, CA: Stanford University Press.

Arendt, Hannah (1958), *The Human Condition*, Chicago, IL: The University of Chicago Press.

Arendt, Hannah ([1951] 1968), *The Origins of Totalitarianism*, London: Harvest/ HBJ.

Arendt, Hannah (1970), *On Violence*, London: Harvest/HBJ.

Arendt, Hannah ([1963] 2009), *On Revolution*, London: Penguin.

Aristotle (1995), 'Politics', in Jonathan Barnes (ed.), *The Complete Works of Aristotle. The Revised Oxford Translation, Volume Two*, Princeton, NJ: Princeton University Press, pp. 1986–2129.

Aumont, Jacques (1994), *The Image*, trans. Claire Pajackowska, London: The British Film Institute.

Austin, M. M. and P. Vidal-Naquet (1977), *Economic and Social History of Ancient Greece: An Introduction*, trans. M. M. Austin, Berkley, CA: University of California Press.

Bakunin, Mikhail (1953), *The Political Philosophy of Bakunin: Scientific Anarchism*, G. P. Maximoff (ed.), London: Macmillan.

Balibar, Étienne (2002), *Politics and the Other Scene*, trans. Christine Jones, James Swenson and Chris Turner, London: Verso.

Ball, Terence (1979), 'Marx and Darwin: a reconsideration', *Political Theory*, 7: 4 (November), 469–83.

Bataille, Georges (1957), *L'Érotisme*, Paris: Minuit.

Bataille, Georges (1976), 'La souveraineté', in Georges Bataille (ed.), *La Part Maudite, Oeuvres Complètes, VIII*, Paris: Gallimard, pp. 243–456.

Bataille, Georges (1988a), *Inner Experience*, trans. Leslie Anne Bolt, New York, NY: SUNY Press.

Bataille, Georges (1988b), *Œuvres Complètes, XII: Articles 2, 1950–1961*, Paris: Gallimard.

Baudrillard, Jean (1975), *The Mirror of Production*, trans. Mark Poster, St. Louis, MO: Telos Press.

Baudrillard, Jean (1981), *For a Critique of the Political Economy of the Sign*, trans. Charles Levin, St. Louis, MO: Telos Press.

Baxi, Uppendra (2008), *The Future of Human Rights*, 3rd edition, New Delhi: Oxford University Press.

Beatty, John (2006), 'Chance variation: Darwin on orchids', *Philosophy of Science*, 73: 5, 629–41.

Benhabib, Seyla (2004), *The Rights of Others: Aliens, Residents and Citizens*, Cambridge: Cambridge University Press.

Benjamin, Andrew (2008), 'Particularity and exceptions: on Jews and animals', *South Atlantic Quarterly*, 107: 1 (Winter), 71–87.

Benjamin, Andrew (2010), *Place, Commonality and Judgement: Continental*

Philosophy and the Ancient Greeks, London and New York, NY: Continuum.

Benjamin, Walter (1996), 'Critique of violence', *Selected Writings. Volume One: 1913–1926*, Cambridge, MA: Harvard University Press, pp. 236–52.

Benveniste, Emile (1966), *Problèmes de Linguistique Générale, I*, Paris: Gallimard.

Bernstein, J. M. (2004), 'Bare life, bearing witness: Auschwitz and the pornography of horror', *Parallax*, 10: 1, 2–16.

Bickermann, Elias (1929), 'Die römische Kaiserapotheose', *Archive für Religionwissenschaft*, 27, 1–34.

Bigo, Didier (2008), 'Globalized (in)security: the field and the ban-opticon', in D. Bigo and A. Tsoukala (eds), *Terror, Insecurity and Liberty: Illiberal Practices of Liberal Regimes after 9/11*, Abingdon: Routledge, pp. 10–48.

Birmingham, Peg (2011), 'The subject of rights: on the declaration of the human', *Epochē*, 16: 1 (Fall), 139–56.

Booth, Ken (1991), 'Security and emancipation', *Review of International Studies*, 17: 4, 313–26.

Borradori, Gionvanna (2004), *Philosophy in a Time of Terror: Dialogues with Jürgen Habermas and Jacques Derrida*, Chicago, IL: University of Chicago Press.

Brown, Wendy (2004), '"The most we can hope for . . .": human rights and the politics of fatalism', *The South Atlantic Quarterly*, 103: 2/3 (Spring/Summer), 451–63.

Brown, Wendy (2010), *Walled States, Waning Sovereignty*, New York, NY: Zone Books.

Buch, Robert (2007), 'Seeing the impossibility of seeing or the visibility of the undead: Giorgio Agamben's gorgon', *Germanic Review*, 82: 2, 179–96.

Bui, Doan (2012), 'Les indigènes oubliés', *Le Nouvel Observateur*, 2497 (13 September), 50–1.

Bull, Malcolm (1998), 'Slavery and the multiple self', *New Left Review*, 231: 1, 95–131.

Butler, Judith (2006), 'Critique, coercion, and sacred life in Benjamin's "critique of violence"', in Hent de Vries and Lawrence E. Sullivan (eds), *Political Theologies: Public Religions in a Post-Secular World*, New York, NY: Fordham University Press, pp. 201–19.

Canguilhem, Georges (1979), *Le Normal et le Pathologique*, 4th edition, Paris: Presses Universitaires de France.

Canguilhem, Georges (1992), *La Connaissance de la Vie*, Paris: J. Vrin.

Cavarero, Adriana (2009), *Horrorism: Naming Contemporary Violence*, trans. W. McCuaig, New York, NY: Columbia University Press.

Chandler, David (2008), 'Human security: the dog that didn't bark', *Security Dialogue*, 39: 4, 427–38.

Chandler, David (2009), 'The ideological (mis)use of human rights', in

Michael Goodhart (ed.), *Human Rights: Politics and Practice*, Oxford: Oxford University Press, pp. 109–25.

Chanter, Tina (2010), 'Antigone's liminality: Hegel's radical purification of tragedy and the naturalization of slavery', in Kimberly Hutchings and Tuija Pulkkinen (eds), *Hegel's Philosophy and Feminist Thought: Beyond Antigone?* New York, NY: Palgrave Macmillan, pp. 61–85.

Connolly, William E. (2007), 'The complexities of sovereignty', in M. Calarco and S. DeCaroli (eds), *Giorgio Agamben: Sovereignty & Life*, Stanford CA: Stanford University Press, pp. 23–42.

Darwin, Charles (1981), *The Descent of Man, and Selection in Relation to Sex*, John Tyler Bonner and Robert M. May (intro), Princeton, NJ: Princeton University Press.

Debord, Guy (1994), *The Society of the Spectacle*, trans. Donald Nicholson-Smith, New York, NY: Zone Books.

De la Durantaye, Leland (2009), *Giorgio Agamben: A Critical Introduction*, Stanford, CA: Stanford University Press.

Dembour, Marie-Bénédicte and Marie Martin (ed.) (2011), *Are Human Rights for Migrants?: Critical Reflections on the Status of Irregular Migrants in Europe and the United States*, Abingdon: Routledge.

Derrida, Jacques (1967), 'Violence et métaphysique: essai sur la pensée d'Emmanuel Levinas', in Jacques Derrida (ed.), *L'Écriture et la Différence*, Paris: Seuil, pp. 117–228.

Derrida, Jacques (1990), 'Force of law: the "mystical foundation of authority"', trans. Mary Quaintance, *Cardozo Law Revue*, 11: 5–6, 920–1045.

Derrida, Jacques (1994), *Spectres of Marx*, trans. Peggy Kamuf, New York, NY: Routledge.

Derrida, Jacques (1998), *Archive Fever: A Freudian Impression*, trans. Eric Prenowitz, Chicago, IL: University of Chicago Press.

Derrida, Jacques (2002), 'Declarations of independence', trans. Elizabeth Rottenberg (ed.), *Negotiations: Interventions and Interviews, 1971–2001*, Stanford, CA: Stanford University Press, pp. 46–54.

Derrida, Jacques (2005), *Rogues: Two Essays on Reason*, trans. P.-A. Brault and M. Naas, Stanford, CA: Stanford University Press.

Derrida, Jacques (2009), *The Beast and the Sovereign, Volume One*, trans. G. Bennington, Chicago, IL: The University of Chicago Press.

Dillon, Michael (1996), *Politics of Security: Towards a Political Philosophy of Continental Thought*, London: Routledge.

Donnelly, Jack (2003), *Universal Human Rights: In Theory and Practice*, 2nd edition, Ithaca, NY: Cornell University Press.

Douzinas, Costas (2000), *The End of Human Rights: Critical Legal Thought at the Turn of the Century*, Oxford: Hart.

Edkins, Jenny and Véronique Pin-Fat (2005), 'Through the wire: relations of power and relations of violence', *Millennium – Journal of International Studies*, 34: 1, 1–24.

Esposito, Roberto (2008), *Bios: Biopolitics and Philosophy*, trans. Timothy Campbell, Minneapolis, MN: University of Minnesota Press.

Esposito, Roberto (2009), *Communitas: The Origin and Destiny of Community*, trans. Timothy Campbell, Stanford, CA: Stanford University Press.

Esposito, Roberto (2011), *Immunitas: The Protection and Negation of Life*, trans. Zakiya Hanafi, Cambridge: Polity Press.

Fassin, Didier and Mariella Pandolfini (2010), 'Introduction: military and humanitarian government in the age of intervention', in D. Fassin and M. Pandolfini (eds), *Contemporary States of Emergency: The Politics of Military and Humanitarian Interventions*, New York, NY: Zone Books, pp. 9–25.

Finley, M. I. (1980), *Ancient Slavery and Modern Ideology*, New York, NY: Viking Press.

Finley, M. I. (1985), *The Ancient Economy*, 2nd edition, London: The Hogarth Press.

Fisher, N. R. E. (1995), *Slavery in Classical Greece*, London: Bristol Classical Press.

Fitzpatrick, Peter (2005), 'Bare sovereignty: *Homo Sacer* and the insistence of law', in A. Norris (ed.), *Politics, Metaphysics, and Death: Essays on Giorgio Agamben's Homo Sacer*, Durham, NC: Duke University Press, pp. 49–73.

Foucault, Michel (1982), *The Order of Things: An Archaeology of the Human Sciences*, London: Tavistock.

Foucault, Michel (1998), *The History of Sexuality, Volume One: The Will to Knowledge*, trans. Robert Hurley, London: Penguin.

Foucault, Michel (2000), *Ethics: Subjectivity and Truth. The Essential Works of Michel Foucault 1954–1984, Volume One*, Paul Rabinow (ed.), London: Penguin.

Foucault, Michel (2002), *Power: Essential Works of Foucault 1954–1984, Volume Three*, Robert Hurley (trans.) and James Faubion (ed.), London: Penguin.

Foucault, Michel (2003), *Society Must Be Defended: Lectures at the College de France, 1975–1976*, David Macey (trans.) and Mauro Bertani and Alessandro Fontana (eds), London: Penguin.

Foucault, Michel (2007), *Security, Territory, Population: Lectures at the Collège de France, 1977–1978*, Michel Senelart (ed.) and Grahame Burchell (trans.), Basingstoke: Palgrave Macmillan.

Friedländer, Paul (1964), *Plato. An Introduction*, trans. H. Meyerhoff, New York, NY: Harper.

Garlan, Yvon (1988), *Slavery in Ancient Greece*, trans. Janet Lloyd, Ithaca, NY: Cornell University Press.

Giroux, Henry A. (2006), *Beyond the Spectacle of Terrorism: Global Uncertainty and the Challenge of the New Media*, Boulder, CO: Paradigm Books.

Guild, Elspeth (2010), *Security and Migration in the 21st Century*, Cambridge: Polity Press.

Gündoğdu, Ayten (2012), 'Potentialities of human rights: Agamben and the narrative of fated necessity', *Contemporary Political Theory*, 11: 1, 2–22.

Habermas, Jürgen (2003), *The Future of Human Nature*, Cambridge: Polity Press.

Hardt, Michael and Antonio Negri (2000), *Empire*, Cambridge, MA: Harvard University Press.

Hegel, Georg Wilhelm Friedrich (1979), *Phenomenology of Spirit*, trans. A. V. Miller, Oxford: Oxford University Press.

Hegel, Georg Wilhelm Friedrich (1991), *The Encyclopaedia Logic: Part I of the Encyclopaedia of Philosophical Sciences* with the *Zusätze*, trans. T. F. Geraets, W. A. Suchting and H. S. Harris, Indianapolis/Cambridge: Hackett Publishing Company.

Hegel, Georg Wilhelm Friedrich (1993), *Lectures on the Philosophy of World History: Introduction*, trans. H. B. Nisbet, Cambridge: Cambridge University Press.

Heidegger, Martin (1975), *Poetry, Language, Thought*, trans. Albert Hofstadter, New York, NY: Harper and Row, Harper Colophon Books.

Heidegger, Martin (1982), *On the Way to Language*, trans. Peter D. Hertz, New York, NY: Harper and Row Perennial Library.

Heidegger, Martin (1993), 'Letter on humanism', in David Farrell Krell (ed.), *Martin Heidegger Basic Writings: From Being and Time (1927) to The Task of Thinking (1964)*, London: Routledge, pp. 213–65.

Heidegger, Martin (1999), *Ontology: The Hermeneutics of Facticity*, trans. John van Buren, Bloomington, IN: Indiana University Press.

Hobbes, Thomas ([1651] 1968), *Leviathan*, C. B. Macpherson (ed.), London: Penguin.

Horowitz, Asher (2002), '"By a hair's breadth" critique, transcendence and the ethical in Adorno and Levinas', *Philosophy and Social Criticism* 28: 2, 213–48.

Huysmans, Jeff (2006), *The Politics of Insecurity: Fear, Migration, and Asylum in the EU*, Abingdon: Routledge.

International Committee of the Fourth International (ICFI) (2002), 'Life inside an Australian detention centre', online article, accessed 23 August 2011. http://www.wsws.org/articles/2002/feb2002/mari-f07.shtml

Ignatieff, Michael (2003), *Human Rights as Politics and Idolatry*, with K. Anthony Appiah, David A. Hollinger, Thomas W. Laqueur and Diane F. Orentlicher, Princeton, NJ: Princeton University Press.

Ignatieff, Michael (2005), *The Lesser Evil: Political Ethics in an Age of Terror*, Edinburgh: Edinburgh University Press.

Jacob, François (1970), *La Logique du Vivant: Une Histoire de Hérédité*, Paris: Gallimard.

Kaldor, Mary (2007), *Human Security*, Cambridge: Polity Press.

Kant, Immanuel (1970), *Critique of Pure Reason*, trans. Norman Kemp Smith, London and Basingstoke: Macmillan.

Kantorowicz, Ernst Hartwig (1957), *The King's Two Bodies: A Study in Mediaeval Political Theology*, Princeton, NJ: Princeton University Press.

La Boétie, Estienne de (1983), *Discours de la Servitude Volontaire*, Simone Goyard Fabre (chronologie, introduction, bibliographie, notes), Paris: Flammarion.

Lacan, Jacques (1973), *Le Séminaire: Livre 20: Encore*, Paris: Seuil.

LaCapra, Dominick (2003), 'Approaching limit events: siting Agamben', in M. Bernard-Donals and R. Glejzer (eds), *Witnessing the Disaster: Essays and Representation on the Holocaust*, Madison, WI: University of Wisconsin Press, pp. 262–304.

Laclau, Ernesto (2007), 'Bare life or social indeterminacy?', in Matthew Calarco and Steven DeCaroli (eds), *Giorgio Agamben: Sovereignty & Life*, Stanford, CA: Stanford University Press, pp. 11–22.

Lechte, John (2007), *Fifty Key Contemporary Thinkers: From Structuralism to Post-Humanism*, 2nd edition, London: Routledge.

Lechte, John (2012), *Genealogy and Ontology of the Western Image and its Digital Future*, New York, NY: Routledge.

Lechte, John and Saul Newman (2012), 'Agamben, Arendt and human rights: bearing witness to the human', *European Journal of Social Theory*, 15: 4, 505–21.

Lefort, Claude (1988), *Democracy and Political Theory*, trans. D. Macey, Minneapolis, MN: University of Minnesota Press.

Levinas, Emmanuel (1989), *The Levinas Reader*, Sean Hand (ed.), Oxford: Blackwell.

Levinas, Emmanuel (1993), *Outside the Subject*, trans. Michael B. Smith, London: The Athlone Press.

Levinas, Emmanuel (1998), *Otherwise Than Being, or Beyond Essence*, trans. Alphonso Lingis, Pittsburgh, PN: Duquensne University Press.

Levinas, Emmanuel (1999), *Alterity and Transcendence*, trans. Michael B. Smith, New York, NY: Columbia University Press.

Lévi-Strauss, Claude (1974), *Tristes Tropiques*, trans. John Weightman and Doreen Weightman, New York, NY: Atheneum.

Levy, Carl (2010), 'Refugees, Europe, camps/state of exception: "into the zone", the European Union and extraterritorial processing of migrants, refugees, and asylum-seekers (theories and practice)', *Refugee Survey Quarterly*, 29: 1, 92–119.

Luhmann, Niklas (1998), *Observations on Modernity*, trans. William Whobrey, Stanford, CA: Stanford University Press.

Marmor, Andrei (2011), *Philosophy of Law*, Princeton, NJ: Princeton University Press.

Mason, Stephen F. (1962), *A History of the Sciences*, New York, NY: Collier.

May, Todd (2008), 'Equality among the refugees: a Rancièrean view of Montréal's sans-status Algerians', *Anarchist Studies*, 16: 2, 121–34.

Mesnard, Philippe (2004), 'The political philosophy of Giorgio Agamben: a critical evaluation', *Totalitarian Movements and Political Religions*, 5: 1 (Summer), 139–57.

Mills, Catherine (2004), 'Agamben's messianic politics: biopolitics, abandonment and happy life', *Contretemps*, 5 (December), 42–62, online article, accessed 13 September 2012. http://sydney.edu.au/contretemps/index.html

Mondzain, Marie-José (2005), *Image, Icon, Economy: The Byzantine Origins of the Contemporary Imaginary*, trans. Rico Franses, Stanford, CA: Stanford University Press.

Mouffe, Chantal (2000), *The Democratic Paradox*, New York, NY: Verso.

Mouffe, Chantal (2005), *On the Political*, New York, NY: Routledge.

Mouffe, Chantal (ed.) (1999), *The Challenge of Carl Schmitt*, London: Verso.

Nancy, Jean-Luc (1991), *The Inoperative Community*, trans. Peter Connor, Lisa Garbus, Michael Holland and Simona Sawhney, Minneapolis, MN: University of Minnesota Press.

Nancy, Jean-Luc (2003), *Au fond des images*, Paris: Galilée.

Negri, Antonio (1999), *Insurgencies: Constituent Power and the Modern State*, trans. M. Boscagli, Minneapolis, MN: University of Minnesota Press.

Norris, Andrew (2005), 'The exemplary exception: philosophical and political decisions in Giorgio Agamben's *Homo Sacer*', in A. Norris (ed.), *Politics, Metaphysics, and Death: Essays on Giorgio Agamben's Homo Sacer*, Durham, NC: Duke University Press, pp. 262–79.

Ojakanges, Mika (2005), 'Impossible dialogue on bio-power: Agamben and Foucault', *Foucault Studies*, 2 (May), 5–28.

Owens, Patricia (2009), 'Reclaiming "bare life"?: against Agamben on refugees', *International Relations*, 23: 4, 567–82.

Rancière, Jacques (1999), *Disagreement: Politics and Philosophy*, trans. Julie Rose, Minneapolis, MN: University of Minnesota Press.

Rancière, Jacques (2004), 'Who is the subject of the Rights of Man?' *The South Atlantic Quarterly*, 103: 2–3, 298–310.

Rousseau, Jean-Jacques (1969), *Émile*, in *Oeuvres Complètes*, *IV*, Paris: Gallimard, 'Bibliothèque de la pléiade'.

Sartre, Jean-Paul (1962), *Imagination: A Psychological Critique*, trans. Forrest Williams, Ann Arbor, MI: The University of Michigan Press.

Sartre, Jean-Paul (2004), *The Imaginary: A Phenomenological Psychology of the Imagination*, trans. Jonathan Webber, London and New York, NY: Routledge.

Schmitt, Carl (2007), *The Concept of the Political*, trans. G. Schwab, Chicago, IL: University of Chicago Press.

Smith, Anthony (1971), *Theories of Nationalism*, London and New York, NY: Torchbook Library.

Sofsky, Wolfgang (2003), *Violence: Terrorism, Genocide, War*, trans. A. Bell, London: Granta Books.

Sophocles (1974), *Antigone*, trans. E. F. Watling, London: Penguin.

Sorel, Georges (1961), *Reflections on Violence*, trans. T. E. Hulme and J. Roth, New York, NY: Collier Books

Stiegler, Bernard (1998), *Technics and Time: The Fault of Epimetheus*, trans. Richard Beardsworth and George Collins, Stanford, CA: Stanford University Press.

Stiegler, Bernard (2001), *Le Technique et le Temps 3. Le Temps du Cinema et la Question du Mal-Etre*, Paris: Galilée.

Stirner, Max ([1845] 1995), *The Ego and Its Own*, trans. David Leopold, Cambridge: Cambridge University Press.

Suvák, Vladislav (2000), 'The essence of truth (*aletheia*) and the Western tradition in the thought of Heidegger and Patocka', *Thinking Fundamentals, IWM Junior Visiting Fellows Conferences* (proceedings) 9: 4, 1–18, online conference article, accessed 25 July 2012. http://www.iwm.at/publ-jvc/jc-09-04.pdf

Tambakaki, Paulina (2010), *Human Rights, or Citizenship?* Abingdon: Birkbeck Law Press.

ten Bos, René (2005), 'On the possibility of formless life', *Ephemera*, 5: 1, 26–44.

Tirman, John (2006), 'Immigration and insecurity: post-9/11 fear in the United States', online article, accessed 22 August 2011. http://borderbattles.ssrc.org/Tirman/

Tucker, Robert C. (ed.) (1978), *The Marx-Engels Reader*, 2nd edition, New York and London: W. W. Norton & Co.

United Nations Educational, Scientific and Cultural Organization (UNESCO) (1997), 'Universal declaration on the human genome and human rights', online webpage, accessed 30 May 2012. http://portal.unesco.org/en/ev.php-URL_ID=13177&URL_DO=DO_TOPIC&URL_SECTION=201.html

United Nations (UN) (2005), 'In larger freedom: towards development, security and human rights for all', online report, accessed 19 August 2011. http://www.un.org/largerfreedom/contents.htm

Vernant, Jean-Pierre (1978), *Myth et pensée chez les Grecs, II*, Paris: Maspero.

Verschuer, Otmar Freiherr von (ed.) (1942), *État et Santé, Cahiers de l'Institut Allemand*, Paris: F. Sorlot.

Vincent, Andrew (2010), *The Politics of Human Rights*, Oxford: Oxford University Press.

Virno, Paolo (1996), 'Virtuosity and revolution: the political theory of exodus', in P. Virno and M. Hardt (eds), *Radical Thought in Italy: A Potential Politics*, trans. M. Boscagli, Cesare Casarino, Paul Colilli, Ed Emory, Michael Hardt, and Michael Turits, Minneapolis, MN: University of Minnesota Press, pp. 189–212.

Virno, Paolo (2002), 'General intellect, exodus, multitude', online interview with Paolo Virno [published in *Archipélago*, 54], accessed 24 July 2012. http://www.generation-online.org/p/fpvirno2.htm

Waldron, Jeremy (2003), 'Security and liberty: the image of balance', *The Journal of Political Philosophy*, 11: 2, 191–210.

Watkin, William (2010), *The Literary Agamben: Adventures in Logopoiesis*, London and New York, NY: Continuum.

Weizman, Eyal (2011), *The Least of All Possible Evils: Humanitarian Violence from Arendt to Gaza*, London: Verso.

Zahavi, Dan (2003), 'How to investigate subjectivity: Natorp and Heidegger on reflection', *Continental Philosophy Review*, 36: 2, 155–76.

Ziarek, Ewa (2008), 'Bare life on strike: notes on the biopolitics of race and gender', South Atlantic Quarterly, 107: 1, 89–105.

Žižek, Slavoj (2008), *Violence: Six Sideways Reflections*, London: Profile Books.

INDEX

Abu Ghraib, 141, 147–8
Adorno, T., 86
Agamben, G.
  the ban, 16, 51, 61, 63, 77–8, 82, 113, 119, 125
  criticisms of *see Chapter Five esp.* 96–115
  critique of human rights, ix–x, 3–9, 19, 51–2
  gesture, 11, 82–9, 125, 144–5, 159
  glory, 90–2, 134, 151
  homo sacer, 3, 51, 60–3, 75n5, 82–3, 95n10, 104–7, 112–13, 172
  language, 50, 52, 77–88, 94n2, 144–6, 150–1, 159, 180, 186n3
  oikonomia, 90–1, 134, 149
  paradigms, 98–100, 110, 117n2
  poetry, 86, 88–9, 151
  singularities, 86, 134–5
  sovereignty, 105–12
  state of exception, ix, 4, 12, 63, 65–6, 68–70, 72, 75n12, 106, 122, 125, 127, 132, 183
anarchism, 129, 131, 133–4, 172
Antelme, R., 83
Antigone (Sophocles), 41–4
Arendt, H.
  critique of human rights, vii–viii, 17–18, 27–34, 97, 115
  public sphere, 27–34, 77, 126
  necessity, viii, 29–35, 47n6, 48n7, 49, 51, 63, 95n11, 114, 163, 167–8, 185
  'right to have rights', vii, ix, 9, 23, 33, 35, 41, 51–2, 183
  violence, 95n11, 173–4
  vita activa, 31

Aristotle
  bios and *zoē*, viii, 17, 39, 49, 103–4
  see also slavery
Auschwitz, 86, 98–100, 150; *see also* camps

Balibar, E., 176
bare life *see Chapter Three*
  biological life, 47, 52–3, 59–60, 63–5, 71, 73–4, 84, 89, 91, 103–4, 119, 160n1, 164, 168, 180
  economic theory, 54
  quantification, 53, 55–6, 65, 84
  survival, 6, 21n10, 29–30, 32, 41, 53–4, 56–9, 63, 114
Barthes, R., 155, 158
Bartleby the Scrivener (Melville), 125
Bataille, G., 20n2, 21n11, 90, 93, 161n10
  sovereignty, 137n10, 165–9
Baudrillard, J., 64, 75n3
bearing witness, 85–6
Benhabib, S., 16
Benjamin, A., 43, 63, 75n5
Benjamin, W.
  'divine violence', 131–3, 137n10,n11, 169, 172
  legal violence, 66, 127, 169–72
Benveniste, E., 52, 79, 86–7, 145
Bergson, H., 150
Bichat, M. F. X., 57, 74n2
biometrics, 155
biopolitics, x, 6, 14, 51–3, 58, 62–3, 65, 71, 96, 100, 107, 117, 119, 123–4
bios and *zoē*, viii, ix–x, 5, 8, 17, 39, 49–53, 62, 65, 68, 84, 89, 91, 96, 98, 103–4, 116, 133, 151